HANDBOOKS TO PRINTING

PHOTOLITHO-OFFSET

PHOTOLITHO - OFFSET

By
ERIC CHAMBERS
A.M.I.O.P., A.R.P.S., F.R.S.A.

LONDON · ERNEST BENN LIMITED

FIRST PUBLISHED 1967 BY ERNEST BENN LIMITED
BOUVERIE HOUSE · FLEET STREET · LONDON · EC4
DISTRIBUTED IN CANADA BY
THE GENERAL PUBLISHING CO LTD · TORONTO
© ERIC CHAMBERS 1967
PRINTED IN GREAT BRITAIN

About the author:

Senior Lecturer; Head of School of Photomechanical, Lithographic and Finishing Processes, Department of Printing Technology, Manchester College of Art and Design

Honorary Technical Adviser the Society of Lithographic Artists, Designers, Engravers and Process Workers

Technical Consultant in the Industry

Member of the Advisory Committee and the Moderating Committee for Graphic Reproduction (325) and Examiner City and Guilds of London Institute

Preface

THE BIGGEST single factor about technical education today is that there is not enough of it! The technological revolution which has overtaken printing methods during the past two decades is causing this shortcoming to be rectified and has revealed the need for technicians and technologists possessing wide knowledge of the industry.

The new conception of a Craft Course, outlined in the Government White Paper (Cmnd. 1254, January 1961), is a course designed to bring the average apprentice to a predetermined standard of competence in the practice of his own craft in three or more years. A Craft Certificate, although a complete qualification in itself, can serve as a stepping-stone to a higher award – the Advanced Craft Certificate, which implies specialist or advanced skills in addition to fundamental craft knowledge.

A 'technician' is the term applied to a wide range of responsible jobs involving a higher level of technical knowledge than that generally needed by a craftsman. For instance, the application of scientific and mechanical principles in solving day-to-day workshop problems. A 'technologist' has been defined as one who is trained 'to apply scientific methods to the analysis and solution of technological problems, requiring the exercise of original thought and judgement . . . and the supervision of the technical and administrative work of others'.

The technician and the technologist benefit from knowledge and experience of basic craft skills and processes. This is necessary before applying the mechanical and scientific principles which govern the various craft methods and affect the behaviour of materials, electronic and other control systems, associated with production techniques.

The purpose of this book is to further the knowledge of all interested in Graphic Reproduction and in particular to assist apprentices and students in obtaining the Basic Craft Certificate (325) of the City and Guilds of London Institute, and also to provide the stepping-stone to further achievement and success in the Institute of Printing and advanced level examinations.

It may seem something of an anomaly that the word 'school' is derived from the Greek work meaning 'leisure', but this testifies to mankind's old conviction and experience in the past that education unfits man for productive work. The man of education, however limited, shunned heavy toil – the plough, the potter's wheel, all forms of manual labour were not for him. The spectre of the 'educated proletariat' haunted the early educators, with the danger of an educated class too numerous for the few available job opportunities for educated people, and too highly educated for honest work.

This state of affairs is, fortunately, past history. Today there is a shortage of trained and educated people. Our economic progress and standing in the world depend more and more upon increasing the supply, both in quantity and quality, of trained and educated personnel. Knowledge – rather than 'labour' or 'capital' – is fast becoming the central and the most productive resource of our society. The question is not 'How many trained and educated people can a society afford?' but increasingly 'How many people who are not trained and educated can a society afford?'

Learning and education cannot be carried on in a vacuum; they are part of a general culture, a common way of living. The aim must be to teach how to think rather than what to think and in that respect the most important part of one's education is that which we give ourselves, bearing in mind that the object of education is to teach us how to live as individuals and as useful and active members of a community.

Earlier in our history the need was for people who could read and write; now the demand is for technically trained people. If the paramount need of yesterday was for literacy in the community, the comparable need today is for the technically trained and efficient. G. B. Shaw has said that there are only two qualities in this world, efficiency and inefficiency, and only two sorts of people, the efficient and the inefficient. If the perusal of the following pages increases the former and decreases the latter then the effort of writing this book has been well worth while.

E. C.

Contents

Illustrations

Lithoprintex senior – showing micrometer setting,
dials and notch bars   *Jacket cover*

In text

Acknowledgements

THE LONGER we live the more we realise that life is a system of relations rather than a positive and independent existence. We cannot, in the nature of things, wallow in our own egotism because we soon learn that we are as much, or more, dependent on others as they are on us. In this age of vastly accumulated knowledge and mass systems of communication it is scarcely possible for anyone to write or say anything to which a parallel could not somewhere, in part, be found. There is some consolation in the thought of Ruskin that the virtue of originality that men so strain after is not newness, as they vainly think. There is nothing new; it is only genuineness!

My sincere thanks are due to very many friends and associations which, directly or indirectly, have contributed to the production of this book. The City and Guilds of London Institute and the following organisations have been most helpful in providing information and the illustrations used in the text:

Agfa-Gevaert Ltd; Griffins Supplies Ltd; Hunter-Penrose-Littlejohn Ltd; J. J. Huber Ltd; W. H. Howson Ltd; Kodak Ltd; Pershke Price Service Organisation; Pictorial Machinery Ltd.

I wish to record my special appreciation to my wife and family for their unstinted help and co-operation in proof-reading, etc., and particularly to my daughter, Sheila, who typed (and corrected!) the whole of the manuscript. Also to my colleague, Mr J. T. Astley, for his advice and contribution when preparing the text matter, and for his valuable help in preparing the illustrations. The Sage of China was surely right when he observed that a good picture is better than a thousand words.

E. C.

I

The Planographic Process

INVENTION

IT WAS in 1798 that Alois Senefelder, aged 27, discovered, by a happy accident, the process of lithography. He was practising the difficult task of writing in reverse on a piece of Kelheim stone, which consists mainly of smooth calcium carbonate and which can be resurfaced and polished without difficulty. He was using this medium to acquire the skill for copperplate handwriting. His mother, entering his workshop, asked him to note the items of clothes being given to a laundrywoman for cleaning. Senefelder, without ink and paper, used the greasy acid resist – the etching ground of the copper plate – to list the items on the clean polished surface of the Kelheim stone. The greasy ink would not wash off the stone with water, and, acting on an impulse, he etched the stone surface with his copperplate etching solution, reasoning that the etch would be resisted by the etching ground of wax, soap and lampblack. On covering the edges of the stone with wax and applying dilute nitric acid to the surface, it dissolved away, leaving the greasy image behind. Some accounts give the date of this discovery as 1796, but Senefelder himself refers to his invention as taking place in 1798.

Such accidental discoveries are never made except by men on the lookout for new ways of realising old ambitions. Roast pork, the steam engine, and penicillin are instances of discoveries that fell into the unsuspecting laps of persons who knew what use could be made of them. The kettle boils as it has already boiled in a thousand kitchens, but not until a James Watt, observing the unremarkable phenomenon, cries 'Eureka!' can a steam-engine be envisaged; and not until Senefelder saw what had happened to a chance scribble on a smooth slab of stone could lithography become a cheap, efficient, and marvellously flexible technique for reproduction.

Senefelder patented the process, invented a printing press, chalks, printing inks and transfer papers, and wrote a comprehensive treatise on the new reproductive method. The world knows the result. Delacroix, Goya, Daumier, Vuillard, Degas, Lautrec and many others seized the opportunity to pour out prints. Lithography became a craze, not because it produced new effects but because it achieved old effects cheaply and quickly. Then the inventive minds of artists such as Matisse, Picasso, Pennell and Nevinson realised that there were more adventurous things to do with the new medium than merely to run off replicas of an original drawing. There were ways of scraping, texturing and juggling on the stone surface that were beyond the reach of other print-makers' methods. In the field of art a new lithographic era began. The print ceased to be a reproductive and became a creative process. Thus, the forerunner of autolithography.

At the end of his book Senefelder expressed the desire that his invention, lithography (stone writing), should be 'spread over the whole world, bringing much good to humanity through many excellent productions, and that it may work towards man's greater culture but never be misused for evil purposes'.

In his initial experiments with transferring, he used a weak gum–nitric acid–water solution, finding that the stone so treated would not transfer the greasy ink to the surface. Further work showed him that when the greasy soap or wax was applied direct to the stone and the surface damped and inked, the ink only adhered to the wax lines, the remainder repelling the ink on the roller. Senefelder realised that the stone had two definite chemical qualities. Firstly the chemical affinity of a clean polished stone for grease and secondly the complete repulsion of applied grease by water or gum solution retained in the porous stone. Thus, a planographic process was evolved, prints being pulled on Senefelder's new press from a stone which had no sunken or raised areas, as applied hitherto, to mark the distinction between image and non-image areas.

BASIC PRINCIPLES

A DESIGN in a greasy pencil or ink containing soap among other constituents is traced or transferred on a lithographic stone, which is 'etched' by being covered over for a few minutes with a solution of gum arabic, acidified with nitric acid. The nitric acid decomposes the soap which has commenced to penetrate the stone, and liberates the fatty acid, which clogs the pores of the stone, making it completely impermeable. At the same time, the nitric acid liberates the acid of the gum arabic in a soluble form. This penetrates the areas of the stone not covered with any greasy substance, becoming insoluble when dry, but capable of swelling by absorbing water. Water will no longer remove it. When the stone is moistened, the water is retained by the acid liberated from the gum. The acid fills the pores of the stone in the light areas of the image, and is repelled by the areas where the fatty acid has penetrated the stone, even though by this time the fatty substances forming the black areas have been washed away by the use of suitable solvents. When the moist stone is inked up, the ink is repelled by all the parts which retain water and is deposited solely on those parts which formed part of the original image. If additions are required to the image, it is necessary to 're-sensitise' the stone by eliminating from it the insoluble products originating from the gum, which stop penetration by any greasy substance. This can be done by the use of dilute acetic acid.

Lithographic stone is calcium carbonate, $CaCO_3$, and the best is found in Solnhofen and Kelheim in Bavaria. It was used in a thickness varying from two to five inches and was prepared as to its surface in different ways, according to the character of the work which was to be produced on it.

The original procedure was as follows, with crayon, pen work, and engraved work being the three methods used. If the stone was to be engraved, the surface was ground smooth with sand and water and then polished with pumice and water-of-ayr stone. If the pen was to be used, a smooth surface was also required; but if a crayon drawing was to be made on the stone, the surface was ground with a grain the fineness of which varied with the nature of the subject that was to be put on the stone. If a subject which was bold in effects was to be printed, the stone would usually be grained coarsely; but if the subject was to be finely worked, the grain would correspondingly fine.

Lithographic Crayon Work

IN MAKING a crayon drawing the artist works with a lithographic crayon, which is black in colour and greasy in nature. The grain given to the stone serves the same purpose as the grain in crayon paper and catches the particles of crayon. The light and shade of a drawing is thus produced on the stone in the same manner as it is on a sheet of crayon paper. Light or heavy tones may be obtained by the difference of pressure of the hand in manipulating the crayon, or by variation of the crayons used, either soft or hard. The stone is then etched with an acid of about two parts of nitric to forty to sixty parts of dissolved gum arabic; the mixture being lightly sponged over the stone. The greasy lithographic ink on the top of the grain resists the acid, but the bare stone, at the bottom of the grain, absorbs the solution readily, as the action of the acid and the gum arabic gives to the stone the property of absorbing and holding water. Although the parts which have been etched are slightly below the surface of the stone, the depression is very slight and the principle of printing does not rest upon this depression. To all intents and purposes it is a plane surface throughout, hence the name, planographic printing.

The operation of printing consists, first, in damping the stone – with a wet sponge in hand-press printing or with a wet roller in power-press work. The water will be taken up by the etched portions, but will be repelled by the greasy crayon ink of the drawing on the stone. If a lithographic roller charged with ink is then passed over the stone, the parts which have not been touched by the crayon will resist the ink, but the drawing, being greasy, will have affinity for the printing ink and will take it up readily. After a very careful inking-in, the impression is pulled. The process of wetting and inking must be repeated for each impression.

Beautiful results in chiaroscuro were obtained in lithographic crayon work and many artists of renown have used this process. The tones are not quite continuous to the eye, but sufficiently so to give an agreeable effect. The finer the grain the more nearly continuous will be the tone.

Lithographic Pen Work

A LITHOGRAPHIC pen, similar to a fine writing pen, is used for drawing the design on the stone and especially prepared greasy lithographic ink is used on the pen. But little black and white work is done by this method. It is in colour work by this process that pen work becomes chiefly valuable. Sometimes a brush is used instead of a pen.

Engraved Work

A SMOOTH stone and a sharp needle in a wooden handle, held in the same manner as a pencil, comprise the material required for lithographic engraved work. The stone has first been prepared by etching with acid and gum arabic, so that if it were wet and inked up it would resist the ink over the whole surface. In working the design by scraping with a needle, the preparation on the stone is removed and the slight depressions which are made in the stone hold ink partly because they are below the surface, and print in the same manner as an intaglio plate, and partly because the ink-resisting preparation has been removed from the stone by the needle point. The edition is not printed from this engraving, but by the transfer process, which plays a most important part in this art.

Transfer Process

IMPRESSIONS ARE pulled from the engraving on the stone by rubbing greasy lithographic transfer ink into the lines by means of a wooden block covered with felt. These impressions are pulled on the hand press on prepared transfer paper, such as a china paper, and are carefully laid on another sheet, supported on a board, and are held to it by pricking with a point through the two papers. The sheets are removed from the board and put face down on another stone and run through the lithographic hand press. The paper is soaked off and the stone is etched; it is then ready for printing. Transfers of pen or crayon work are made in a similar manner.

By means of the transfer process hundreds of copies of a single design or many different designs may be put on one stone. Steel or copper plates in lines may be transferred in the same manner, but if the engraving is very deep it is difficult to prevent the spreading of the great quantity of ink drawn out of the lines of the engraved metal plate and subjected to the heavy pressure of the transfer press. An ink must be especially prepared to overcome this difficulty.

Billheads, business cards, letter-heads, stock certificates, and similar commercial work were the chief products of lithographic engraving.

Many experiments have been made to substitute another material for lithographic stone. The great weight of the stones, their extreme costliness; the danger of breaking, thereby not only entailing the loss of the stone, but possibly of some valuable drawing; the cost of transportation and storage were factors that, soon after the invention of the process, made it clear that the discovery of a substitute material was imperative. Nevertheless, it was many years before the problem was solved.

Aluminium and zinc are both in general use today as substitutes, with other mediums, for lithographic stone. The principle of printing is identical with that of lithography already described. It is planographic printing dependent chiefly on the repulsion of greasy ink and water. The preparation of the plates and the technique throughout are sufficiently varied from the manipulation of stone so that it has taken many decades to bring to a successful solution what seemed at first a simple matter.

THE TECHNIQUE OF LITHOGRAPHY

THE CHEMICAL principle on which the formation of the lithographic image is based, is the antipathy of grease to water. In lithography, the printing and non-printing areas are at approximately the same level in the printing image carrier, ink adhering only to the printing areas. The basic principle, subject to limitations when considering the finer points, is that oil and water do not mix.

What happens when a greasy ink comes into contact with a newly polished stone? Senefelder erroneously assumed that the grease sinks into the stone, but, in fact, the chemical composition of the parts of the stone contacted is changed. The ink contains fatty acids; that is, fats and oils with an acid reaction; for example, stearic and oleic acids which form a calcium oleate or stearate. This is insoluble in water and has grease-attracting properties. Thus a new chemical compound is formed which is incorporated in the surface of the stone. The stone has a water–grease affinity, but water and grease have a strong antipathy for each other.

A stone with a greasy ink in certain areas, when treated with water, will retain the water, excepting in the parts covered with ink, where the water will be strongly repelled. A solution of gum arabic (gum acacia) will *desensitise* the stone, that is, remove its affinity for grease. Dissolved in water, the arabic acid, when allowed to dry on the stone, makes it insoluble in water and with no affinity for grease.

If the stone thus treated is water washed, the soluble residue of the gum solution will wash away and the calcium arabinate, being insoluble in water, remains. Thus, by 'gumming-up' a stone holding a greasy design, the whole surface, apart from the design area, can be desensitised, and the design will repel the gum solution. The next stage is to wash off the gum, leaving the calcium arabinate, and to pass an ink-charged matt leather roller over the dampened stone. The greasy ink will be repelled by the damp stone and attracted by the image design, which will in process be 'rolled up'.

Etching. Finely powdered, acid-resisting resin, dusted over the dried image, will partly adhere to it, and a weak solution of nitric acid, if applied, would not affect the image, but would 'etch' the stone, calcium nitrate forming and carbon dioxide being given off in small bubbles. Treating with water removes the calcium nitrate, leaving the stone more porous, slightly roughened and minus the covering of calcium arabinate. To desensitise the stone, it must be again gummed up and dried, the gum arabic again being repelled by the ink image.

Washing Out. When dry, turpentine is washed over the stone to dissolve and remove the ink and resin, thus exposing the calcium oleate compound beneath. After the gum has been washed off, the surface is then re-inked, using a 'nap', or rough leather roller. If 'washing-out' were omitted, the resin would cause trouble by causing the paper to 'pluck', owing to the resin sticking to the paper when printing. Also, if left, the deposit of resin, plus the ink coating on top of it, would cause a gradual thickening and blurring of the result.

After etching it is necessary to gum up the stone thoroughly with a thick layer of gum, and dry quickly. The reason being that the action of the nitric acid is to eat away the desensitised layer of calcium arabinate and a further coating of gum is required to desensitise the stone again.

Litho stone is a natural formation of limestone arising from deposits which occurred during the Jurassic age of geology. It is, in fact, a stratified rock substance of slabs of calcium carbonate (97%) plus about 3% of magnesium carbonate. The stones are especially suitable for lithographic printing, absorbing grease readily, being porous enough to hold moisture, yet providing a smooth working surface. They were quarried in sizes up to 44 × 62 inches, and were often from 3 to 5 inches thick, weighing more than half a ton. It is obvious why, with the introduction of zinc and aluminium, the stones are rarely used today! The method of preparing the stone for printing is also time-consuming, involving a mechanical operation in which a smaller stone, or a flat metallic jigger or levigator, consisting of a heavy circular disc of cast iron with holes pierced through it, is rubbed in a continuous series of circular movements evenly over the surface. A grinding paste or abrasive of sieved sand and clean water, etc., is applied through the holes of the levigator, until the stone is perfectly clean and level. Graining, and if necessary polishing, is carried out in a similar manner using a smaller piece of stone and suitable sand. Solids and lines require a polished surface; crayon drawings require a grain to suit the result desired. The grade range is from 36 grain to 200 grain. Abrasive materials include silver sand, flint, aluminium oxide, powdered glass and carborundum.

Alternatives to stone

ZINC AND aluminium are generally used in sheets varying from 5 to 25 thousandths of an inch in thickness. Compared with litho stone, they lack porosity and require treatment in order to create a satisfactory printing surface.

The element zinc, Zn, is a hard, tough, close-textured, bluish-white metal with an atomic weight of 65·38 and a melting point of 419° C. It occurs as calamine, $ZnCO_3$, and zinc blende, ZnS, and is extracted by roasting the ore to form the oxide, which is then reduced with carbon, and the resulting zinc distilled. It is malleable at 100–200° C and is unaffected by alkalis, but will dissolve in dilute solutions of most acids. It should be noted, however, that both zinc and aluminium will dissolve in caustic solutions, such as lye, caustic soda and caustic cyanide, which should be avoided for cleaning purposes.

The element aluminium, Al, is a light, white metal, ductile and malleable; atomic weight 26·98; melting point 658·7° C. It occurs widely in nature in clays, etc., and is extracted mainly from bauxite by electrolysis of a molten mixture of purified bauxite and cryolite. It is unaffected by most acids but is vigorously attacked by alkalis.

The principles underlying lithographic printing were thoroughly studied and evaluated by F. J. Tritton, who published his findings in the September 1932 issue of the *Journal of the Society of Chemical Industries*. His findings were as follows:

'In the case of metal plates lithography is based essentially on the adsorption (concentration of a substance on a surface, such as molecules of a gas or of a dissolved or suspended substance on the surface of a solid) of fatty acids by the metal, while the non-image areas are kept free from ink by gum arabic, which is apparently also adsorbed on to the metal. The chemical action of sensitizers has been examined, and they have been shown to produce basic substances on the face of the plates, which substances are therefore capable of adsorbing fatty acids. Lithographic etches produce non-polar deposits not capable of adsorbing an acid, while both contact angle and lithographic experiments have been used to demonstrate that, in the absence of adsorption, water is capable of displacing greases from the surface of litho plates; thus for the first time it is possible to explain the real difference between grease receptive and water receptive lithographic surfaces. The majority of etches form films of aluminium phosphate or zinc aluminium phosphate on these two metals.'

My revered tutor in Manchester, C. W. Gamble, lucidly stated the different meanings of adsorption and absorption. 'Adsorption means the adhesion of the substance to the surface of the body, whilst the word absorption is intended to convey that one body fills up the interstices of another body, as water fills up a sponge.'

Gum arabic is a gum that is exuded from certain species of acacia, and is hygroscopic, attracting and holding moisture. The term *desensitise* is used to describe its action. When dampened it renders the surface of the plate or stone insensitive to grease, its function for both materials being the same, but the principle of adhesion differing. With litho stone the gum is absorbed into the stone, quite deeply, which also applies to the ink image, resulting in a strong, relatively indestructible, hydrophilic, grease-repelling surface in the non-image parts. Weak nitric acid application increases the hold of the gum on the stone by opening up the pores to enable the gum to penetrate more thoroughly. It is suggested that the chemical reactions between the gum etch and the stone is secondary to the strong physical bond which occurs. This is noted in particular when grinding a stone and preparing it for another image.

The surface of zinc and aluminium is not penetrated by acacia gum. In this instance the gum forms an adsorbed film on the surface. The adhesion is limited, and is more easily removed than on stone, by abrasion or chemical action. Thus metal plates are not as robust as stone in standing up to rough or careless treatment. Gum arabic is not of itself an effective desensitiser of plates and its efficiency is improved by the addition of phosphoric acid to convert it to arabic acid, which is adsorbed closer to the surface of the plate. It should be observed that in the instance of metal plates the desensitising is carried out, to a greater extent, by the chemical reaction between the acid and the gum and the plate surface. A few drops of phenol (carbolic acid C_6H_5OH) added to the gum solution prevents it losing its desensitising qualities by going sour.

Zinc and aluminium, in thin metal sheets, are in general use today. They are thin and flexible, to wrap easily around the cylinder. The thickness depends upon the machine size, for example, 0·030 in. for 17 in. × 22 in. presses and 0·025 in. for 52 in. × 76 in. machines. Some plates are as thin as 0·004 in. for small offset work. Plates 0·030 in. thick were used on older type presses. Uniform thickness is essential, with a gauge tolerance for the larger size plates of ±0·001 in. Whilst the use of zinc plates is more general, aluminium plates are being increasingly employed, with anodised aluminium widely used for offset work in this country.

The two metals have many similarities, with little difference in cost. Zinc is the more grease-receptive, making it better suited for drawn work. It also stretches more before breaking – this stretchability being sometimes useful to correct mis-register. Zinc plates can stretch permanently when fastened round the cylinder for printing, and if one plate goes more than the others in colour work, register problems arise. Aluminium has a similar hardness for printing purposes and is less than half the weight of zinc, but, whilst less cumbersome, also requires greater care in handling to avoid kinks which, once formed, cannot be entirely eliminated. Being more water-receptive than zinc, aluminium can be more completely desensitised and it runs clean and sharp on the press. Where the chloride content of the water is high, aluminium plates tend to oxide and scum. Being the whiter and brighter metal allows fine detail to be more visible to the printer on aluminium plates. This, plus its resistance to stretch and lightness, are distinct advantages.

Apart from zinc and aluminium, other metals have been introduced. Chromium, plated on steel or alloyed to form stainless steel, is used for bimetallic and trimetallic plates where maximum water wettability is required. Copper and brass, which have higher contact angles than chromium, and therefore form very good image materials where minimum water wettability is required, are used for multimetal plates. Nickel and nickel-phosphide for non-image areas and paper 'plates' are recent innovations. The latter is a speciality product of the paper mills and includes resins for dimensional stability, fine grain coating, with special gelatins and synthetic materials incorporated. On removal from the package, the required image for printing is typed, drawn, or printed in position.

HISTORY AND DEVELOPMENT

SINCE SENEFELDER established the basic principles of planographic printing in 1798 many hundreds of people have contributed to the progress and development of photomechanical methods. A brief mention of outstanding dates and contributors is shown overleaf.

1727	J. H. Schulze	Discovered that chemical compounds of silver are sensitive to light.
1798	Alois Senefelder	Invented Lithography.
1802	Thomas Wedgwood and Sir Humphry Davy	Investigated the light sensitive properties of silver salts. Prints on paper coated with silver nitrate and silver chloride (unfixed).
1804	H. W. Eberland	Grained metal plates with an abrasive.
1813 (1824–26)	Joseph Nicéphore Niépce	Experimented with sensitising lithographic stones. Earliest photographs using camera obscura; bitumen prints on metal etched to give intaglio plates.
1819	John Herschell	Showed that sodium thiosulphate constituted an effective fixing agent, providing the means for removing unexposed silver salts from developed images.
1839	Mungo Ponton	Permanent image on bichromated paper.
	Louis Daguerre	Daguerreotype and practical photography evolved. Mercury development of silver iodide latent image.
	Hullmandel	Colour lithographic process.
	Dr Andrew Fyfe	Key image on litho-stone with silver phosphate.
1840/ 1841	Fox Talbot	Calotype process. Negatives printed on salted paper sensitised with silver nitrate using silver iodide and gallic acid for increased sensitivity and fixing with hypo. Latent image developed to a negative used for positive printing – thus the real beginning of practical photography.
1841	Joseph Dixon	Direct photolithography using dichromated gum.
1851	Frederick Scott Archer	Welt collodion photography.
1852– 1858	Fox Talbot	Photoglyphy. An early form of photogravure: experiments connected with dichromated gelatin: first screen experiments using a gauze to produce a dot formation.
1852	Barreswil, Davanne, Lemercier and Lerebours	Direct photolitho by bitumen of Judea developed with turpentine.
1854	Paul Pretsch	Swelled gelatin process.
1855	Louise Alphonse Poitevin	Advocated the use of dichromated colloids of gelatin, glue, albumen, or gum for the formation of printing images. Direct photolitho with gelatin. Film inked after wetting. (first patent for collotype).
	A. J. Berchtold	First vignetted contact screen.
1859	W. Osborne of Melbourne	Photolitho transfer to stone using dichromated gelatin and albumen.
	E. I. Asser of Amsterdam	Photolitho transfer. Dichromated starch on unsized paper, exposed, heated, moistened and rolled up.
1860	Colonel Sir Henry James and Captain Scott	Photozincography. Photolitho transfer from a developed gelatin image.

1861	J. Clerk Maxwell	Three-colour photography by additive synthesis.
1864	W. B. Woodbury	Woodburytype lead mould made from high gelatin relief. Prints on paper in coloured gelatin.
1865	Tessié du Motay	Photo-collotype. Exposed gelatin film damped and inked. With C. R. Maréchal early collotype on copper base.
	Sir Joseph W. Swan	Carbon method of photographic printing.
	E. and J. Bullock	Suggested use of a ruled screen in the camera.
1868	Louis Ducos du Hauron	Patent for three colour printing, after establishing the principle of subtractive synthesis in 1862.
1868/ 1869	Dr Josef Albert	Basic collotype on glass plate.
1869/ 1870	Ernest Edwards	Heliotype, Collotype with dichromated gelatin, chrome alum stripped film.
1871	Dr R. L. Maddox	Gelatin Dry Plate. Photographic emulsion.
1872	C. Gillot	Line etching process relief printing.
1873	John Burgess	Manufactured commercial gelatinobromide dry plates and *Herman Vogel* introduced dyes to colour sensitise.
1878	Charles Petit and F. E. Ives	Patented independently systems of obtaining halftone relief images.
1879	Karl Klic	Resin dust grained photogravure.
1882	George Meisenbach	Halftone process with single line screen.
1886	F. E. Ives	Introduced the cross-line screen and, in 1890, the Kromskop projection and viewing instruments.
1890	Karl Klic	Rotogravure using crossline screen.
1893	Louis and Max Levy	Patented a halftone screen made by a combination of engraving and etching.
1894	Max Levy	Expounded the diffraction theory of halftone photography.
1895	Etienne Deville	Postulated the penumbral theory of halftone reproduction.
1901	F. R. Vandyke	Patented the Vandyke Reversal Process.
1902	A. Schulze	Devised the rhomboid halftone screen.
1904	Ira Rubel	Introduced offset printing on paper.
1907	M. M. Lumiere	Autochrome screen plate.
1908	W. C. Huebner and G. Bleistein	Three patents for a step-and-repeat machine.
1910	Dr Edward Mertens	Rotary intaglio halftone.

II

Planning and Imposition

TYPE FACES AND SIZES

THERE ARE literally thousands of type faces used in printing, and the first distinction is to be made between capital letters and small letters. Capitals are termed *caps* or *upper case* and the small letters are called *lower case*. Type is also classified according to its size and the style of letter that it carries. Large letters are called *display* or *headline* type and the small sizes are called *body* or *text* type. The setting of type is called *composition* and the assembling and arranging of type into pages or formes is known as *make-up*. Positioning and spacing the pages so that they will print correctly in relationship to each other on the printing press is known as *imposition*, and the smooth iron-topped table on which formes are imposed and locked-up is called an *imposing* table or *stone*.

A normal series of foundry types consists of sizes 6 to 72 points. The full range of type sizes is 3 to 144 points. The British-American point system is based on a *pica* of 0·16604 in., which is divided into twelve equal parts, termed *points*, each measuring 0·013837 in. For practical purposes the *pica* is assumed to be 0·166 in., giving six picas to the inch with the *point* 0·014 in. Thus 12 points = 1 pica, 6 picas = 1 in. (0·996 of an inch).

Leads and *slugs* are strips of line-spacing materials. If less than six points in thickness they are known as *leads*; if six points or over they are classified as *slugs*.

Quads and *spaces* are the separation material used between letters and words. The *em quad* is the square of a given body size; the *en quad* is half the square width and the *thick space* and *middle space* are a third and a quarter respectively of the width of the *em quad*.

Type faces are grouped into *families*. Each family has a name and certain basic family resemblances – some families have dozens of different type faces (Caslon, Bodoni, Baskerville, Plantin, etc.).

A final classification is the different kinds or groups of type faces of which there are, in the main, six different groups. Roman, Gothic, Script, Text, Italic and Contemporary.

Roman type faces are easy to read in the smaller type sizes and therefore are often used for the text of newspapers, magazines and books.

They are divided into two classifications – *modern* and *old style*, with the main difference being found in the *serifs* (the cross-strokes at the ends of the main lines). The old style letter has soft, rounded serifs, the modern letter has heavier shadings, with thin, clean-cut hairlines. Script and cursive type faces are generally grouped together. Scripts have little connecting links or *kerns* combining the letters to give the appearance of handwriting. Cursive letters are without these *kerns*. Italics are slanting letters and *swash* letters are similar to italics, but embellished by additional swirls and curves known as swashes. Gothic letters are constructed of lines of even weight, perfectly plain without serifs, and could be called block letters. Roman letters, on the other hand, are composed of a series of thick and thin lines.

Text type faces are of the style worked almost exclusively by Gutenberg and are sometimes known as 'Old English'. Leading the contemporary field are the *square serif* and the *sans serif*. These are new styles, with the sans serif being a kind of gothic type without serifs but of perfect geometric proportions and the last word in simplicity. The square serif is in essence the same serif with serifs added, having the same even strokes and splendid geometric proportions.

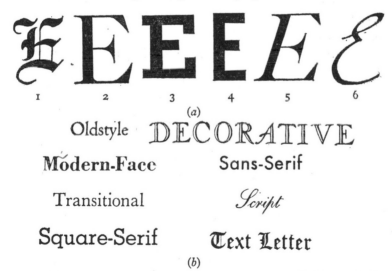

(*a*)

Oldstyle   DECORATIVE

Modern-Face   Sans-Serif

Transitional   *Script*

Square-Serif   Text Letter

(*b*)

Fig. 1 (*a*) 1 Text; 2 Roman; 3 Contemporary; 4 Gothic; 5 Italic; 6 Script. (*b*) Type faces

STANDARD PAPER SIZES

THE BRITISH Standard – B.S. 3176 (1959) and 730 (1960) – sizes of printing and writing papers are shown on the following page.

Foolscap 13½ in. × 17 in.

Foolscap, Oblong Double
    13½ in. × 34 in.

Pinched Post 14½ in. × 18½ in.

Large Post 16½ in. × 21 in.

Foolscap, Double 17 in. × 27 in.

Foolscap, Quad 27 in × 34 in.

Post 15¼ in. × 19 in.

Post, Double 19 in. × 30½ in.

Large Post, Double 21 in. × 33 in.

Demy 17½ in. × 22½ in.

Demy, Double 22½ in. × 35 in.

Medium 18 in. × 23 in.

Royal 20 in. × 25 in.

Crown 15 in × 20 in.

Crown, Double 20 in. × 30 in.

Imperial 22 in. × 30 in.

Demy, Quad 35 in. × 45 in.

Medium, Double 23 in. × 36 in.

Royal, Double 25 in. × 40 in.

Crown, Quad 30 in. × 40 in.

Imperial, Double 30 in. × 44 in.

Note: Double and quadruple sizes are exact multiples of the standard sizes. To find a double size the rule is to double the smaller dimension: For an oblong double size, double the larger dimension, and in quadruple size, double each dimension. Thus large sheets are based on multiples of standard sizes and a double size sheet implies a sheet twice the area of a 'broadside' or standard size sheet. Also a quadruple-size sheet implies four times the area of a standard size sheet.

Sub-divisions

Folio – given size	one half sheet; found by dividing the long side by two.
Quarto (4to)	one quarter sheet; found by dividing both dimensions by two.
Octavo (8vo)	one eighth sheet; found by dividing the long side by four and the short side by two.
Sextodecimo (16mo)	one sixteenth part of the sheet found by dividing both sides by four.
Trigesimo-secundo (32mo)	32 leaves or 64 pages; folded in eight, long way of sheet; in four, short way of sheet.
Sexto	size indicated is one sixth part of a sheet, the long dimension being divided by three and the short dimension by two.
Long Octavo	When specified as 'long', the sheet is divided in the opposite way – the long side divided by two and the short side by four.
Double	Refers to the fact that the short dimension of a broadsheet is multiplied by two.
Quad	Denotes that both sides of the sheet are multiplied by two.

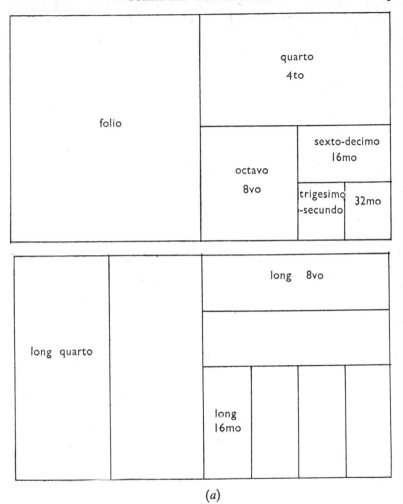

(*a*)

Fig. 2 (*a*) Common sub-division of a broadside sheet

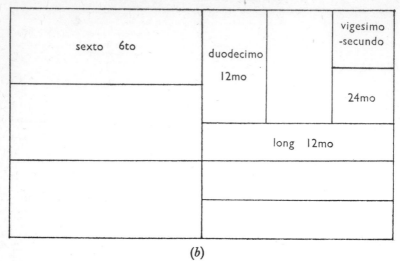

(b)

Fig. 2 (b) Further sub-division of a paper sheet

International Paper Sizes (D.I.N. – Deutsche Industrie Normen)

MANY EUROPEAN countries have accepted these standards and the B.S.I. are using the new 'A' standard for stationery and pamphlets. The three sizes are A (printing and stationery); B (posters and wall charts); C (envelopes).

The basic size is 'AO', which has an area of one square metre, with its sides in the ratio of $1/\sqrt{2}$. All other sizes are multiples or sub-divisions of this, as shown in the diagram. The other series 'B' and 'C' have basic sizes of 917 mm. × 1297 mm. and 1000 mm. × 1414 mm., respectively. This gives three basic sizes, compared with the present British sizes, which number over a dozen.

CODE	TRIMMED SIZE	
	Millimetres	Inches (approx.)
4Ao	1682 × 2378	66 × 93½
2Ao	1189 × 1682	47 × 66
Ao	841 × 1189 (1 sq. m)	33 × 47
A1	594 × 841	23½ × 33
A2	420 × 594	16½ × 23½
A3	297 × 420	11½ × 16½
A4	210 × 297	8½ × 11½
A5	148 × 210	6 × 8½
A6	105 × 148	4 × 6
A7	74 × 105	3 × 4
A8	52 × 74	2 × 3
A9	37 × 52	1½ × 2
A10	26 × 37	1 × 1½

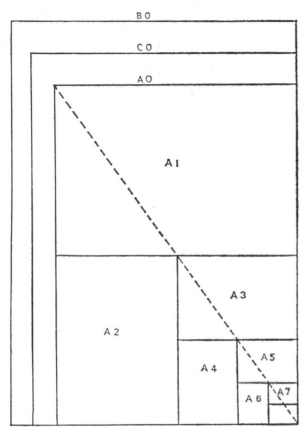

Fig. 3 Sub-divisions of international (D.I.N.) paper sizes

The arrangement of pages on the printed sheet is dictated by the requirements of the finishing process. The order and position of the pages depend upon the number of pages, the type of paper whether hand or machine folding applies, plus, in bookwork, the peculiarities of a particular folding machine and the method of binding. In lithography the arrangement of work, before the negatives or positives are printed, goes under the broad classification of planning; in letterpress work the older term imposition is used.

PRINT TERMINOLOGY

GENERAL TERMINOLOGY relative to the above includes the terms and expressions, together with their meanings as shown overleaf.

Backing-up (or perfecting) – Printing on the second side of a sheet already printed on its first side.

Backing pages – Pages printed back to back – such as the even folio (8) backing to the odd folio (7).

Bleed – Work which runs off the edge of the page.

Broadside – A full sheet of standard size paper or any full sheet which has not been sub-divided.

Facing pages – Pages facing each other when the sheet is folded – such as the odd folio (23) facing the even folio (22).

Folio – The page number or the half-size of a standard sheet.

Foredge – The edge of a page opposite the back – margin formed when the sheet is folded and trimmed.

Gripper edge – The space required on the edge of the paper that enters the machine first, to accommodate the grippers of the press.

Gutter – The margin between the sides of the two pairs of pages positioned side by side (two foredges).

Heads – The amount of space between two pages positioned head to head, including the trim.

Tails – The amount of space between two pages laid foot to foot, including the trim.

Sheet work is the term used to indicate that two formes are used to print the sheet, sometimes called 'work and back'. Half-sheet work, often called 'work and turn', means that all the pages of a sheet are planned in one unit. 'Work and twist' is a method used with either of the above methods, as it has nothing to do with backing-up. The sheet is either turned right round, presenting a new pair of lay-edges to grippers and side-lay, or partly turned. Tumbler impositions are used when the job pecularities make the normal half-sheet work impracticable.

In preparing a layout sheet it is essential to know whether the pages are to be guillotined clean or whether a trim is required between pages to allow for folding or bleeding. Allowance must also be made in book-work for trim, and thus the positioning of pages on a press plate to give correct page sequence. Accurate and even margins are essential.

'Work and turn' printing infers the printing of both sides of the stock from one plate. This is done by first printing half the run on one side of the paper, then reversing the paper from left to right, by turning it over sideways, to complete the printing.

'Work and tumble' printing means that impressions are printed on both sides of the sheet from the same plate or forme as above, with the difference that in 'work and turn' the sheets turn over from left to right, the side guide being changed but not the gripper edge. For 'work and tumble' both edges of the paper are fed to the gripper, top edge then bottom edge.

'Work and twist' printing indicates that after the work has gone through the press once, the paper is both tumbled over top to bottom and also twisted around so that the left-hand side becomes the right-hand side. This involves a considerable time factor in registering on the press, hence unless a long run is contemplated, this method is uneconomical.

With sheet work, after one side of a sheet has been printed, the forme is removed and the second forme, to print the reverse side of the sheet, is positioned on the press. Thus with a 'work and tumble' job, the paper must be carefully squared by cutting before the printing run. This means adjusting the gripper on the press, which with the extra work of cutting and preparing is again time consuming.

LAYOUT AND IMPOSITION

THE SIMPLEST layout of pages would be a 4-page folder like the following:

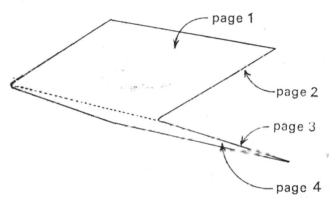

Fig. 4A A sheet of paper folded to form a 4-page folder

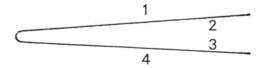

Fig. 4B Side view of 4-page folder

Pages 1 and 4 would be on the outside and pages 2 and 3 on the inside. Pages 1 and 4 are therefore known as outside pages, pages 2 and 3 as inside pages. More pages could be added by taking further sheets and folding in a similar manner.

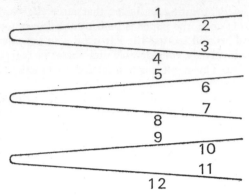

Fig. 5 Side view of 4-page folder when further
4-page sections have been added

The pages can be grouped in two columns, as follows:

Outside	Inside
1	2
4	3
5	6
8	7
9	10
12	11
13	14
16	15

This can be continued as required; the outside pages will always be on one side of a sheet, or one half of a half-sheet scheme, the inside pages being on the other side of the sheet, or the other half of a half-sheet scheme.

The arrangement of pages depends on the manner in which the sheet is to be folded. For convenience, the basic rules are based on hand folding. When folding the long edge of the sheet is at right angles to the body of the person folding the sheet and rests on a flat table in front of this person. The sheet is laid face down, with page one positioned at the left-hand, bottom corner. The right-hand side is then brought over to meet the left-hand side. The folded sheet is turned, with page 1 still at the left hand. The folding is then repeated. The number of folds is limited by the bulk of the paper and the size of the pages.

The layouts used here show the actual printed sheet, which is done to simplify procedure and prevent any confusion of thought. This is contrary to the usual imposition schemes shown in typographical text books, which always show the arrangement of the type – itself the printing surface. In lithography, with negatives and positives, planning can take place at either stage.

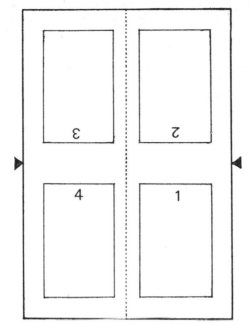

Fig. 6 An imposition scheme for half-sheet work. The four pages are upright. The sheet when printed on both sides will be cut into two at the point indicated by the black triangle

Basic rules for a 4-page half-sheet working are as follows:

(*a*) Page 1 is in the bottom right-hand corner with the foot towards the outside of the sheet.

(*b*) Page 2 is at the opposite corner on the same long side of the sheet.

(*c*) Pages 3 and 4 follow in the same direction as 1 and 2 which, in this instance, is anticlockwise.

(*d*) The first and last pages are always a pair.

(*e*) The centre pair of pages are head to head with the front and back pages.

(*f*) Each pair of pages, added together, total one more than the number of pages in the layout. In a 4-page layout this is five, in an 8-page layout this would be nine.

(*g*) Inside pages are in one half of the layout, with all the outside pages in the other half.

(*h*) The long edge of the sheet is the gripper edge. This edge is still gripped when the sheet is turned and backed up.

From the above basic 4-page half-sheet work layout it is possible to build up 8-, 16-, 32-, 64- and 128-page layouts if so required. It is quite impossible, for example, to memorise a 128-page layout if this particular number of pages is not in regular use. But it is relatively simple to remember a few basic rules in conjunction with the 4-page layout.

The sheet for 4 pages has been drawn in the upright position. For an 8-page layout the sheet should be shown with the long edge in the horizontal position.

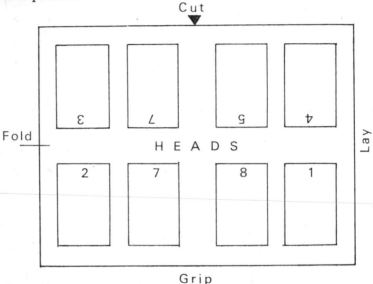

Fig. 7 Eight-page upright printed half-sheet work

The cut for the sheet must be marked on the long side. The outside pages are laid out on the right-hand half of the sheet, exactly as the pages in the 4-page layout. The page numbers have been doubled and for the original odd page numbers, where this applies, one is deducted from the product. When the outside pages have been laid, then the basic rules are used. Rule (*b*) gives page 2 in the opposite corner to page 1, on the same long edge. The top left-hand corner is the position for page 3, because it is obvious from the sequence of pages 1 and 2 that they are in a clockwise direction. An additional guiding principle (rule (*i*)) can be useful here.

(*i*) The second quarter of the layout follows the first quarter, but in the opposite directional sequence.

In the 8-page layout 1, 2, 3, 4 are clockwise, therefore it follows that 5, 6, 7, 8 must be anticlockwise. This is uncomplicated, because the positions of 5 and 8 have already been fixed. A check shows that each pair of pages adds up to nine. The first and last pages are together, the centre pages are in a pair and head to head with the first and last pages.

Automatically it is a natural step forward to consider a 16-page layout.

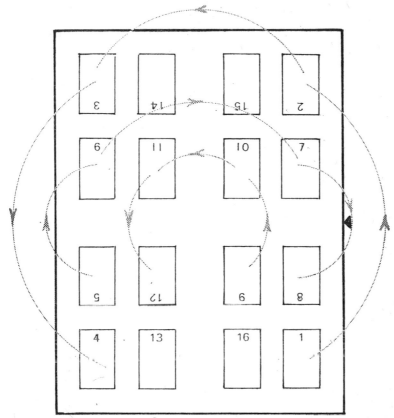

Fig. 8 Sixteen-page half-sheet work showing clockwise and anticlockwise arrangement of page positions

The sheet is drawn upright with the lower half, the outside pages following the layout of the 8-page scheme.

When landscape pages are arranged, the layout is slightly different because certain rules do not apply. On reflection, it is possible to follow the sequence of the page numbers (Fig. 9).

Rule (b) cannot be followed because page 2 is on the same side, that is, the short side and not the long side as before. This is peculiar to this particular page layout. The other rules will apply, that is, first and last pages pair, the inside pages pair, and the pairs of page numbers add up to one more than the total number of pages in the layout. In this layout

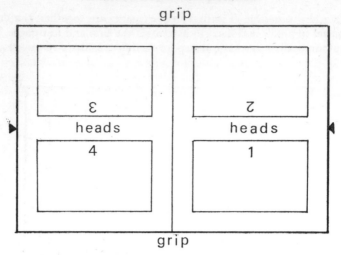

Fig. 9 Four-page landscape printed half-sheet work

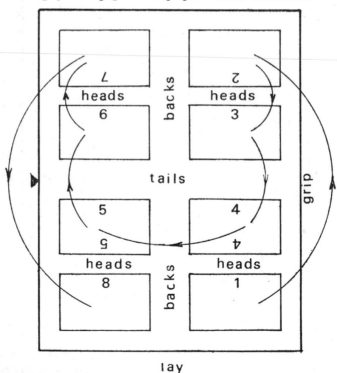

Fig. 10 Eight-page landscape printed half-sheet work

the two grip edges are marked. This is because the scheme is called a 'work and tumble', the sheet being turned over so that the opposite long edge becomes the gripper edge and with the same short side still being the side lay edge. An 8-page landscape can be laid out from this basic 4-page scheme in the same way as a 4-page upright to an 8-page upright.

With the outside pages positioned, it is possible to fit in the inside pages – 2, 3, 6 and 7. Page 2 is on the same side, opposite corner to page 1. The corner on the short side must have the last page, that is, page 8, because pages 1 and 8 are paired. It follows that page 2 must now be on the long side on the opposite corner to page 1. The position of page 3 is now undecided, but the only logical position is between pages 2 and 4. The same sequence can be used to allocate the position of pages 6 and 7. Alternatively, the page position can be determined by checking that the pairs of pages add up to 9.

Work that is of a very large page size may not be a practical proposition to print half-sheet work, neither is this always convenient for short-run work. Sheet work can be made from the half-sheet work layout, by laying the pages out in the same way, but putting all the outside pages on one plate, and all the inside pages on another plate.

A 12-page layout scheme can be treated in many different ways, being, for instance, printed half-sheet work, then cut and folded as a 4-page and an 8-page section. The 8-page section, being the heavier, fits into the 4-page section.

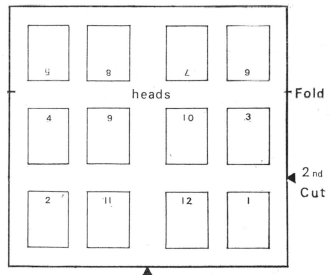

Fig. 11 Twelve-page upright with offcut. The sheet is cut as indicated to fold as 8-page and 4-page sections

If the 12-page layout is folded as a complete sheet, then there are as many layout schemes possible as there are ways of folding the paper. With a 12-page scheme it is only necessary to visualise the paper being folded, and then to apply the appropriate rules as shown in the following series of diagrams.

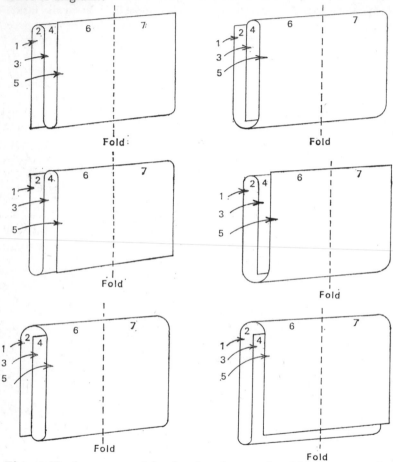

Fig. 12 Twelve-page upright showing six ways in which paper can be folded. The arrows point to pages that face away from the viewer

To ensure that all the pages are square, and in the correct relationship to each other and the sheet edges, accurate marking equipment is required. An accurate marking-up light table with T-square and guide edges is essential. This enables both layout and patched-up photographic material to be checked for backing-up, etc.

III
Preparation of Copy for Reproduction

SUITABILITY OF COPY

THE CONSIDERATION of originals for reproduction has been discussed previously.* Copy is classified into two main groups, either line or tone. Line copy includes pen-and-ink drawings, scraper boards, technical illustrations, engineers' plans and reproduction proofs from type matter. Artwork is preferred one third, one half to twice the size of the final reproduction size. This minimises slight imperfections and crudeness in the original. Copy should not be prepared too large for the copyboard and, if possible, should not exceed 25 to 50% reduction or enlargement. Fine line and crayon drawings are, for preference, drawn to be reproduced same size. The surface drawn upon should be smooth and white. All lines should be solid black, firmly drawn with sharp, clean edges and thickness of lines should allow for reduction in size. The photographic material for line reproduction is designed to distinguish only between jet black and pure white. Contrast values less positive can result in imperfect reproductions. Instructions should be on an overlay or written in blue pencil. Whites on solids are more sharply and clearly reproduced by camera or chemical reversal methods from black on white copy. Dot or stipple tints can be inserted on the copy by the use of adhesive materials or added in reproduction by using strip film, printing in, flashing, etc. Ben Day tinting mediums are not often used today.

Tone copy is generally in the form of black-and-white bromide prints. These should be black, not toned, on smooth white paper with good detail in both shadows and highlights. Fluorescent and high-gloss paper is not normally required and unglazed glossy paper is suitable. Ivory, cream and other off-white surfaces should be avoided and the more textured and duller the surface, the less brilliance and detail will be obtained in the negative. Some smooth, semi-matt prints give fair results, but, in general, sepia tone prints, matt-surface prints and hand-coloured prints should be avoided.

THE AIRBRUSH

THE RETOUCHING of copy is a highly skilled process. If the retoucher knows his job he will select only the obvious and crucial areas

* Eric Chambers, *Camera and Process Work*, Chapter 3, Ernest Benn, 1964.

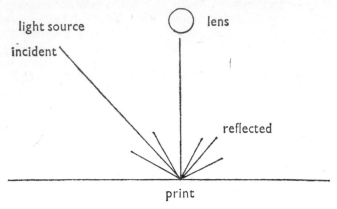

Fig. 13A Light scatter by uneven surface

for correction and treat them with minimum effect. It is easy to over-retouch and produce an artificial rendering of the subject. A good retoucher knows from experience just how much emphasis is required to obtain the correct amount of detail and contrast. The air brush is an indispensable tool in the hands of the retoucher. Watercolour, either transparent or opaque, dye, lacquer or other medium, is placed in the cup attached to the airbrush and pressure for spraying is provided by a small compressor. The proper use of the airbrush is characterised by its ability to apply colour in soft, subtle tonal gradation, ranging from the lightest discernible tint to a dense opaque solid.

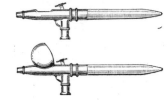

Fig. 13B Standard model (A 504) and large Reservoir air brush (model E 504). The Aero-graph–De Vilbiss Company Ltd

The two basic types of airbrush are the single-action and the double-action type. With the first, the medium flow is done by one action – pressing down on the finger lever. A flow regulator is incorporated for fine or coarse effects with a fixed spray pattern. The double-action airbrush controls the spray action by two actions – pressing down the finger lever and pulling back to control the spray pattern – the further back the coarser the spray. As the airbrush is held further away from the work and the finger lever pulled back a wider band of spray pattern with the edges fading more gradually would result. If a sharp edge of colour is required, a mask of paper or acetate is cut to the required shape and positioned before air brushing. To soften the edge, raise the mask slightly off the surface when spraying. Complicated areas to be air brushed require the use of friskets – sheets of thin tracing of frisket-paper, covered with rubber cement, laid over the image. The frisket is cut away and removed from the part to be airbrushed, and the area sprayed. Masking tape and liquid friskets, which are painted on the print and peeled off after use, are also used.

The air pressure required for spraying water colours is from 20 to 30 pounds per square inch and 35 to 40 pounds for process black and white, designers' colours or oil colours. It is inadvisable to use a higher pressure than is necessary to atomise finely the material being sprayed as the higher the pressure, the greater the risk of lifting stencils, friskets and the like. The air supply should be maintained at a uniform pressure, otherwise the texture obtained will be uneven because the atomisation coarsens as the pressure drops. The nearer the instrument is held to the surface, the sharper and narrower will be the lines produced. For very fine lines the air brush may even touch the paper lightly if it is held at a slight angle.

KROMO-LITE, BOURGES AND COLOTONE OVERLAYS

SPECIAL PROCESSES for the elimination of backgrounds and high-lights have been discussed in *Camera and Process Work* (page 124), including the Kemart and the Fluorographic process. The Kromo Lite method of Eastern Graphic Arts Supply is an American method worthy of note. The artist simply uses Kromo-Lite, a colourless solution, instead of water in mixing his medium. This dries exactly as if prepared with water. The latter, mixed with opaque white, is used only where the Kromo-Lite solution has been applied and it is required to eliminate the screen by drop-out. The design is prepared by the artist and before being reproduced on the camera it is sprayed with Kromo-Lite spray solution – which turns the grey wash drawing to a greenish yellow. After processing, a restorer returns it to its original colour. The negative is exposed and screened in the normal way. The screen is then removed and the subject exposed as a line negative using a special filter. This filter causes the yellow portions of the copy to reproduce as black, that is, to absorb the light, thus having no effect on the work. The white areas of the copy reflect light and thus on development the screen dot formation is here eliminated giving a complete highlight halftone negative.

The Bourges Process is the invention of Albert R. Bourges in America. The method seeks to co-ordinate art preparation and the processes preparatory to printing and it covers a whole range of subjects. By the use of a grey Solotone overlay sheet of the required density, and by removing the grey coating for the highlight areas, it is possible, by overlaying the sheet on the copy before photographing, to add to, or change, the background completely. Solotone sheets are made of different tonal values for white and grey effects. The sheet is taped to the copy and areas not required to be altered are removed with a special wedged-shaped stylus aided by a liquid Coloremover which softens the coating. The process can be used for drop-outs and for line and halftone combinations using a special, clear, acetate sheet on which to prepare the line work, as a separate transparent overlay. For duotone work, separate Solotone grey and white sheets may be used for each colour, removing the coating of these sheets over areas which are to remain unaltered. For example, the foreground can be made lighter on the black plate using a white sheet and a 50% grey sheet substituted to deepen the sky before making the negative for the blue plate. The coating is removed over areas that are to remain unchanged. Added detail, in the form of spraying and drawing with black and white Solotone liquids or pencils, can be carried out on the coating of the sheets.

Pre-separated colour art work can be prepared using Bourges Colotone overlays, which are sheets of dimensionally stable acetate coated with removable colour films. These Bourges sheets are available in standard process colours – yellow, magneta and cyan. A matching range of 60 colours, consisting of 12 basic inks made in 10, 30, 50, 70 and 100% values, are made. Liquid colours and modelling pencils giving the full strength of these colours are used to model tones and gradations on the sheets. Adhesive sheets are made primarily for layout and spot colour separation overlays. Overlay Colotone sheets are made for general separation copy work and for colour correction of transparencies and artwork. By superimposing the separate coloured overlays, the artist has a visual check on colour values and colour renderings which equate with the actual printing colour. The overlays can be used with transparencies, by attaching the coloured transparent sheets behind the transparency, to correct local colour by making it brighter or warmer or cooler. They can also be utilised to increase contrast and correct the overall colour balance.

For line separation copy, Transopaque is marketed. This is a transparent red-orange coated sheet on a high quality 0·005 in. plastic. The material has the same photographic quality as black, but allows the artist to see through the overlay as he is working. It is removable, a wedge-shaped stylus taking away the colour cleanly and sharply and a fine point, steel wool, etc., can be used to produce fine lines and textures.

The artist removes the coating for the areas where he does not want the colour, using the stylus, the Coloremover, etc., according to the line effect desired. There is also a Transopaque liquid which can be used in brush or pen to add fine line detail. The sheet can also be utilised as part of the copy where a dot tint is to be recorded. When photographed it will appear a clear and transparent window on the negative, over which a mechanical tint can be positioned before printing down.

CONVERSION METHODS FROM TYPE

IN THE past the majority of copy preparation or composition for reproduction originated in metal type for letterpress or direct printing. Hand composing and mechanical typesetting were exclusively part of the letterpress method of printing. The advent of photocomposition with the development of the Fotosetter, the Linofilm, the Monophoto, the Photon, the Justowriter, etc., has changed this. With the growth of offset and gravure photocomposition has made rapid advances, and a knowledge of these methods, which is outside the scope of this book, should be obtained because they hold the key, with tabular and electronic methods, to the future.

In a general sense conversion is any change, transition, or transfer of type or image from one medium to another. The most common conversion from letterpress is made from a good reproduction proof, which becomes copy and is photographed in the normal way for plate-making. Transparent proofs are sometimes pulled and dusted with powdered iron oxide to give opacity. Also translucent proofs pulled on a special light-weight baryta-coated paper, which has a base of alpha cellulose and an emulsion coating of gelatin and pure precipitated barium sulphate. A contact negative is made from this translucent proof in a vacuum or contact printing frame.

The Brightype (Ludlow) method is a fairly recent innovation. The method is based on direct photography from the type forme. The forme – containing type and blocks – is surface cleaned and tin plated with a small electroplating hand brush and sprayed with a special non-reflecting, quick-drying, black lacquer. The printing face is then polished to remove the lacquer from it, and positioned on the Brightype camera board, the chase is clamped and the unit raised to a vertical position and photographed. The light source, consisting of an array of incandescent bulbs rotating around the camera lens, gives sharp, even, frontal illumination of the reflecting metal surface of the type forme.

Negative Conversion. Reproduction proofs on paper can be transferred into same-size negatives without the medium of a camera or a darkroom. The process, evolved by the Printing Arts Research Laboratories Inc., California, consists in making a repro-proof and covering with a sheet of special film. The combination is placed in a vacuum platen and briefly heated to about 140° F, after which the negative is developed by wiping over with a clearing solution and it is then ready for printing down to a litho plate. A special low-tack ink contains chemicals which act on the film emulsion. The ink has a slight penetrating action on glycerine composition and urethane rollers which should be replaced by rubber or polyvinyl rollers of the type suitable for use with glycol inks. The heat releases chemicals from the ink which penetrate the film emulsion in the areas where it has direct contact and the chemicals make the emulsion dissolvable so that the image area becomes translucent when the clearing solution is applied. The heat is administered for about thirty to fifty seconds and the chemicals, transferred to the emulsion from the ink, are loosened by the clearing solution and wiped away to leave clear areas on the orange-coloured film, through which exposures can be made. The definition is sharp and grainless and dries immediately. It is wiped with a hardening agent, to protect it from scratches and abrasions, before printing down to metal. The repro. proof should be placed in the platen and heated in contact with the special plastic film within twenty minutes of being pulled in the low tack ink.

The Cronapress Conversion System is also simple and straightforward. The metal relief image to be converted to film is first placed on the vibration platform of the Du Pont Cronapress No. 1 clarifying machine and a sheet of Cronapress conversion film, which consists of a cellular, pressure-sensitive coating on one side of a 0·05 mm. sheet of clear Cronar polyester film base, is placed emulsion side down on the relief metal plate or forme. The thin coating is opaque (milky white) in appearance and is not light sensitive. A vacuum frame covered with a 'mylar' polyester film and a frame containing over 10,000 tiny steel or lead balls are locked into position over the conversion film and metal plate or forme. Vacuum is applied to bring the respective surfaces into intimate contact and conversion takes place by vibration created by the machine's motor and eccentric cams setting the circular balls into action. The bouncing balls strike the conversion film surface at random, resulting in millions of impacts before conversion is complete (6–8 minutes). Each ball makes a mark on every impact and whilst each weighs only a small fraction of an ounce this point contact produces a momentary pressure of about 3 tons per square inch. The contacts completely overlap to ensure overall controlled pressure which collapses the cellular coating where it is in contact with the type or screen dot, fusing the coating together to produce translucent areas. The conversion film covering the nonprinting areas of the relief image remains opaque or unclarified. The final result is a high-fidelity reproduction of the relief areas of the metal plate or forme with a transparent image area and a milky-white background. After the conversion time is over, the clarifier switches off automatically. The vacuum pump is switched off and the converted film is peeled from the surface of the relief metal giving a low-density range negative, the background density of which is increased for contact printing to 4·0 by applying a special black dye (supplied by DuPont) to the layer side of the film. A broad soft brush is used for this purpose and the dye is absorbed and dries in about 45 seconds on the sponge-like surface. To make the dye permanent it is treated with a wad of cotton wool soaked in a special stabilising solution for about 30 seconds. The principle is that the cells of the unclarified areas of the film, which are still white and opaque, absorb the dye, making the film dense black and opaque, whilst the transparent image areas remain clear and transparent because the cellular structure has been removed by friction with the bouncing balls and therefore absorbs no black dye. The stabiliser makes the dye water insoluble, so that the film can be quickly rinsed in water, swabbed to remove residual dye from the film surface and dried. The dry conversion film negative is now ready for printing to metal, or for contact printing to positive form for deep etch plate making.

Scotchprint. This printing stock conversion system has been intro-duced by 3M-Minnesota Mining and Manufacturing Co. Ltd. The material is a grainless translucent plastic film base, coated with a matt ink-receptive surface. It is dimensionally stable and is not light sensitive, so that it keeps indefinitely without stretching, shrinking, curling, 'cracking' or tearing and takes pen, pencil, typing, erasing, rubber cement, ink or wax. Sheet sizes are 9 in. × 12 in., 12 in. × 18 in. and 20 in. × 24 in., with a thickness of 0·0025 in.

The letterpress forme is positioned on the proofing press and the proof pulled at a slow but uniform speed to assure best ink transfer on the coated (matt) side of the Scotchprint. A short, thick, dense ink is recommended, with hard underpacking which must not contain emboss-ing from previous formes. To obtain maximum detail from a good forme, pack the press with quality manila underpacking and back up the Scotchprint with acetate or more Scotchprint. Synthetic rollers are pre-ferred for inking because of their durability and uniformity under varied temperature and humidity conditions. Minor imperfections in the proof can be corrected using a pen or brush. Drying time is slightly longer than for paper and warm air up to 110° F can be used.

Make the contact film on a high contrast (lith) orthochromatic film, exposing so that the light passes through the Scotchprint proof to the sensitive film. Exposure is about 50% more than for normal film to film contacting; develop using 'lith' developer in the usual manner. The result is a negative, obtained quickly and easily without the use of a camera. The Scotchprint image can be used with autopositive material and a yellow filter (four times normal exposure) to transpose from black to white, and it can also be reproduced on the camera, positioned on black, non-glossy paper, to enlarge or reduce the image.

The material is dimensionally stable to a temperature of 150° F. Infra-red heating units should not be used for drying because differential heating occurs between printed and non-printed areas causing warping of the sheet. Subject matter for reproduction can be typed on Scotchprint using IBM Electric typewriter – PF-75 ribbon (silk and nylon ribbons unsuitable) – and adjusting to minimum pressure to prevent slurring of characters. With the Friden Justowriter the standard polyethylene carbon ribbon is used and with the Varityper the Variclear 1900 ribbon, using minimum pressure and backing up the Scotchprint with a sheet of bond stock.

LAYOUT AND PLANNING OF ARTWORK

ORIGINALS FOR reproduction should include register marks, which are used to check the fit of negatives, positives and plates in colour work, assist in double printing on metal, enable plates to be registered on the press and used for checking the fit and register of superimpositioned multicolour proofs. Register marks should be centred and at right angles to the subject. The kind indicated, which can be used for negatives or positives, is preferred.

Fig. 14 Register marks

Register ticks should also be included with the subject matter to assist the plate maker and pressman in positioning the printing correctly on the paper. Horizontal and vertical centres with corner trim marks are essential. These should not be thick and clumsy but as finely drawn as possible.

The term 'copy' describes all elements of the artwork used to produce the final printed sheet, and a layout is required of the complete job. This may be a visual rough or something quite comprehensive. The main point is that it must be accurate with regard to size and position of the various elements of the job. It provides a blueprint of what the completed job will be like, and, with the layout, a folding dummy of the actual paper stock, cut, folded and finished in accordance with the required specifications, should be prepared. This assists in assessing bleeds, margins and binding requirements, etc. A duplicate of the final layout, either a tracing or photostat copy, should be pasted in position in the dummy, so that the final completed job can be visualised.

It is recommended and desirable that all artwork should, as far as possible, be assembled into a single master composite copy. This key drawing or paste-up, as it is often called, should at least include all type pulls, line lettering and art work and the various sections should be brought to the required size by, if necessary, making copy negatives and reduced or enlarged bromide prints and tipping them in position. This also applies to portions requiring transposing or reversing from black to white. To assure accuracy, centre marks should be drawn on each paste-

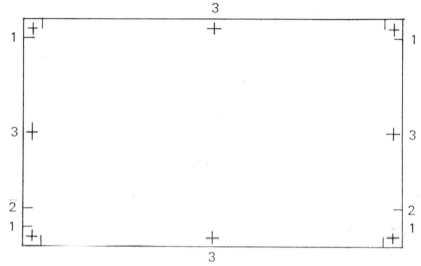

Fig. 15 Plate guide indications: 1, Trim margins; 2, Distance from gripper edge for job and sheet squaring-up; 3, Centre marks

up and everything on the composite original squared-up relative to the centre marks and rechecked with the base centre marks.

Continuous tone copy is usually treated as separate artwork. Its position on the composite paste-up can be indicated by outlining and filling-in the area where it is to be positioned in black or red. Peculiar shapes can be outlined from a camera tracing made to the correct size from the art work, or a photostat copy is tipped in position, and inked-in to give a transparent window on the line negative. Alternatively, the image may be camera traced on a red translucent film, which is then cut-out to the required shape and positioned on the paste-up for line negative making. The halftone negative is then made and stripped in position on the line film, or it may be taped in position on the line negative or positive before printing to metal. With this latter procedure, there is always a risk of out of contact resulting. Register marks are essential and should be on the separate art work to serve as a final guide for positioning on the key line negative. In some instances the halftone image, where close register is apparent, could be double printed into position when printing to metal.

A further alternative procedure would be to make the halftone negative to the required size, leaving a slightly larger dot in the high-light and shadow areas. From this screened negative, make a bromide contact print and tip in position on the paste-up, reproducing dot for dot as line copy with the remainder of the art work. An advantage is that the artist can, if necessary, retouch the screen print, adding highlights and shadows, or even over-drawing line work if required.

The production of line and halftone combination work can often be simplified by the use of overlays prepared in the art department. An overlay consists of two or more elements that are not positioned next to each other but are arranged over each other. Instead of preparing the line and tonal areas together on one piece of drawing board, production is made easier if the tonal areas or photograph are separate on a board and the line work on an overlay of tracing paper, cloth or acetate sheeting. Register marks and centre marks must be positioned accurately on both, or all, copies. In colour work, where a colour has to be eliminated to permit another colour to print in that position, it is necessary for the artist to allow a slight overlap to assist register and fit on the press. This overlap should be the absolute minimum, consistent with doing the job required.

The use and application of shading mediums have been discussed in *Camera and Process Work*, pages 17 and 153. More recently pre-process adhesive tints applied to the original have found favour. Often these are applied by the artist or the retoucher, and Zip-a-Tone and Craftint are two such mediums. The former are tints which have been printed on to a transparent sheet with an adhesive backing for attaching them to the drawing or photo print. This, in turn, is covered with a protective backing which peels off. The tint is cut to shape and positioned on the copy, or it is stuck down first and then trimmed. With Craftints, stumps and scrapers are used to remove unwanted tint from certain areas of the copy. They are supplied with a black dot or line on a transparent back-ground for overlaying white areas, and with opaque white elements on a transparent background for overlaying black areas to give the reverse effect. They can also be used as negative material for direct printing down to plates. Care must be taken to ensure that they are laid perfectly flat, otherwise they will reproduce unevenly owing to flare, caused by the camera lighting being reflected at varying angles from the uneven surface and causing light scatter through the lens system on to the light sensitive emulsion.

IV

The Photolitho Retouching Department

THE ARTIST who prepares and retouches art work for reproduction, works in close association and contact with the artist who is designated photolitho retoucher. This latter person is concerned with the product of the camera department and his job is, in the main, to correct and improve the quality of negatives and positives. In the smaller workshops the two jobs are interchangeable, and often the same person functions,

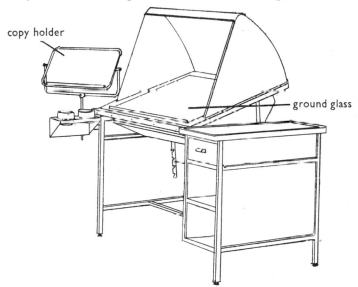

copy holder

ground glass

Fig. 16 Retouching unit

through necessity, in both capacities. The litho artist or retoucher is concerned with tone and colour values and, because something over eighty per cent of his work is concerned with colour reproduction, this chapter deals mainly with the consideration of colour correction, which is only briefly mentioned in the subsequent chapter relating to the camera department. The actual technique of dot reduction and correction is the same for both monochrome and colour work.

EQUIPMENT

THE RETOUCHING room should, for preference, be painted a neutral grey, illuminated with cool, white fluorescent lighting, and fitted with colour viewers, which have a colour temperature of 3000–4500°K; standard light tables fitted with squared, machined edges and a stainless steel T-square are necessary equipment. Dot-etching benches with sinks, suitably lined to withstand chemicals and water, with good

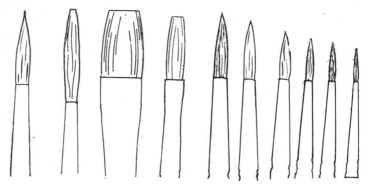

Fig. 17A Chisel-edge brushes ($\frac{1}{8}$ in., $\frac{1}{4}$ in., $\frac{1}{2}$ in.); nos. 1–7, round-tip-brushes

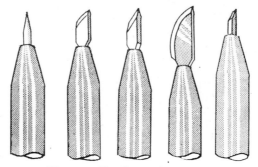

Fig. 17B Needles and scrapers

illumination, are essential. Pocket magnifiers of 10 times to 20 times magnification are required for judging dot size and a transmission densitometer should be available. This measures the amount of light passing through selected areas of the negatives or positives. A density of 0·00 represents a completely transparent area, whilst a density of 3·00 records opaque metallic silver. These values are calibrated to a logarithmic scale and the density numbers are the logarithm of the ratio of the percentage of the incident light that is transmitted through the negative.

An area with a recorded density of 0·30 will transmit twice as much light as a 0·60 area, and five times as much as a 1·00 density area. An area with a density of 2·00 transmits only one-tenth of the light that a density area of 1·00 will transmit.

Additional equipment should include an airbrush, for use in connection with continuous tone negatives and positives complete with frisket-paper for masking-out and vignetting. Scrapers and retouching knives are useful for scribing, removing the emulsion, cutting sharp edges, etc. Ruling-pens, rulers, protractors and the usual drawing equipment and materials employed by the commercial artist should be in evidence, including stumps, pencils, graphite powder, red and neutral grey dyes, opaque medium, staging lacquers and resists, etching solutions and a plentiful supply of red sable and camel's hair brushes. Medium-size brushes, such as numbers 4, 5 and 6, are in most demand. Litho crayons and tint sheets, such as Ben Day Medium, or their commercial equivalent, and abrasive erasers and abrasive pastes for local reduction of density are useful accessories. Rapidograph pens are indispensable for the quick, neat and accurate positioning of register marks on copy and layout, etc.

THE NEED FOR CORRECTION

IT IS unfortunate that none of the known methods of colour reproduction will give a true rendering of all colours without some form of correction. The transmission values of available filters allied to the dyes used in the sensitisation of photographic material are not perfect but in actual practice they are sufficiently close to theoretical requirements and are not the cause of any real errors in colour rendering. The Kromscop experiment of F. E. Ives proved conclusively that if errors in colour rendition were only caused by filter limitations the amount of correction required would be negligible, if any.

Nevertheless colour correction is essential for good colour reproduction, and in the instance of the trichromatic theory of printing the basic cause is the spectral impurity of synthetic pigments. The most unsatisfactory colour is the cyan which reflects a certain proportion of yellow and red which should be completely absorbed. If all red light were completely absorbed by the cyan ink it would not be necessary to correct the magenta printed negative in the green regions. Greens produced by the available cyan and yellow pigment without any correction of the magenta printer negative reproduce much darker than required, and in some instances even produce browns.

In like manner magenta inks which should absorb all the green and reflect blue and red light completely actually absorb some of the blue and red rays and reflect a percentage of green, resulting in degraded purples and reds.

The yellow inks are generally very satisfactory. They reflect about 98% of the green and red light and are by far the nearest to the theoretical spectral reflection and absorption requirements.

Approximate Reflection Curves of Printing Inks (Fig. 18)

Yellow ink is the most correct, but correction on the yellow printing plate is extensive because the high blue absorption of the magenta and some blue absorption of the cyan means reducing the corresponding areas in the yellow plate to prevent excessive yellow or brown appearing on the final result.

Magenta ink is reasonably correct in red reflection with unwanted blue absorption (equivalent to yellow). Thus a high degree of correction is needed in areas required to print cyan, so that red areas which over-print cyan must be reduced and some reduction in the areas of excessive blue absorption is required.

The cyan ink spectrophotometric curve is the worst of all with insufficient blue and green reflection, that is, unwanted blue absorption and much more green absorption, equivalent to yellow and magenta elements respectively. These limitations are corrected on the other two printing records as they cannot be carried out on the cyan. Because of this the cyan record involves the least amount of work.

It is also a fact that apart from limitations in absorption and reflection characteristics trichromatic inks are in themselves not sufficiently transparent to give the correct theoretical colour values when superimposed one on top of the other. When tints are formed from dots of the three inks lying side by side the resulting colour may be said to be formed by the addition of light. Where larger dots overlap, the effect upon the eye is produced partly by addition and partially subtractively; and if the inks are less and less transparent in their layers the top colour of the superimposed dots will have the greatest effect upon the resulting colour.

Another factor which influences the correction required is the use of the glass crossline screen. Perfect reproduction from highlight to solid is not possible using this medium on account of loss of detail, particularly in the lighter tones due to diffraction, and tonal gradations between these extremes may not be reproduced in their correct values, although the end densities in the negative may be approximately correct in dot size. Thus it may be necessary to correct for tone values as well as colour values.

Methods of reproduction vary from one establishment to another. Thus hard and fast rules of standardisation cannot be laid down. The use of colour charts is not recommended unless the inks, paper and machinery used in producing the charts are identical with those used on the job. Thus the cost of producing such charts in a lithographic

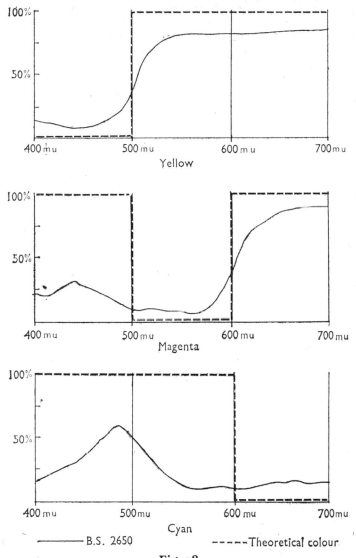

Yellow

Magenta

Cyan

———— B.S. 2650   −−−−−Theoretical colour

Fig. 18

establishment where there is an infinite variety of work could be a very
costly business. The use of colour charts presupposes the standardisation of all presswork and the running of standard colours which is a very
laudable suggestion but not always a practical proposition because jobs
are often required to be printed in non-standard colours.

It is therefore apparent that if it were possible to make printing pigments and colour filters to carry out the work that is desirable there would be no need for colour correction. It is generally agreed that each filter should transmit in that region of the spectrum where the corresponding printing colour absorbs. Although this ideal is not fully realised the fact remains that very acceptable results can be obtained using either wide-band (trichromatic) or narrow-cut filters. Again panchromatic emulsion has not uniform sensitivity throughout the visible spectrum, the relative sensitivity being lower in the green or blue-green region where the human eye has high sensitivity. In actual practical application it is found that filter and emulsion limitations are very minor factors in reproduction procedure, the main consideration being the use of printing colours having a spectral composition far from the ideal requirement. This, plus the ever-present problem of degradation of tone value, necessitates the use of correction techniques.

In photo-engraving, using the orthodox methods of etching and fine etching, the colour etcher makes the required correction on the copper plates whilst etching to obtain the depth essential in the particular type of printing. In the postwar years many methods of photographic colour correction have been evolved which, in general, may be utilised for all the graphic reproduction processes. Before being able to appreciate the value of masking techniques it is necessary to understand the methods employed in hand correction; and in particular those applications peculiar to photolithography and photogravure. The system evolved for these processes was to make whatever corrections were required on the negatives and positives; this highly-skilled job being performed by the retoucher. Aptitude, ability and experience make a good retoucher; this cannot be acquired by a purely theoretical approach. Good eyesight, colour sense and training as an artist are the requisite fundamentals before the basic principles of reproduction may be practised.

A high percentage of work for reproduction uses non-standard colours, particularly in the instance of the packaging industry where solid colours employed to reproduce line work, such as type matter or lettering, may also be used to reproduce tone values in the job. A typical example would be a biscuit wrapper in which the biscuit illustrations may be reproduced in buff, brown and black with any bloom or warmth on the biscuits being provided by a tint of vermilion red, with the red and black being used for solid lettering and type matter on the body of the wrapper. Colour correction, due to the inability of cyan and magenta inks to behave as desired, does not arise in this instance, but there will still be a need for correction. This kind of work could present many problems if correction were purely photographic and it would be far easier to execute by hand.

Every original for reproduction must be treated individually and, because a different style or technique may have been used in making it, reproduced by the particular method which suits the job best. This ability to discriminate is often the key to the successful reproduction of certain types of copy. Also the requirements of the printer as to the method of printing and plate preparation will dictate the way in which the job is to be produced.

In lithography there are three main methods of preparing work for the platemaker – direct, indirect, and indirect for deep-etch. For direct off-set printing the first negatives are made without the prism-reading laterally reversed on the emulsion side. These negatives are retouched and then printed-down on to plate using dichromated albumen as the light sensitive colloid. Although particularly suited for certain types of work the press-life of such plates is limited and the dot formation not so sharp and hard as from other methods. With the indirect method the first negatives are made as formerly and they may be in continuous-tone or in dot formation. After retouching, a set of positives are produced either by contact or in the camera. From these positives a set of final negatives are made for printing-down in dichromated albumen. Obviously this method provides a threefold opportunity for increasing, erasing or reducing the printing value of any tones. Nevertheless since the negatives are printed-down by the surface method, as applies in direct reproduction, press-life is still limited. This procedure is often adopted when reproducing difficult copy which cannot be sited on the studio camera, such as large originals, art gallery work and subjects in relief, etc., from which continuous-tone negatives must first be made.

With the indirect method for deep-etch the first negatives may be continuous-tone (contone) or halftone. They are retouched as fully as possible after which halftone positives are made either in the camera or by contact and the full correction of tonal gradation and colour values is done chemically by reducing the size of the dots to the required dimensions. The positives are printed-down by the deep-etch method of plate-making which creates a plate with firm hard dot fringes of good printability, sharpness and long press-life.

BASIC METHODS OF RETOUCHING

THE THREE basic methods of retouching employed are the use of pencil, the application of dye and the alteration of tone values by chemical means. In workshop application the skilled retoucher also devises and introduces various other means and methods to reproduce the character of the original. For instance, he would not reproduce a large softly drawn chalk drawing by applying opaque paint on the highlights between the chalk lines. Soft edges are necessary and these can be most successfully obtained by using a medium similar to the one used by the artist in making the sketch, namely pencil and chalk applied between the lines to reduce the printing intensity of the highlights.

The modern approach to the reproduction of pencil and chalk drawings is by making in the first instance a 'contone' negative from which a dot positive is made using a magenta contact screen. The range of the negative is adjusted so that the purest highlights are 'dropped out' or eliminated in exposing the positive. It is interesting to note that some of the finest fascimile reproductions of Augustus John's sketches were reproduced from direct wet collodion halftone negatives, coated with matt varnish and retouched with pencil and litho chalk and printed-down on to fairly rough grained plates. When viewed with a magnifying glass the dot formation was atrocious, being scrappy and broken, but the resulting impressions were first-class. Thus it follows that it is the end product that matters and no aesthetic considerations can be applied to retouching since it is the end that justifies the means.

For the application of pencil retouching on negatives special plates and films are manufactured which have a matt surface, but if ordinary photographic material is used several types of varnish may be applied to give the necessary 'tooth' to hold the graphite. Ellis's shading medium, Autotype retouching medium, and Kodak retouching medium are three of the many proprietary varnishes that can be purchased for use on continuous-tone images. Also a solution of resin in methylated spirits may be applied with a clean piece of chamois leather. This is rotated on the negative until the surface becomes tacky. These retouching mediums have a very fine grain and if the character of the original is coarse, or for direct application to halftone negatives, matt varnish would be the most suitable ground for the pencil or chalk retouching. This varnish may be purchased as a proprietary brand, but it can be made by dissolving gum benzoin and gum sandarac in benzine and ether respectively, bringing the two resultant solutions together to form the varnish. The structure of the grain may be adjusted by adding more benzine or ether. If ether is added the varnish will dry quicker and the grain will be coarsened.

Correction by the Use of Dye as a Medium

ASSUMING THE original to be comprised of varying gradated tints it can be pre-supposed that some of these tints would perhaps need a smaller amount of yellow, magenta or cyan than is recorded in the original negatives. Dye could be applied with a brush so that in local areas any subsequent exposure would be reduced, so that in the positive the corresponding dots would be reduced in size. Sometimes when direct halftone screen negatives are made these are retouched with dye. Obviously the results obtained are not as good as when dye is applied to 'contone' negatives because if any great increase in density is required there is a danger of finishing up with grey dots on the positives. A combination of dye work on the dot negatives is, with a reasonable amount of dot etching on the positives, sufficient to ensure all necessary correction without encountering this difficulty.

It is realised that the introduction of the halftone screen is always accompanied by a degradation of tonal separation particularly in the highlight areas. Thus with monochrome, as with colour reproduction, correction is required.

Chemical Method of Tonal Correction

BASICALLY THE method of chemical retouching is the process of dissolving away unwanted density in silver deposits. To a degree this can be controlled, under certain conditions, and a reasonable amount of local reduction can be accomplished. Reducing agents for continuous-tone work on either negative or positive can be grouped into three general headings and formulae may be obtained by consulting *Camera and Process Work* (page 81). The *subtractive* method attacks the least deposits of metallic silver first, thereby increasing the contrast. Farmer's reducer consists of potassium ferricyanide, sodium thiosulphate (hypo) and water.

A *proportional reducer*, as its name implies, reduces the silver uniformly throughout all tone values. A negative thus treated will retain its original contrast range but will lose overall density. Potassium permanganate, sulphuric acid, ammonium persulphate and water are the constituents of such a reducer.

A *super-proportional reducer* is one which attacks the heavier densities of silver first, thus lowering contrast as well as density. They are often called highlight reducers and consist of ammonium persulphate, sulphuric acid and water.

With images in dot formation the subtractive reducer is the one usually employed. Because of the obvious advantages of the indirect method for deep-etch plate-making, colour and tonal correction by dot etching has become routine procedure – of which more will be said later. It is sufficient to say at the moment that chemical reduction on the negative increases printing saturation and values, whereas reduction on the positive lightens and decreases printing values. It is obvious that every job has its own peculiar characteristics which must be dealt with on merit. However, it should be possible to initiate a routine which introduces a degree of standardisation.

Assuming that a job is to be printed in six colours and reproduced by the indirect method of, firstly, continuous-tone negatives followed by camera positives. The negatives would be laid out on the illuminated glass-topped retouching table and studied against the original artwork in order to decide the corrections to be done on the negatives and after-wards on the positives. They are then checked for contrast range on the densitometer, the end densities being recorded for the guidance of the operator when exposing the camera positives. Reduction in density is carried out, working in rotation through the negatives, so that by the time the last negative is finished the first negatives have been washed and dried and ready for subsequent operations.

Local Reduction

THE NEGATIVE is thoroughly wetted so that there is a complete absorption of moisture throughout the emulsion. Whilst the negative is soaking the retoucher takes two shallow glass jars with wide necks and fills one with a solution of hypo (approximately 55% solution) and the other with a solution of potassium ferricyanide (30%); with constant practice it will be found that the retoucher will vary the strength of the ferricyanide solution to suit his requirements. Some retouchers often keep a large crystal of solid ferricyanide on their retouching bench and stroke it with their brush for picking out areas of absolute solid on the negative or pure highlights on the positive.

Before work is started it is necessary to evaluate the job against the colours to be used in printing and for this purpose a set of colour tabs are provided by the pressman. Taking up the yellow tab and observing the yellow negative, it is noticed that on the original sketch a yellow tint and a strong purple, which may be adjacent to each other, show on the negative as having more yellow coming through the purple than occurs on the actual yellow tint. Thus it is obvious that if the yellow is allowed to remain under the purple the resulting colour will be degraded towards brown, and at a later stage this will have to be eradicated. The strength of the yellow tint on the copy, against the printing ink colour tab, will also indicate that the quantity of light passing through the negative is not sufficient to give the required size of dot on the positive. Therefore the negative will need to be reduced in that particular area.

The procedure is to dab the negative all over with a chamois leather to remove the surplus moisture and apply hypo solution, either with a pad of soft cotton wadding or a soft sponge. Some retouchers prefer to harden the emulsion before reduction, but if reasonable care is exercised the emulsion will not suffer damage. Enough time is spent in correction techniques without extending it with operations which, at best, are only a protection against careless treatment.

A soft red sable brush, dipped into the ferricyanide solution, is applied to the hypo impregnated emulsion and reduction takes place. When the required density is reached hypo solution is again applied and dabbed off with the chamois leather. It will be found that quite a high degree of control can be exercised with the use of the leather; for since the negative emulsion is soaked in hypo, which has a higher density than water, the ferricyanide is not inclined to run but remains in situ. Large areas are reduced more evenly if the strength of cyanide is reduced and the brush applied in a circular movement. In like manner the whole area of the negative is treated and corrections made, generally to areas requiring additional printing values. Pure solids can be added later on the positive, so only those tones in the highlights and near-shadows need be observed and treated. Systematically each negative is thus checked and corrected against the appropriate colour tab.

Application of Dye

WHEN ALL the negatives have been checked and corrected they are, in rotation, washed and dried. The yellow is now subjected to further treatment – this time areas are observed that require the printing value reducing. For this purpose a neutral black dye is applied carefully and smoothly with a brush. Some retouchers prefer to have available several jars in which tints of five, three, two and one per cent solutions of dye are ready mixed. Others prefer full-strength dye, reducing to the strength required by diluting on a piece of glass before applying to any particular area of the negative.

The final stage in the correction of the negative is to paint out all pure highlights, and areas similar to the purple patch appearing on the yellow negative, with an opaque paint, two very good proprietary brands being Vanguard Liquid Photopaque and Plumtree opaque. Registration marks, cuts and folds can then be scribed into the emulsion; the work areas ruled down to size and white borders painted off.

The negatives are forwarded to the camera room where the operator will make either contact screen positives, or halftone positives using a transmission holder on the camera, in which to position the negatives used in conjunction with an orthodox glass ruled screen. Camera positives, it should be stated, dot etch much better than either direct halftone contact positives or magenta or grey contact screen positives. In practice a 90% dot in situ on a correctly exposed camera positive is capable of being reduced down chemically to a 10% dot without loss of opacity, i.e. printing density. It is advisable that such positives are made using small stops in the lens aperture combined with relatively long exposures, because positives made with larger stops and correspondingly short exposures tend to lack the required etching range.

Contact positives from original direct halftone negatives can be employed when excessive chemical correction is unnecessary on the positives. This is due to the fact that it is only a feasible proposition to reduce a 90% dot to about a 60% dot. Further treatment would result in a grey dot formation which would prove unsatisfactory for printing-down to metal.

Maximum dot reduction can best be obtained when, in making the dot positives by contact from halftone negatives, the screen negatives are fully exposed and developed. This added density requires an increase in exposure and development time to obtain satisfactory dot positives which develop out as black metallic silver right through to the base of the emulsion.

Dot Etching of Positives

THE PROCEDURE of chemical reduction is similar to that performed on the negatives with the exception that when reducing the positives the actual printing value is diminished. Reduction can be done locally, or the whole positive may be reduced by immersion in the solution. Any areas not requiring etching may be staged out with cellulose lacquer. An improvement in the dot etching properties of the positives can be effected by tanning the gelatin in proportion to the silver image, resulting in a greater degree of lateral etching without loss of density. This process is known as rehalogenisation, or metallising. The formulae published by J. S. Mertle consists of copper sulphate 1 oz; potassium bromide 1 oz; ammonium bichromate 80 grains; hydrochloric acid ½ oz; water to make 40 oz.

The positive, after development, fixation and washing, is bleached in the above-mentioned bath, washed again until the yellow bichromate stain is eliminated and then re-developed in the original developer. This operation is carried out in a strong normal lighting. It is noticed that the dots on the positive take on a slight relief which is helpful in staging – either with a brush or a greasy crayon.

Avoiding Dot Reduction Trouble

BEFORE DOT reducing the emulsion must be thoroughly washed and dried evenly to prevent uneven etching. To obtain trouble-free positives for dot etching it is worth while taking every care and precaution. A fixing bath free from hardener should be used and washing must be thorough. Afterwards, place in water containing a wetting agent and pass through a dilute acetic acid wash before drying. Soak in a dish of water containing a wetting agent before commencing to etch. The emulsion will not stand rough handling but it should etch smoothly and evenly.

It is realised that only training, experience and practice can make a competent retoucher. Each job must be treated on its own individual merit and often requires special treatment. The table appended for four- and six-colour work is, however, based upon general practical considerations, and will be found useful if it is understood it forms a guide for general average requirements.

Printing colour	Delete on the negative	On the positive reduce the printing value	On the positive make solid	Remarks
Yellow	Purples Blues Magenta-tints Highlights	Blue-Greys Pinks Blacks to 60%	Strong Yellows Yellow-Greens Orange-Browns	Tones from 50% to 100% must be accentuated otherwise there will be a lack of drawing detail.
Pink	Cold Greens Cold Blue Highlights	Cold Greys Bright cool Yellows	Reds that require extra saturation	The highlight end of the scale should be over-emphasised since small differences in light tints are not easily discernible. If left as recorded in the negative they will tend to add weight to the red instead of adding roundness which is its true function.
Red	Yellows Greens Blues (excepting very warm Blues) Greys and Highlights	Pale Purples Pale Browns Lighter Flesh Tints Black to 50%	Extremely deep Red areas. Otherwise solids will stand out too much	If reds require greying they should be darkened by the addition of black and not blue.
Light Blue	Very bright colours opposed to Blue Highlights			It is necessary to emphasise the differences between tints at the light end of the scale. However this negative can often be left without a great deal of retouching. The light tints are balanced by the choice of light blue when passing the proof. The fact that blue in tint form is inclined to appear grey can be very useful.
Dark Blue	Very light Blues Flesh Tints Yellows Reds Light Greys Highlights	Pale Purples Pale Browns Very light Greens Black to 70%	Only Blues require full colour saturation with very deep Blue-Greens	
Black	All bright colours			Functions as a modelling colour for those areas requiring depth and extra contrast. With fine screen work black may be used alone to produce some greys. Black with yellow makes a deep olive green when surrounded by other colours. In this connection it may be used as a colour to give clean bright results. With fine work, such as greatly reduced carpet reproductions and textile patterns, black with red makes a brown; black and yellow makes a green, whilst black and blue gives a deeper blue.

V

Preparation and Assembly for Platemaking

IT IS essential that the printed image should be positioned straight and parallel on the plate. The side guides or cylinders can be adjusted or changed on the press but this is time-consuming and should not be necessary. This kind of press make-ready should be avoided by careful and accurate work before printing-down on the layout table and in photo-composing and stripping.

WET AND DRY STRIPPING

THE TERMS stripping and assembly have come to mean one and the same thing. In actuality a stripping film is a thin membrane attached to a heavier support and the membrane with its photographic image is removed from its base and positioned on a new support. Stripping is also the general term used for splicing cut films together to serve the same purpose as a strip-film assembly. Pressure-sensitive clear cellophane tape is then used to hold the films in position.

 With wet stripping, after washing the stripping layer is detached from its support, and, for face-down mounting on the final support (glass, film, etc.), it is sufficient to press the stripped layer, image side downwards, on to the support using a rubber squeegee. The emulsion layer will itself provide adequate adhesion. With face-up stripping a stripping cement is first applied to the base support, the stripped layer attached image side upwards and pressed firmly in position using a rubber squeegee.

 Dry stripping is preferable for colour work, assuring better dimensional stability of the image than applies with wet stripping. After washing the film is dried and then detached from its support. The procedure followed for face-down stripping is to immerse the stripped layer for 10 seconds in a 15% aqueous solution of glacial acetic acid, moisten the base support with water and press the stripped layer in position using a rubber squeegee to secure complete adhesion. When the image side has to be positioned upwards, follow the same procedure, first applying stripping film cement to the mounting support. The mounting support should be perfectly clean and free from grease. Sheets of glass should be cleaned using French Chalk and any greasiness removed by immersion in a 15% aqueous solution of glacial acetic acid followed by thorough washing in clean water.

EQUIPMENT AND TOOLS

A STRIPPING bench, layout and lining-up tables are essential requirements. The former provides the illuminated working surface on which the various images can be positioned to the layout. The working surface should be smooth plate glass, grained on the underside to diffuse the lighting, which consists of several fluorescent tubes, of a standard colour temperature to give a white light. The tubes should be located at a distance from the glass top to give an even distribution of light. This can be helped by the use of internal reflectors and diffusers to improve the

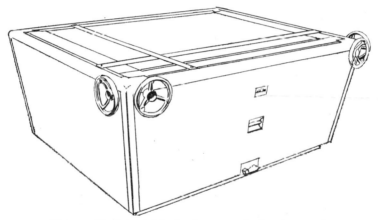

Fig. 19 Register table for layout and planning work

quality of the light. A straight edge on two or all sides is essential. Modern layout and lining-up tables are in many respects similar to stripping benches or shiners, with straight edges often in the form of steel rules, and micrometer-adjustable. Ruling, locating and scribing attachments are also necessary.

Ruling pens, compasses, dividers, plastic triangles, protractors, irregular curves, T-squares, straight-edges, razor blades and knives are part of the general range of tools required. Also needles, to mark the location for register when transferring a film to a predetermined position, and scribers for cutting and scribing lines in films.

Plastic sheets are often preferred to glass sheets for assembly work.

They are available in several forms of acetate film, vinyl film and polyester base material, all in several thicknesses. Low-shrink acetate film (acetate butyrate) is fairly cheap and reasonably dimensionally stable. Vinyl sheeting is preferred, having a higher dimensional stability and providing a substantial working base o·o10 in.). Polyester sheets are also most suitable and dimensionally stable and accurate.

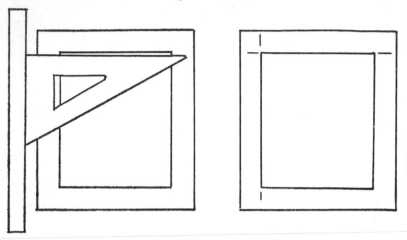

Fig. 20 Squaring-up procedure

Opaquing and Squaring-up

OPAQUING IS used for spotting out pinholes, edge lines and other undesirable marking on the negatives. It is applied with a brush, usually on the emulsion side, oftimes on the back of the negatives. Black opaque water paint is made of finely ground lamp black or graphite and dries very smoothly and evenly. It therefore gives good contact between the negative and plate when printing down. A drawback is that it doesn't wash off very easily and is inclined to leave stains. Red opaque is less expensive, covers large areas better than black opaque and is easier to remove with less likelihood to stain. It is thicker, and lies more unevenly, and unless carefully applied, results in out-of-contact between the two surfaces in printing. Also areas treated with red opaque soon develop pinholes.

Turpentine opaque is very suitable on glass negatives. It is thinner than red opaque, dries perfectly flat and is not liable to develop pinholes. It can be removed from the image with cotton wool, moistened with turpentine, carbon tetrachloride or petrol, without softening the emulsion or dissolving water opaque in close proximity.

Halftone areas can be squared-up and corrected and ruled-up for size (cropped) using a ruling pen filled with opaque colour, up to the work area, and then painting out the remaining background areas. Masking foils and pressure-sensitive cellophane or polyester tapes in red, brown and black are also used. The metal foils of tin or aluminium are about one-thousandth of an inch in thickness and are supplied in rolls. Glycerine is applied to the underside and the foil is squeegeed in position after having been cut to shape and size, using a sharp point with the assistance of a straight-edge. Sellotape or Scotch tape is a fast and effective means for masking and joining films together. The red and brown tapes are translucent and therefore assist the operator who can see clearly the sections masked out and check for accuracy and position.

In colour reproduction it is helpful to the pressman if colour tabs,

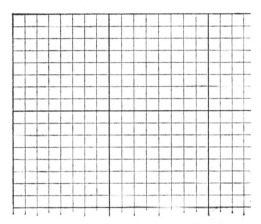

Fig. 21 Grid lines for assembly work

showing small rectangular areas of solid colour, are left in position in the trim areas of the sheet. These show the colours already printed and provide a guide for the pressman in assessing whether he is carrying the full weight of ink. The use of a grey scale is also indispensable in giving the pressman a quick visual check of the ink control and density for each colour, as any tendency towards filling in shadow detail or blinding highlight area would be soon noticed and rectified.

Assembly work is often done on the shiner with the layout or dummy underneath a clear plastic sheeting or acetate film, on to which the various negatives or positives are positioned and located, with strips of clear tape or stripped into position using stripping film technique. A grid of small, clear squares, each square separated by a thin opaque line, is also a most useful accessory for accurate assembly and register work. This six point, or larger, unit square grid can be positioned between the dummy and the clear acetate film. The assembly of images prior to printing is termed a flat. This can be prepared using one of many different methods, according to the nature of the job.

For example the assembly is prepared on a sheet of goldenrod Ulano Rubylith or Amberlith masking and stripping film, which serves either as a drawing base to indicate the image positionings on the printing layout, or as a support on which to assemble the various elements of the job, or, finally, to function as a mask to prevent the printing light from reaching the non-printing areas of the work during the printing on metal stage.

A common procedure for non-intricate work is to make a film flat by attaching the various separate elements together with strips of clear Sellotape directly over the prepared layout. For more complicated work

Fig. 22 Image assembly on masking film

complementary flats are prepared. This often applies with close-fitting text matter and numerous small illustrations, which would be difficult or impossible to strip in close proximity one with the other. Two separate flats are assembled over the layout each containing various sections of the complete work. The complementary sections are exposed successfully in register with each other, to pre-located register marks on each flat which correspond with each other, so as to produce a combined overprint, by double exposure technique, on the same sensitised press plate.

For close and accurate assembly the blue key method is recommended. For colour work blue key images are photographically printed-down to a set of sensitised plate glass or plastic sheets made from a master key flat, which consists of an assembly which includes all the location detail necessary to register the images on each flat. Acetate and, for preference, the higher-priced vinyl and polyester plastic sheeting, which are more dimensionally stable, are now often used for preparing the blue key which serves as a clear guide for accurately locating each image. The colour is transparent to the printing illuminant and therefore the blue key image does not record when printing down to metal. As stated, the tendency in this country is for images requiring superimposition to be over-printed in position on metal to register marks or, in the instance of colour transparencies, for them to be re-copied to the correct sizes, or colour prints made to the required sizes, and in both methods the artist assembles the various sections together as a photomontage, so that the

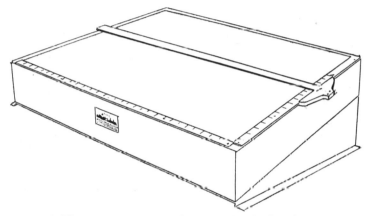

Fig. 23 Bench-type illuminated stripping desk

various elements fit together to make a single composite copy for reproducing on the camera. Whilst this is also done in other countries, the American system favours stripping, employing different techniques to suit the type of job involved.

One method is to make a key ink print on an albumen surface plate, pull the requisite number of impressions on goldenrod or orange sheets and strip the negatives from the various colours into their respective positions, face-up on the light table, holding them in place temporarily with tape. The flat is then turned over and windows cut into the sheet, so that the printing areas of the image are exposed. The individual images are then permanently stuck down and the tape removed from the emulsion side of the negative.

When preparing blue key images the plastic sheets or plate glass must first be thoroughly cleaned to de-grease and remove any foreign matter. Fine pumice powder can be used for this purpose, and after washing, coat with a fish glue and ammonium dichromate solution, whirling at about 40 r.p.m. Exposure approximates to normal platemaking time and development follows under running water assisted, if necessary, by light circular rubbing with cotton wool. After washing immerse in a blue dye solution such as Methylene or Toluidin Blue and if register marks, etc., are required to print, treat locally with potassium permanganate, which converts them to a dark brown colour. Wash and dry, and if a protective coating is required on which to strip, coat with a thin clear varnish. Wet or dry strip film technique can be utilised. An alternative method to obtain the set-offs is to make the key images in ferroprussiate blue. This is done by coating with ferric ammonium citrate

Fig. 24 Fluorescent illuminated light table for retouching
and stripping

and potassium ferricyanide. These solutions are made separately as 20% solutions and mixed – prior to coating, whirling and drying in the usual way – in the ratio of three parts of the former to one part of the latter. The 'ferric' salt is reduced by exposure to the 'ferrous' state, and when immersed in a 1% hydrochloric acid solution, ferro-ferricyanide (Berlin blue) is formed, resulting from the reaction between the ferrous salts and the ferricyanide. During exposure the image appears blue and then fades after approx. three minutes. Exposure should be continued for up to ten minutes. Citric acid added to the ferric ammonium citrate solution acts as a stabiliser and increases the intensity of the blue image. Ammonium dichromate, added to the potassium ferricyanide solution, whilst tending to increase the exposure, prevents the background from turning blue during development.

BLUE-KEY REGISTER

THE MODERN trend in publicity work is to combine separate originals, either in monochrome or especially in colour, to produce a composite illustration. The work is done either from reflection copy or from 35 mm or larger transparencies. Reproduction is by the indirect method and, without resorting to specialised equipment, blue-key technique provides a satisfactory method of procedure. For photolithography, screen positives are made from the continuous tone separation negatives (if colour), whilst for photo-engraving screen negatives would be made after first making continuous tone positives. Screening is carried out using lith type stripping film with strictly standardised procedure to assist registration and fit, using an acid-hardening fixer and, for preference, dry stripping technique in place of wet stripping.

An accurate layout of the proposed finished composite is placed under the glass plate on the light table on to which the positives will be stripped in position. One positive is selected from each colour set which shows the boldest detail and outline, usually the cyan or black printer. They are coated with stripping film lacquer and thinners and stripped, when dry, into position over the layout on to the clear sheet glass, which has been prepared with a stripping film cement. This now forms a 'master' to provide a blue-key image on the other glass plates. Blue-key plates can be prepared using Kodak Blue-Toning method by making a positive from the composite on Kodak Autopositive film from which contact negatives are made which are bleached and toned to give the final blue-key plates. Alternatively, using the Kodalith reversal method a negative is made on lith material from which contact positives are made and chemically reversed and bleached with the resulting negatives dyed to produce the blue-key plates.

With the blue-toning method, from the composite assembly a positive is made on Autopositive Film to give a laterally reversed positive. If ordinary material were used a negative would result. The positive requires an exposure of about 3 minutes using a photoflood bulb at 3 feet distance, exposing through a Kodak S58/2 flexible yellow filter. Develop in lith developer for 2 minutes at 68° F (20° C). From this positive make the required number of negatives on high contrast material, developing in hydroquinone caustic developer, and after washing bleach in a bath of potassium ferricyanide (2 oz), sulphuric acid ($\frac{1}{2}$ oz) and water made up to 80 oz. After thorough washing tone pale blue in a bath of ferric ammonium citrate ($\frac{1}{4}$ oz), sulphuric acid ($\frac{1}{2}$ oz), and water to 80 oz. Rinse before drying.

Using the Etch-Bleach method a contact negative is made from the strip-up combination using 'lith' material and exposing for about 8 seconds at 3 feet from a 25-watt bulb. The required number of contacts are made on lith type plates, developed, passed into the stopbath and etch-bleached in the usual manner in a solution of equal parts of (A) copper sulphate (9 oz), citric acid (12 oz), potassium bromide (260 gr) and water to 80 fl. oz and (solution B) a 3% hydrogen peroxide solution (10 vol.). During this stage the room light is switched on and the bleaching softens and removes from the glass the developed areas. The operation is continued until all the silver image is removed. Rinse and swab with cotton wool to remove all traces of softened gelatin. Fix the bleached plate in a hardening fixing bath, wash and immerse in a $\frac{1}{2}$% solution of blue crystals dissolved in very weak ($\frac{1}{2}$%) acetic acid until a pale blue image is produced (I.C.I. soluble Paper Blue 3M200 is suitable). The dye image will disperse if washed, thus a quick rinse, immerse in a 5% solution of acetic acid and dry. Coat with lacquer to prevent emulsion swelling. The blue-key impressions on the glass plates make the positioning of the various images, comprising, for instance, a composite colour set, simple and accurate. The blue image, being transparent to actinic light, will not print.

A further alternative method would be to coat a sheet of glass with dichromated fish glue, print down on to it, processing in a similar manner to normal metal printing procedure. The exception being to dye the image in a solution of blue crystals in place of methyl violet dye.

STRIPPING AND POSITIONING

THE EMULSION of a sheet of stripping film will peel easily from its support after a short immersion in lukewarm water. A suitable cement for adhering it to the new support consists of 6 oz gelatin, 1 oz fish glue, 4 oz glacial acetic acid, water to make 80 oz. Dry plates can be stripped using 1 oz sodium fluoride, 8 oz formalin, 20 oz water; and in the dry condition, by first immersing for about one minute in a solution of 1 oz potassium carbonate, $\frac{1}{2}$ oz glycerine, $\frac{1}{2}$ oz formalin, 20 oz water. Dab off with a soft chamois leather and allow to dry before stripping. Colour work is stripped on the shiner generally to a blue-key image.

For black-and-white work the procedure in this country is to strip up in page form with an accurate layout or dummy on the shiner top and the clear acetate sheet or glass over-positioned. On this the images are assembled. Another method is to assemble the images on a layout sheet of goldenrod paper or coloured masking film, such as Ulano, ruled to show the correct position for each image. After taping in position, the sheet is turned over and sections cut away corresponding to the printing areas of the images so that these are exposed. The work is centred left to right on the sheet and a space left at the base for gripper margin – i.e. the minimum non-printing space required for the grippers to clamp the paper as it goes through the press.

For example if four pages 8½ in. × 11 in. are to run on a 20 in × 22 in. press using standard size 17 in. × 22 in. paper. On a sheet the size of the printing plate, rule a 17 in. × 22 in. rectangle to represent the paper stock size. Centre it left to right with at least 1¼ in. from the base of the sheet to provide the necessary gripper margin. Using the squaring-up equipment or a T-square and triangle, divide the 17 in. × 22 in. rectangle into four equal parts to give the 8½ in. × 11 in. pages. Draw lines across the rectangle through the centre of all four pages to provide register lines in centring and squaring-up the negatives. Similar register marks are made on the negatives before stripping.

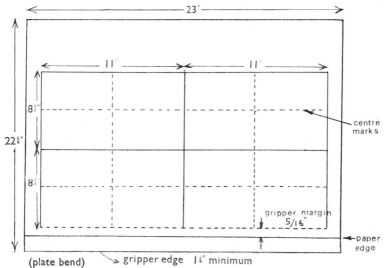

Fig. 25 Four-page layout – sheet size 17 in. × 22 in.

When the layout or dummy has been ruled to show the sizes of each page, the next step is to refer to the imposition chart to see the order of the pages. This consists of a layout which is the exact size of the finished job, folded as it will be in the bindery after printing, with the pages numbered in the correct sequence. It is unfolded and placed alongside the stripping base, to be used as a guide in positioning the images on the stripping flat. The required areas are then numbered to correspond with the imposition chart – with the proviso that it should be remembered that for surface printing where no prism is used, the negatives will be reversed left to right (laterally) when the plate is printed, to give a right reading image on the plate. After offsetting on the blanket it is right reading on the paper. Thus a negative on the right side of the flat will print on the left side of the plate and vice versa. Therefore the page numbers on the dummy should be reversed, i.e. reading left to right when compared with the imposition chart. This does not apply in the case of negatives laterally reversed for positive making for deep etch plate making but applies when stripping in position positives made from such negatives.

In bookwork, at least $\frac{1}{8}$ in to $\frac{1}{4}$ in. must be allowed for trim on the top, bottom and outside margin, which is the side opposite the fold of each page. This should be shown on the layout; also if illustrations are to bleed off the sheet, the trim must be shown very accurately to prevent the bleed subject over-running into the next page. In printing, the sheet registers against a set of pins which square it and position it correctly

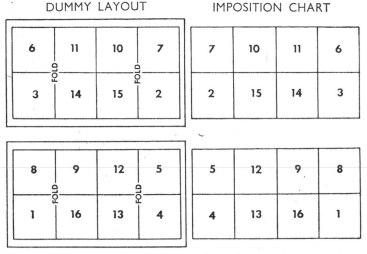

Fig. 26 Sixteen-page sheetwise imposition (back-up) printing from two plates

for printing. There are front guides and side guides. Obviously, since the paper may vary in size, to assure register the same edges of the sheets must be fed to the guides each time the work is run through the press. It is a good point to indicate on the layout which sides of the sheet are to be fed to the guides.

The gripper edge, which designates the side of the sheet to be fed to the front guides, must always be marked, but it is also a good point to indicate the side guide edge of the layout so that in the work that follows the operators can work from these two sides. In general the right-hand side of the layout is considered to be the guide side, but when the paper is turned for backing, the machine minder may move the side guide to the opposite side of the press so that for back-up pages the left-hand side of the stripped-up assembly could well be the guide side.

Accurate Positioning

THE NEGATIVES should be located on the flat and accurately positioned so that the negative register marks match exactly the corresponding marks on the layout sheet. With Ulano Rubylith or Goldenplast orange masking plastic sheets, for better dimensional stability, the positioning is done with red cellulose tape. Guide marks and centre marks are cut into the flat. The sheet is turned over and the sheet cut away, using a sharp knife, in the areas covering the required printing portions of the assembled negatives. During this operation, a strip of clear acetate film inserted between the negative and the sheet will prevent the knife cutting into the negatives. The Amberlith or orange mask should be cut a fraction from the working area of the film and this small area filled-in by opaquing. Where the windows have not been cut into the sheet, the yellow or orange colour of the sheeting will effectively prevent any penetration by the illuminant when printing down. Clear tape is used to firmly attach the images to the cut-out windows; the flat is then turned over to its correct position and the Sellotape, used to hold the images temporarily in situ, is removed from the film side.

DOUBLE PRINTING

THIS IS often done direct on to the metal plate by having identical register marks on both negatives and by stopping out on one negative all the subject matter appearing on the other negative and vice versa. The two images are then registered in position and exposed one after the other on the same sensitised metal sheet.

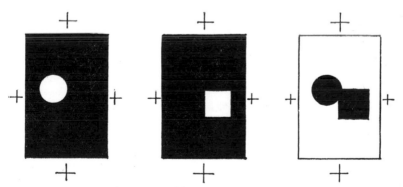

Fig. 27 Double printing in register

Sometimes with a strip-up job it is not possible to position, by stripping-in, one section of the job because of its intricate nature. When the main work has been stripped on to one sheet, position another clear sheet over it and fit the insert on the clear sheet in exact register with the main flat. Draw or cut crossmark register ticks in exact juxtaposition on both sheets. The platemaker can then match the register marks when he overprints the insert image on to the main job.

Alternatively, by photographic procedure the subject matter from both films can be combined into a single film. This is also done when detail is in very close proximity, especially close-fitting line and half-tone work and furthermore it eliminates out-of-contact possibilities. If

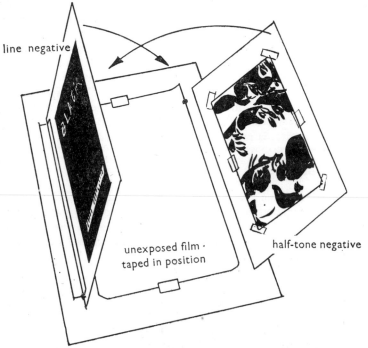

line negative

unexposed film · taped in position

half-tone negative

Fig. 28 Flap method of registering

the flap method is used, a sheet of metal is placed on the base of the contact printing frame, a piece of white paper placed on it, and the two negatives for double printing are then carefully registered to each other in position on the white paper. Each negative is then taped to the metal sheet, one on the left side and the other on the right side so that they are hinged to the metal base. Under darkroom safelight conditions the white paper is removed and the unexposed film positioned face-up and taped down securely to the metal base. The first flap negative is positioned on the film, the frame closed, the air extracted and the first exposure made. The vacuum contact is released and the second hinged negative positioned on the sensitised film. The second exposure is then made and the film developed in the normal way. When double printing from positives, it is necessary to mask-out each positive in the areas where the other positive is required to print to prevent pre-exposure of the emulsion.

Punch register and three-point lay register systems are methods in general use. The two films for double printing are first registered together over a light table, taped together and punched to give the register locations. Using peg or pin locations in the printing frame which match the punched holes, the successive exposure of each nega-

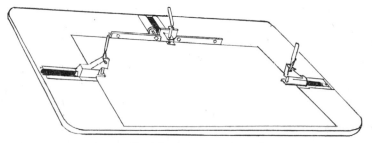

Fig. 29 Kodak pin bar register frame

tive on the sensitised film results in the perfect register of the two images. The sensitive film is punched and located on the pins and the negatives, similarly punched out, are also positioned, in turn, on the pins prior to exposure.

Side register or three point register is done by first registering and taping the images together over the light table and trimming the adjoining horizontal and vertical edges of the assembly to form a right angle. This edge is used for locating the job in the contact frame. Each negative is positioned for printing against locating studs or a right angle edging, against which the sensitive film has been taped face-up. The negatives in turn are taped down in correct position before closing the vacuum frame, exhausting the air and exposing.

Astrafoil (D.E.P. Ltd)

ASTRAFOIL SHEETS of proved dimensional stability are used for planning and assembling. The key drawing is printed down photomechanically and dyed-up in a Blue Astrafoil Film Dye, using the blue key lines as a guide for positioning. The Astrafoil coating is supplied in liquid form in both high and low viscosities. Whirler coat the Astrafoil. If preferred a coating powder is available which is mixed with ammonium dichromate sensitiser or, alternatively, Diapos presensitised Astrafoil material, which requires only contact printing. Development is effected with ammonia fumes.

VI

Duplicate Images

MULTIPLE REPRODUCTION

IN THE early days of lithography duplicate images were made by 'hand-transferring', in which the drawn image on the prepared stone was inked-up and impressions pulled on transfer paper. These were then transferred to a larger stone to form the printing surface. Exact register was something of a problem and detail was generally lacking in some impressions, compared with the original image on the stone. The introduction of photography solved many of these problems in that bromide prints could be made from a master negative, patched-up in position, colour separated, or altered as required, and a further negative or negatives made for single or multiple printing to metal.

Today methods such as multi-positive and multi-negative systems using Astrafoil techniques, etc., are used.

STEP-AND-REPEAT WORK

STEP-AND-REPEAT camera projectors and printing down equipment are available to cover a wide application and built to ensure absolute accuracy. They are expensive pieces of apparatus and when not available the pin system can be used for making multiple exposures when printing down to metal. A clear piece of plastic film with a punch and pegs to fit the punched holes is required with masking tape and a blue ballpoint pen. A layout is prepared on the plastic sheet and gripper marks are drawn at the base and punched out. The plastic sheet is then positioned over the metal plate and taped in position. Using the pen, scribe on the plate through the punched holes the gripper hole outlines which have been punched in the centre of the gripper marks on the plastic sheet. If holes are punched on the gripper edge of the plate, as on the plastic sheet, the sheet can be pegged to the plate.

In multiple exposing on the plate the register marks are matched to the cross lines drawn on the sheet as indicated in Fig. 30. The film image is moved to the new position after each exposure and all other areas of the plate masked out during the exposure. Alternatively, for greater accuracy, as shown in the diagram, holes can be punched into the plastic sheet and the image pegged to the sheet each time it is moved. After the exposure and re-alignment of the image, the platemaker must carefully mask out portions not to be exposed. This method makes it unnecessary to line up visually the register marks with the plastic sheet ruling when repositioning after each exposure.

A further method for repeating the work on the plate is to position the negatives on one side of the plastic sheet in the normal layout manner and include a double set of register marks as illustrated. These are used in platemaking to position the images on the plate. The platemaker either pin punctures the marks through the plastic sheet and marks

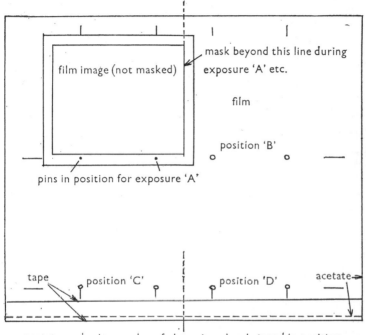

Fig. 30 Hand register method for duplicate images

them in pencil on the plate when he prints the first image, or he develops them out on the plate after the first exposure. This enables him to make one exposure and then move the flat to a new location making a further exposure from the same negatives. If a double print is required the same registration marks are used.

Where multiple repeats are required with great precision step-and-repeat machines are necessary. These are most versatile, and can be used for multi-negative work for postage stamps, labels, cheque backgrounds and the like; also for interlocking designs for book covers and textile work. Scroll and elaborate rosette designs can be stepped-up and combined in bromide prints to make enlarged copy which, when reduced in reproduction, equals copper-plate engraving results.

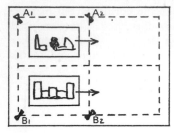 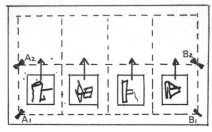

Fig. 31 Layout for double printing. Uncovered areas masked during each exposure

EQUIPMENT FOR SIMPLE AND INVOLVED STEPPING

THERE ARE many makes of step-and-repeat projector for producing photographic multi-images and also step-and-repeat machines for making multi-images on metal plates. All equipment must be accurate and designed on the same basis as a precision machine tool, rigid in construction yet easy to manipulate. Very efficient machines for combining these methods are now in general use.

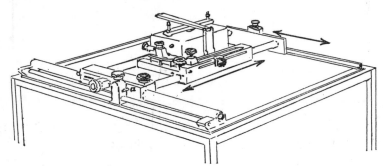

Fig. 32A Huber Fast Stepper – inexpensive and accurate for limited stepping-up

The Lithoprintex Junior Mark II

THE MAXIMUM size of lithographic plate is 38 in. × 50 in. (97 cm. × 127 cm.). The maximum standard size of glass or film for multiple positive or negative images is 30 in. × 40 in. (76 cm. × 102 cm.). Unit-holders for stepping up range from 6½ in. × 8½ in. (16 cm. × 21 cm.) to a maximum of 16 in. × 20 in. (40 cm. × 50 cm.).

The machine has a vertical platen on which a litho plate, or sensitised photographic emulsion, etc., is held firmly in place by vacuum so that a single or multiple image on a photographic film or plate, held in the unit-holder, may be step-and-repeat contact printed to produce multiple images in precisely the required positions accurately. Text and illustration images may be imposed to a required layout, for accurate and precise colour register, etc. Arc lamps, or a 4 kW xenon lamp contained in a

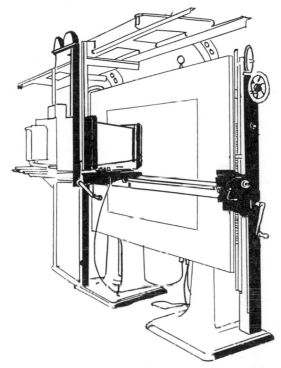

Fig. 32B Step-and-Repeat photocomposing machine –
an all-purpose automatic machine

separate unit, are used for litho plate exposing and a low-power (12-volt tungsten filament) point source lighting for photographic material. Small red safelight bulbs illuminate the setting dials and scales for darkroom working. The images to be stepped are positioned by vertical, partly counter-balanced, vertical and horizontal movement. The unit-holder is firmly secured in a saddle which is easily moved to any desired position on the cross beam and locked. Movements of precise multiples of 1 cm. or 1 in. are made by interlocking the saddle with one of a series of notches in the horizontal notch bar which is carried by the cross beam; finer settings, graduated in divisions of 0·01 mm. or 0·001 in., are made by turning a micrometer screw which traverses the notch bar by the required portion of 1 cm. or 1 in. A vernier scale, used in conjunction with the divisions representing 0·001 on the micrometer control 'drums', permits them to be set to one-tenth of one division.

At the ends of the cross beams are supports attached to the counterbalanced lifting mechanism with notch bars at each side to ensure true parallel location of the cross beam as it is raised and lowered. The same principle, combining notches, micrometer and vernier control providing movement of the notch bars through any part of 1 cm. or 1 in., gives a vertical movement comparable with the horizontal. Indicated by scales, one revolution of the screw produces a movement of 1 mm. or $\frac{1}{10}$ in. and the 'drums' each have 100 peripheral divisions, with handwheels provided for easy and rapid setting. Front and back vacuums are given by electrically driven pumps, an overhead rail carries the arc lamps, which are hooded, and a light integrating meter is supplied. Register marks must be sited on the original. These must number three and must be within $\frac{1}{4}$ in. of the centre lines of the glass plate in either direction. They should be horizontal and vertical, with the two opposed marks in strict alignment, and the third mark, if extended, should cut the line joining the other two exactly at right angles and close to its centre. This point of intersection should also be near the centre of the image. Each unit-holder is made so that negatives or positives may be accurately preregistered – through 90°, 180° or 270° – in readiness for exposing on the machine. Loading and pre-registration are carried out on a separate appliance, thereby enabling subjects to be prepared in advance. A vertical machine has considerable advantage over a horizontal one, both in saving floor space and in permitting easy operational success.

The Lithoprintex Senior Step-and-Repeat Machine

THE MAXIMUM litho plate size is 68 in. × 84 in. and the film size is 54 in. × 77 in., with 7 unit-holder sizes from 8 in. × 10 in. (20 cm. × 25 cm.) to 28 in. × 32 in. (71 cm × 81 cm.). The accuracy of the machine is such that from the same or identical units two or more printing plates can be produced on which the position of any image is duplicated within half of one thousandth of an inch (0·0125 mm.). The precise location and correct interrelationship and accuracy of the stepped images is again guaranteed by the well-tried system of notch bars. The unit-holder is initially located and secured into its appropriate full inch position on the notch bar and the fractional inch settings obtained by turning a hardened and ground steel micrometer screw. A pre-setting device allows the fractional inch position to be altered in readiness for

the next location whilst an exposure is in progress. Machines are supplied with metric or inch calibrations.

The control panel with full instrumentation for all operations is
mounted at the side of the machine and there is a separate register
device for pre-planning and positioning work in holders whilst the
machine is working. A photoelectric light-integrating meter is coupled

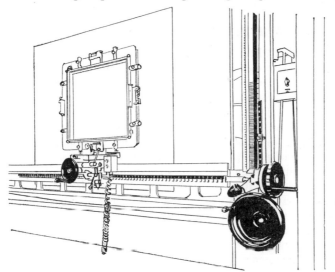

Fig. 33A Lithoprintex Senior

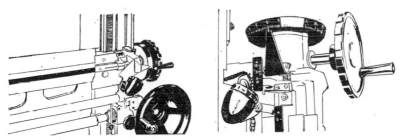

Fig. 33B Lithoprintex Senior – horizontal notch bar, micrometer and
vernier control

to the light source which is a high-powered motorised arc lamp or
pulsed xenon lamp mounted on a counterbalanced support. For photographic work separate hooded illumination is supplied. The holders for
the negatives and positives are equipped with a pre-register device,
operating through 90°, 180° or 270° prior to commencing actual exposing operations. This is invaluable for work and turn, etc. On the control

panel two gauges independently record the vacuum fastening of the subject matter to the machine platen and the contact vacuum of the unit-holder. A safety interlocking device prevents an exposure being made until the correct degree of vacuum is attained.

A model with a completely automatic sequence controlled by the latest fluid logic principles is envisaged.

AUTO STEP-AND-REPEAT MACHINES

STEP-AND-REPEAT projectors are also made for automatic operation. One such projector is the H.P.L. (Hunter-Penrose) Auto Step-and-Repeat Projector which incorporates automatic focusing and full automatic step movement. Once the unit image is positioned in the carrier, registered for size and position on the glass screen, the multiple negative plate or film inserted in the large holder in the darkroom, the control charts inserted in the machine and the lights switched on, the operation of a push-button will set in motion duplicate exposures of the image continuously until a pre-determined number of exposures is completed without further attention of the operator. An accuracy of 0·001 in. (0·025 mm.) is guaranteed and images of subsequent colours will register exactly. By using the push-button control any exposure in the normal sequence can be 'missed' as desired and a second unit image can be exactly projected to fit the missed spaces. The automatic operation can be commenced at any part of the layout and an exposure made to any position on the multi-negative. The machine can, if required, be operated manually and is supplied for inch or metric measurement. Unit plate holders which rotate through 360 degrees are provided to include the following sizes of negatives – 12 in. × 10 in., 8½ in. × 6½ in., 6½ in. × 4¾ in. (25 cm. × 30 cm., 16½ cm. × 21 cm., 12 cm. × 16½ cm.). The maximum multi-negative size is 40 in. × 30 in. (76 cm. × 100 cm.). Range of automatic focus 2½ times enlargement to ⅖ reduction. The illumination may be mercury vapour bulbs, with internal silvered reflectors, controlled by a built-in integrating light meter which automatically corrects any variations of light intensity. The lens diaphragm is set by remote control.

For plate making once the unit image has been registered in the carrier and a lithographic plate and the control charts mounted on the machine, any number of image repeats can be stepped and printed down automatically. The machine will print unit images from 2 in. × 2 in. (5 cm. × 5 cm.) to 24 in. × 20 in. (60 cm. × 50 cm.) on to lithographic plates ranging from Double Demy 36½ in. × 30 in. (93 cm. × 76 cm.), to Extra Quad Demy 53½ in. × 44 in. (136 cm. × 112 cm.), the size of bed being 61 in. × 45½ in. (155 cm. × 115·5 cm.). The negatives in the plate-holders are registered by sighting to an illuminated graticule through a moveable magnifier. Images of any shape or 'lay' can be positioned to the best advantage to avoid waste of paper and card by using the rotating (360 degrees) system supplied. Contact, both for the negative/positive and the lithographic plate, is by vacuum hold and to speed-up exposure time for plate-making a motorised single point 80-amperes arc lamp, photoelectric exposure-meter controlled – with a mirror to increase effective illumination to equal 120 amperes – is a further available source of illumination. A 'point' source filament lamp, also electronically controlled, can be used for photographic plates and films. Control charts, perforated by a special punch, are attached to the drums governing the movement of the negative in the machine.

Multinex Equipment

THE MULTINEX is an automatic machine available in three sizes – Standard, – for multi-negatives only, maximum original $8\frac{1}{4}$ in. × 6 in., maximum multiple plate 25 in. × 25 in.; Universal, for offset plates or multi-negatives, maximum original 9 in. × 12 in., to take plates up to 29 in. × 43 in.; Senior, for offset plates or negatives, maximum original 24 in. × 24 in., to take printing plates up to 80 in. × 102 in. This latter is a punch card model of very advanced design. Approximate speed of operation – photographic materials 350 steps per hour; offset plates 70 steps per hour. The Multinex Standard has two carriages which move in different planes and with an angle of 90° to each other. The film original is mounted on a frame of the upper carriage and the film or plate intended for the multiple negatives is mounted on the lower carriage. Manœuvring of the carriages is effected automatically, according to adjustments of the steps made before the start. When the required number of copies is completed the machine stops automatically and a buzzer sounds to indicate that the job is finished.

A 24-watt tungsten bulb is used for exposure, fitted into the lamp hood of the upper carriage. The rays from the light source are directed on to the film original by a slanted mirror. Movement is by the use of compressed air and all-mechanical movements are guided and controlled by a relay system built into the machine. The electronic exposure control is equipped with a push button unit, consisting of eight push buttons, marked from 0·1 to 5·0, and the exposure time or light value is chosen by depressing one or several of the push buttons. The time range is from 0·1 to 13·2 seconds. For instance, if the desired exposure time is 1·3 seconds, the push buttons marked 0·1, 0·2 and 1·0 are depressed (0·1 + 0·2 + 1·0 = 1·3). There are two limit control contacts on the machine, one for the upper end and one for the lower carriage. The limit control contact for the lower carriage is set for the desired number of exposures in each row (horizontally) whereas the limit control contact for the upper carriage is set for the desired number of rows (vertically). If a copy 2 in. × 2 in. is to be repeated twenty times so that the multiple image consists of four rows each with five copies, the procedure is to move the lower carriage four times, each time followed by an exposure, with the first exposure taking place at the starting position, making a total of five exposures. The carriage will automatically return to its starting position. Simultaneously the upper carriage will move one step length (next row), then the lower carriage will make four movements followed by exposures and then again return to the starting position. Simultaneously the upper carriage will move to a new row, and so on. This continues until the upper carriage has moved three times (to the fourth row) and the lower carriage has moved four times (five exposures) in the last row. If the limit controls are properly set, the machine will then stop.

Adjustment of the limit control contacts is done as follows:

(a) For the lower carriage: 5 in. × 2 in. = 10 in., equal to one side of the multiple negative. The limit control contact is placed about $1\frac{1}{2}$ step lengths before the above-mentioned length (10 in. − 3 in. = 7 in.); i.e. 7 in. on the scale beside the lower carriage.

(b) For the upper carriage: 4 in. × 2 in. = 8 in., equal to the other side of the multiple negative. The limit control contact is placed about $1\frac{1}{2}$ step lengths before the above-mentioned length (8 in. − 3 in. = 5 in.); i.e. 5 in. on the scale beside the upper carriage.

The Multinex Standard has also a built-in device to enable fully automatic copying in a staggered pattern. The device is controlled by two switches on the control panel. After the step length for the lower carriage (horizontal movement) and the upper carriage (vertical movement) have been adjusted, the switch marked 'Normal/Staggering' is put to the 'staggering' position and the switch marked 'Combination' is put to its upper position.

With the Multinex Senior punch card model all step movements, either regular or staggered, are automatic, as are all exposures until the cycle is completed. Details of the layout are punched into a small card and the information fed through a 'reader', which controls movements and exposure. Contact pressure can be varied by an adjustable pneumatic control system and the electronically controlled light source is a 6000-watt xenon lamp. Copying capacity as stated, 70 to 150 offset-steps and 350 film-steps per hour respectively. If a postage-stamp size negative is to be repeated 60 times on film, the multiple negative is ready for developing in 12 minutes. If copying with a xenon lamp directly on to an offset plate the same job is done in about one and a half hours.

The computer side of the machine is now transistored and the machine can be fitted with either a 6 kW water-cooled xenon lamp, or with a 4 kW air-cooled pulsed xenon lamp. For use with photographic film the small tungsten filament lamp is satisfactory. Two motors control the horizontal and vertical drives, for coarse and fine work, with a guaranteed accuracy of 0·001 in. Three table sizes are available, 54 in. × 78 in., 62 in. × 110 in., 70 in. × 100 in., with unit holders up to 24 in. × 24 in. Lead screws with vernier attachment control the setting of step size and in Model 101 the use of a special optical measuring unit gives an accuracy of 0·0002 in.

Rutherford Vertical Composing Machine

THE MODERN use of tape or card is understandable. It is easy to store for repeat orders and it can be used for several colour plates of one order as well as being fast and accurate. The Rutherford Ruth-o-Matic is a vertical photocomposing machine which is governed, in fact, by a roll of plastic tape four inches wide, which is punched using a manual punch, over a punch board containing 140 hole positions. Each number on the tape represents a vertical or horizontal co-ordinate for positioning the plate. All operational information is punched on to the tape and corrections or alterations can be made by hand. The reader, into which the tape is fed, plus the 140 spring-loaded pins, sense the information being fed on the tape, and control the movement. When the sequence of operations is completed the tape is rewound, the vacuum released and the machine returns to starting position. The machine is fully automatic, in many different sizes, with plate sizes, for instance, including 33 in. × 42 in. and 58 in × 78 in. Exposures are set on an electrical timer, and the illumination functions automatically during the machine's operation and last minute changes can be made on the tape with a hand punch. A punched signal can alert the operator to perform a manual function such as inserting a negative or altering its position. The automatic control can be by-passed if required and co-ordinates can be taken from the layout sheet and fed into the reader by dialling settings on the reader control panel.

A recent development is the incorporation of a 1 in. binary tape control for automatic positioning of the machine and automatic exposure cycle. This is punched on a Friden Programatic Flexowriter. The tape is eight-channelled and when punching the operator includes data on exposure and negative number and rotation, plus the five digits needed for horizontal and vertical movement and the direction of travel. A tape reader is used and the individual co-ordinates are stored in relays, five banks of ten for each direction of travel. After each exposure the tape reader reads the information to follow and when stored the digits are projected by read-out tubes. These numbers represent horizontal and vertical movements and are illuminated until the exposure is completed and the machine has moved on to the next setting, thus providing a check against the layout master sheet.

VII

The Principles of Photography

LIGHT

PHOTOGRAPHY CONSISTS in the production by optical means of a physical image and in the formation of a permanent record of the image by chemical means. The optical image is formed in the camera by the lens. This depends upon the illumination – the action of light – and to understand the functioning of a camera it is necessary to know something of the nature of light and the formation of optical images. Light is a form of radiant energy which when reflected from an object enters the eye allowing the object to be observed. Our main source of natural light comes from the sun, and the most common source of artificial light is provided by an electric light bulb.

Much has been written to explain the nature of light. The three main theories of Newton (corpuscular theory), Huygens (wave theory) and the more recent Quantum Theory are outside the scope of this book. It suffices to say that for normal optical considerations the wave theory presents an adequate explanation. The energy, transmitted through space by a form of wave motion of electromagnetic origin, reveals itself in different ways according to the wavelength (from crest to crest), although the speed or velocity through space is the same for all wavelengths – 186,000 miles per second.

It was in 1801 that Herschel discovered that beyond the red end of the visible spectrum were rays which have a heating effect, termed infra-red rays. Almost at the same time Ritter found beyond the violet end of the spectrum invisible rays which could blacken silver chloride, called ultra-violet rays. Since then methods have been evolved of generating, detecting and utilising a huge wide band of electromagnetic waves ranging in wavelength from one-millionth of a millionth of a centimetre to some five hundred miles; including cosmic rays, gamma rays, X-rays, ultra-violet, visible, infra-red, heat rays and wireless waves.

All light has wave-like properties, and light in different parts of the spectrum corresponds to waves of different lengths. Each spectral colour is defined by the wavelength of its light. The units of measurement used are the micron (μ), which is equal to one thousandth of a millimetre; the millimicron (mμ), which is one thousandth of a micron; and the

Ångstrom (Å), which is one ten-thousandth of a micron. The main spectral colours occupy, very approximately, the following wavelength bands; violet 4000–4500 Å and less; blue 4500–4800 Å; blue-green 4800–5100 Å; green 5100–5500 Å; yellow-green 5500–5700 Å; yellow 5700–5900 Å; orange 5900–6300 Å; red 6300–7000 Å. There is a gradual transition from one colour to another throughout the spectrum, which may broadly be divided into equal parts of one-third red, green and blue. This range of colour, called the visible spectrum, occurs in nature as the rainbow.

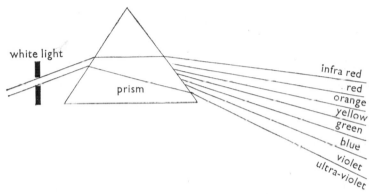

Fig. 34 Spectrum of white light

ILLUMINATION

THE AMOUNT of light striking a surface is called the illumination. A candle was the standard illuminant in days gone by and the light output or luminous intensity was compared to a 'standard candle'. The present day standard of luminous intensity, adopted internationally, consists of one square centimetre of a black body heated to the temperature at which platinum solidifies, having a luminous intensity of 60 candelas. The candela and the old standard candle have approximately the same luminous intensity. Thus it means that a 50 candle-power bulb is 50 times as bright as a standard candle, or as bright as 50 candles. The British unit of illumination is called a lumen per square foot, or a foot-candle; and is the intensity of illumination of a surface at a distance of one foot from a standard candle. The metric unit is the lumen per square metre, or the metre-candle, and 50 metre-candles is the amount of light falling on a surface one metre distant from a 50 c.p. lamp.

The amount of light falling on an object depends upon two factors: the candle-power of the light source and the distance from the source to the object. Here the Law of Inverse Squares operates. This states that 'The action of light varies inversely as the square of the distance from the source to the object'. Illumination varies proportionally with the luminous intensity of the source of light, and inversely as the square of the distance from the source, or:

$$\text{Illumination (in foot-candles)} = \frac{\text{candle power of source}}{\text{(distance from source in feet)}^2}.$$

For example an exposure of 100 seconds is given using double arc lamps 4 feet from the subject, each arc lamp having a 24,000 candle-power light. What would the equivalent exposure be moving the arcs to 6 feet distance?

$$\text{Illumination} = \frac{\text{C.P.}}{\text{(distance)}^2} = \frac{24,000}{(4)^2} = \frac{24,000}{16}$$
$$= 1500 \text{ foot-candles.}$$

With two equal sources of light the

$$\text{total illumination} = 2 \times 1500$$
$$= 3000 \text{ foot-candles.}$$

At a distance of 6 feet

$$\text{Illumination} = \frac{\text{C.P.}}{\text{(distance)}^2} = \frac{24,000}{(6)^2} = \frac{24,000}{36}$$
$$= 666\cdot6 \text{ foot-candles.}$$

$$\text{Total illumination} = 2 \times 666\cdot6 = 1334 \text{ foot-candles.}$$

The new exposure (x) is found as follows:

$$\frac{\text{original C.P. illumination}}{\text{new C.P. illumination}} = \frac{\text{new exposure}}{\text{original exposure}}$$

$$\frac{3000}{1334} = \frac{x}{100}$$
$$1334x = 300,000$$
$$x = 225 \text{ seconds for new exposure.}$$

Reflection

LIGHT FALLING on a flat smooth surface is reflected so that the angle of incidence (the angle between the incident ray and the normal or the perpendicular to the surface at the angle of incidence) is the same as the angle of reflection. The reflected ray is in the same plane as the incident ray and the normal; and this reflection is called specular reflection.

A matt or rough surface causes different parts of a parallel beam of light to meet the surface at different angles, being reflected back at almost any angle to the main plane. Such reflection is known as diffuse or scattered reflection, causing a loss of detail and contrast in reproduction. Some surfaces have both specular and diffuse reflection – such as varnished wood.

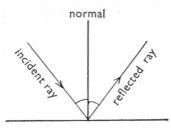

Fig. 35 Specular reflection

Refraction and Critical Angle

REFRACTION OCCURS when a ray of light is bent as it passes at an angle from one medium to another of a different density. When light passes from one transparent medium to another, such as air to glass or water to air, it is bent towards the normal on passing from a rarer to a denser medium, and away from the normal when passing from a denser to a rarer medium. The refractive index of the medium, that is the optical quality, causes different amounts of bending or deviation. When light passes from a denser to a rarer medium it is refracted away from the normal, so that as the incident angle increases it eventually skims along

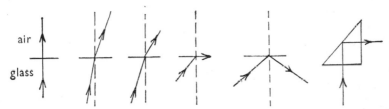

Fig. 36 Refraction – showing on the right, critical angle, total reflection and a reflecting glass prism

the boundary plane between the two substances. This point is known as the critical angle and light striking the boundary at a greater angle is totally reflected. The critical angle for a glass to air surface is 40 degrees, light striking at 45 degrees will be totally reflected.

This characteristic of glass is utilised in the reflecting prism in which a block of glass with non-parallel plane sides causes a change in direction of light toward the base. The amount of refraction, or bending of the light, depends upon the angle of the prism, the angle of incidence of the light, the refractive index of the glass and the wavelength of the light.

Dispersion

THIS OCCURS because the different wavelengths in white light are refracted to various extents. The longer wavelengths (red) are less refracted than the short wavelengths (violet).

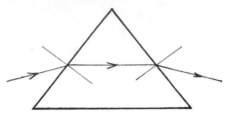

Fig 37 Refraction by glass prism

THE LENS

LENSES USED in graphic work consist of a number of glass elements which are converging or positive (convex) and diverging or negative (concave). Converging lenses converge the light rays emitted by a point object to a single point on the other side of the lens from the source. Diverging lenses spread the light rays so that no real image of the subject point is formed. A lens is a medium whereby a large cone of light from a point may cover a large disc and be refracted so that it is once more concentrated to a point to give a bright, sharp image. Rays of light passing through the centre are not refracted, so that the tangential planes at the centre are parallel. The rays passing through the other parts of the lens are refracted as through a prism with increasing angles as they approach the edge of the lens. The point at which light from a point on the object is converged by a lens is the *focus* and this position depends on the position of the object. With a distant object, such as light from a star, the rays of light are almost parallel and the focal point is called the principal focus.

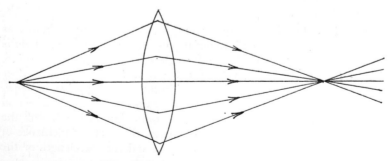

Fig. 38 Refraction of light by a lens

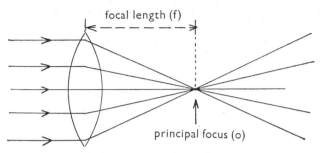

focal length (f)

principal focus (o)

Fig. 39 Refraction by a lens of parallel light

The brightness of the image formed by a lens depends upon (*a*) the amount of light transmitted by the lens and (*b*) the area over which this light has to be spread. The larger the lens aperture, the brighter the image, but the greater the focal length, the dimmer the image. Brightness is proportional to

$$\frac{\text{lens diameter}^2}{\text{focal length}^2}$$

With a corrected lens all rays from a point on the object are refracted and intersect at a point. The point of intersection denotes the position of the image. Rays passing through the centre of the lens are practically unchanged and, as the rays parallel to the axis of the lens are refracted, passing through the principal focus of the lens, these intersections define the position of the image.

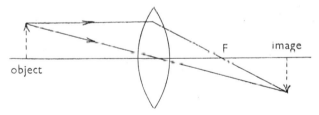

object   F   image

Fig. 40 Geometric construction of an image

Optical principles are discussed in Chapter VI of *Camera and Process Work*. It suffices to say that all optical calculations are derived from the formula of conjugate foci

$$\frac{1}{f} = \frac{1}{u} + \frac{1}{v}$$

when $f =$ the focal length of the lens, $v =$ the distance of the image from the lens and $u =$ the distance of the object from the lens. Magnification (M), the ratio of image size to object size, is expressed as $\dfrac{v}{u}$ and image and object sizes determined as follows:

$$v = f(1 + M) \quad \text{and} \quad u = f\left(1 + \frac{1}{M}\right)$$

LENS ABERRATIONS

SIMPLE LENSES have defects, called aberrations, which will not permit them to create a perfect image. These are due to the fact that the refraction surfaces are not flat but spherical in shape. Thus marginal rays are refracted more strongly than central rays and are therefore not brought to a focus at the same point. Also the edges of the lens, acting as a prism, separate the various spectrum colours forming white light. Because of these defects a sharp image is unobtainable. If the central rays are brought to a focus, the marginal rays are diffuse, and the opposite occurs when the marginal rays are brought to a focus.

Most aberrations are corrected by using a combination of positive and negative (concave) lenses of different types of glass with carefully computed radii of curvature. Two lenses combining a convergent and

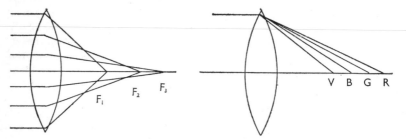

Fig. 41 Lens aberrations – spherical (*left*), chromatic (*right*)

divergent meniscus produce a compound lens called an achromatic or doublet lens, which corrects chromatic aberration for blue, violet and yellow. An aplamat lens, which is free from defects caused by marginal rays, consists of two achromatic lenses in a mount separated by a central opening. An apochromatic lens is further corrected for red radiations. An anastigmatic lens gives a flat field and corrects any spherical shape of the image area which otherwise is non-sharp towards the edges of the image. Curvature of field and coma, which is a form of skewed spherical aberration, are cured by the use of separated elements in the lens.

The main defects are chromatic aberration, spherical aberration and curvilinear distortion. The first is caused by different wavelengths of light being refracted differently, with the shorter wavelengths (violet) being brought to a focus nearer the lens than longer (red) wavelengths. Positive and negative lenses of different glass are combined to cure this fault. With spherical aberration marginal rays are brought to a focus nearer to the lens than rays passing through the centre. Definition is lacking and is corrected by combining positive and negative lenses. Curvilinear distortion occurs when rays reaching the edge of an image use different parts of the lens, according to the position of the aperture or diaphragm opening. If the aperture is in the front element of the lens, barrel distortion takes place, in which a square-shaped object has bowed-out sides. The opposite effect, pin-cushion distortion, occurs when the aperture is behind the lens. With the old-type rapid rectilinear lens the defect was cured by placing the aperture midway between two similar lenses. The modern method is to employ separated elements in the lens barrel.

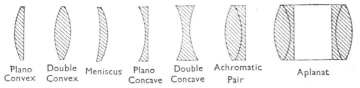

| Plano Convex | Double Convex | Meniscus | Plano Concave | Double Concave | Achromatic Pair | Aplanat |

Fig. 42 Types of lenses

It is not possible in practice for a minute point or line on the object to be reproduced facsimile on the image. No lens is perfect and a fine point is rendered as a small circular area of light, called the *circle of confusion*. Accuracy of focusing and lens quality determine the quality of the result, the smaller the circle of confusion, the better the quality of image definition. At normal viewing (10 in.) a circle of $\frac{1}{100}$ in. in diameter appears to be an absolutely sharp point. The latitude in focusing to obtain critical definition is termed *the depth of focus*. This is increased by decreasing the aperture. The ability of a lens to record detail is carried out by testing with sets of equally spaced black and white lines at different scales. When sharply focused, the *resolving power* of the lens is given as the number of black lines per millimetre which can be separately seen in the image plane. *Acutance* is the term given to the physical measure of image sharpness and involves a comprehensive system embracing the lens and emulsion with associated factors.

Blooming of Lenses

A CERTAIN amount of light reflected from an original will always be lost in passing through the lens system. This is caused by absorption by the glass and reflections from the entry and exit surfaces. The loss caused by absorption is quite small, but the loss of light caused by reflections from the lens surfaces is much more serious. Apart from lengthening exposure, image contrast is reduced and flare spots and ghost images can be produced. Lenses are coated to minimise these defects. Because each colour has a different wavelength and thus a different absorption coefficient, reflections cannot be entirely eliminated and maximum absorption is usually allowed in the middle region of the spectrum. Thus the pale violet colour of the coated lens surface, red and violet being partly reflected. The coating consists of a thin layer of calcium or magnesium, evaporated in a vacuum, on the lens surface. Fluoride is also used for this purpose. The refractive index of the material is about halfway between those of glass and air. This reduces surface reflection from about 5% to something like 1·5% at each surface, reducing the light loss to no more than 15%.

Relative Aperture

LENS-APERTURE readings represent a fraction of the focal length of the lens. Thus $f/16$ using a 16-inch focal length lens would be 1 inch in diameter and $f/8$ would be 2 inches in diameter, 1/8 of 16 = 2. Other factors remaining equal, the amount of exposure using different stops varies directly as the square of the $f/$number.

$f/$no.	8	11·3	16	22·6	32	45·25	64
Relative exposure time	1	2	4	8	16	32	64

The lens aperture is always smaller than the focal length. Process lenses are made to work with maximum efficiency between $f/16$ and $f/32$. It is noted that to avoid the inconvenience of fractions the image brightness produced by a lens is normally defined as:

$$\frac{\text{focal length}}{\text{lens diameter}}$$

which is known as the *relative aperture* of $f/$number of the lens. The formula for image brightness, as has been stated, is proportional to $\frac{(\text{lens diameter})^2}{\text{focal length}}$. This has been inverted to avoid fractions, so that now the $f/$numbers will increase as the brightness diminishes. The lens on a process camera is not used at full aperture for exposure, but only for sizing-up and focusing purposes. The device for decreasing the effective aperture of the lens is the iris *diaphragm*. This consists of a number of thin metal blades which, by rotating a ring in the lens mount, block off portions of the lens, starting from the outer edge. The combined movement of a number of blades equally spaced round the lens makes it possible to leave in the centre of the lens an almost circular hole, the diameter of which depends upon the degree of rotation of the calibrated ring. Separate metal stops (Waterhouse) are sometimes used, which fit into a slit in the lens mount. Brightness varies as the square of the diameter or as the inverse square of the f/number. Since exposure depends upon light intensity and length of exposure, as the brightness is halved by moving from stop to stop (f/16 to f/22), so the exposure time is doubled, in order to keep the total exposure time constant.

Polarisation

LIGHT RAYS, travelling at speed, vibrate in all directions. If the light is made to vibrate in only one direction, it is said to be polarised. A great deal of reflected light is polarised and is a type of glare. By using a polarising glass the glare can be minimised. Polaroid sheets are used in photography to eliminate glare and as sky filters. They produce plane polarised light on transmission, and consist of thin sheets of cellulose nitrate packed with ultramicroscopic doubly-refracting crystals with their optic axes parallel. The crystals produce plane-polarised light by differential absorption of the ordinary and extraordinary rays of light.

SENSITOMETRY

THE PRINCIPLES and rules governing sensitometry are concerned with the study of the photographic properties of continuous tone images, and are concerned with the control of the relationship between the function of exposing the emulsion to light action and the final resulting density, after development and fixation.

It is a fact that the eye does not recognise equal increments in illumination or exposure time, and it has been found experimentally that a series of tone values appear to have the same intervals of brightness only when every step in the series bears approximately the same ratio of illumination to the adjoining step. Thus whereas the difference between a series of increments of 1, 2, 3, 4 etc. would be unrecognised, differences of 1, 2, 4, 8, or 1, 10, 100, 1000 etc., would appear to have approximate equal intervals of brightness as judged by the eye.

1, 2, 4, 8, 16 may also be expressed as 2^0, 2^1, 2^2, 2^3, 2^4, and 1, 10, 100, 1000, 10,000 as 10^0, 10^1, 10^2, 10^3, 10^4.

When the tone value increases in equal intervals, the small index figure, known as the power to which the intensity is raised, also increases in equal values. Mathematically this small index figure is known as the *logarithm* of the corresponding number of the series. Thus 4 is the logarithm of 16 to base 2, or $4 = \log 16$, since $2^4 = 16$. It is also the logarithm of 10,000 to base 10, or $4 = \log_{10} 10,000$. Logarithms are given for any base number, but it is usual to express to base 10, so that this figure is normally omitted in logarithmic data, e.g. $-4 = \log 10,000$. The fact to be observed is that tone values are proportional to the logarithm of intensity; therefore, when representing graph-wise the tone values of an original, in negative or positive form, the unit used should be the logarithm of intensity. Logarithms of numbers between 1 and 10 ($10^0 - 10^1$), and 100 ($10^1 - 10^2$), and 1000 ($10^2 - 10^3$), etc., will lie between 0 and 1, 1 and 2, 2 and 3, etc., respectively. For example, log 20 = 1·30.

The whole number preceding the decimal point of the logarithm is known as the 'characteristic' (1 in the example), and the decimal fraction as the mantissa (0·30 in the example). The characteristic can be written down easily as it is number of figures before the decimal point (2 in the example) less 1 (2 − 1 = 1 in the example). The mantissa is found in a table of logarithms: log 20 = 1·30; log 200 = 2·30; log 2000 = 3·30.

When the log is known and it is the original number which is required, from the same table of logarithms the 'antilogarithm' can be obtained. The characteristic indicates the position of the decimal point: antilog 3·30 = 2000; antilog 2·30 = 200; antilog 1·30 = 20.

Logarithm tables contain detailed instructions which are easy to follow and use. Two applications to remember are as follows:

1. The log of a product is the sum of the logarithms of each factor; e.g. $\log (a \times b) = \log a + \log b$.

2. The log of a quotient is the difference between the log of the integer and the log of the denominator; e.g. $\log (a \div b) = \log a - \log b$.

LOGARITHMIC VALUES

$$\frac{I}{T} = \text{the reciprocal of transmission.}$$

$\frac{I}{T}$	$\log \frac{I}{T}$	$\frac{I}{T}$	$\log \frac{I}{T}$	$\frac{I}{T}$	$\log \frac{I}{T}$
1·00	0·00				
1·12	0·05	11·2	1·05	112	2·05
1·26	0·10	12·6	1·10	126	2·10
1·41	0·15	14·1	1·15	141	2·15
1·58	0·20	15·8	1·20	158	2·20
1·78	0·25	17·8	1·25	178	2·25
2·00	0·30	20·0	1·30	200	2·30
2·24	0·35	22·4	1·35	224	2·35
2·51	0·40	25·1	1·40	251	2·40
2·82	0·45	28·2	1·45	282	2·45
3·16	0·50	31·6	1·50	316	2·50
3·54	0·55	35·4	1·55	354	2·55
3·98	0·60	39·8	1·60	398	2·60
4·47	0·65	44·7	1·65	447	2·65
5·01	0·70	50·1	1·70	501	2·70
5·62	0·75	56·2	1·75	562	2·75
6·31	0·80	63·1	1·80	631	2·80
7·08	0·85	70·8	1·85	708	2·85
7·94	0·90	79·4	1·90	794	2·90
8·91	0·95	89·1	1·95	891	2·95
10·00	1·00	100·0	2·00	1000	3·00

The starting point of sensitometry requires an understanding of sensitometric principles, involving the sensitometric curve. In sensitometry certain terms and units are used, which must be understood. For instance, *luminous intensity* refers to the *luminous flux* emitted by a light source per unit of solid angle (steroadian) in a given direction. Its unit is the *candela*, which is scientifically expressed as '$\frac{1}{100}$ of the luminous intensity emitted per cm.^{2} by a "black body" at the temperature of solidification of platinum (1770° K)'. *Luminous flux* is the amount of energy emitted by a light source as visible radiation per unit of time. Its unit is the lumen (lm.). A light source with a luminous intensity of 1 candela, placed in the centre of a hollow sphere with a diameter of 1 metre, emits a luminous flux of 1 lumen to an area of 1 square metre on the inner surface of the sphere. The surface of the sphere equals $4\pi R^2$. Therefore 1 candela, in this instance, will emit a total luminous flux of $4 \times 3 \cdot 1416$ ($R = 1$ metre), which is $12 \cdot 56$ lumens. A definition of *illumination* is that it is 'the luminous flux at a point of a surface'. The unit used is the *lux*, which is the illumination of 1 lumen per square metre. In this connection it should be noted that whereas the Lux represents an illumination of one lumen per square metre, which is the continental standard, the British standard, which is the *foot candela*, represents an illumination of 1 candela per square foot. Meters can be purchased for measuring the number of Lux (luxmeters) of foot-candela (foot-candela meters).

Exposure is the total amount of light falling on a surface and is the product of the illumination (I) expressed in lux or foot candela; and the exposure time (t) expressed in seconds.

$$E = I \times t \, (It)$$

For standardisation, it is preferred that the unit of exposure is the lux-second (1 lux $\times$ 1 second).

Optical Density

DENSITY IN a photographic context is the standard means of expressing the value of a tone area – its light-stopping ability. The darker a tone, the higher its density. The highlights of a print will have a low density and the shadows a high density. On the negative the same highlights will appear dark and therefore will have a high density. The ability of a silver layer on film to absorb or pass light is expressed in terms of *transmission density*. The term *transmission* refers to the light-passing ability of the silver layer. The term *density* refers to the light-absorbing ability of the layer. The transmission of any tone area is the fraction of incident light transmitted through the area without being absorbed or scattered.

$$T = \frac{It}{Ii}$$

when T = transmission, It = intensity of transmitted light, Ii = intensity of incident light.

Density is equal to the logarithm of $\frac{I}{T}$.

$$D = \log \frac{I}{T} = \log \frac{Ii}{It}.$$

A completely transparent area transmits all the light received, therefore its transparency or transmission is 100%.
Increasing opacity causes a decrease in transmission values.

Transmission, %	Density
100	0·00
10	1·00
1	2·00
0·1	3·00

Transmission (negative measurement)

$$= \frac{\text{intensity of transmitted light}}{\text{intensity of incident light}}$$

Reflection (positive or opaque copy measurement)

$$= \frac{\text{intensity of reflected light}}{\text{intensity of incident light}}$$

CONVERSION DENSITY (D) INTO TRANSMISSION PERCENTAGE ($T\%$)
(0·00 density = 100% transmission)

D	T	D	T	D	T
0·05	89·2	1·05	8·92	2·05	0·89
0·10	79·4	1·10	7·94	2·10	0·79
0·15	70·9	1·15	7·09	2·15	0·71
0·20	63·3	1·20	6·33	2·20	0·63
0·25	56·2	1·25	5·62	2·25	0·56
0·30	50·0	1·30	5·00	2·30	0·50
0·35	44·6	1·35	4·46	2·35	0·45
0·40	39·8	1·40	3·98	2·40	0·40
0·45	35·5	1·45	3·55	2·45	0·36
0·50	31·6	1·50	3·16	2·50	0·32
0·55	28·2	1·55	2·82	2·55	0·28
0·60	25·1	1·60	2·51	2·60	0·25
0·65	22·4	1·65	2·24	2·65	0·22
0·70	20·0	1·70	2·00	2·70	0·20
0·75	17·8	1·75	1·78	2·75	0·18
0·80	15·9	1·80	1·59	2·80	0·16
0·85	14·1	1·85	1·41	2·85	0·14
0·90	12·6	1·90	1·26	2·90	0·13
0·95	11·2	1·95	1·12	2·95	0·11
1·00	10·0	2·00	1·00	3·00	0·10

Using high contrast material, where intense reduction to the metallic state (high blackening) of the emulsion occurs, less than o·1% of the incident light is transmitted. With 'lith' film the dense areas do not transmit more than o·01% of the incident light thus the transmission will be $\dfrac{o·01}{100} = \dfrac{1}{10,000}$.

Reflection Density

THIS IS similar to transmission density. For example when light falls on a bromide print, some of the light is absorbed (dark areas) whilst the remainder is reflected in various directions, depending upon the tone values and surface (smoothness) of the print. The measuring of reflection densities is carried out by illuminating the job at an angle of 45 degrees and measuring the amount of light reflected at 90 degrees to the surface. Transmission density is based upon the transmittance of a tone area and, in the same way, reflection density is based upon reflection from a tone area without involving the question of incident light. It is expressed as the ratio between the amount of light reflected from a given tone area, and the amount reflected either from the white area or from a standard surface.

$$\text{Reflectance} = \frac{Ip}{Ipw}$$

when Ip is the intensity of light reflected from a tone and Ipw represents the intensity of light reflected from white paper. Reflection density has the same relationship to reflectance that transmission density has to transmittance. Transmission density $(DT) = \log I/T$, reflection density $(DR) = \log I/R$. Values, like transmission-density values, are proportional and relative under general viewing conditions to visual tone values and are unaffected by changes in illumination intensity. Readings do not give the value of a tone in terms of light intensity but record how much darker one tone is compared with another; the extreme highlight of the job being the zero point.

The Characteristic Curve

THIS IS named after the men, Hurter and Driffied, who first developed it and is known as the H and D curve or the $D \log E$ curve. It is the basis of all sensitometric control methods. The curves indicate the behaviour of a photographic emulsion diagrammatically and show the relationship between the amount of exposure received by the emulsion, and the opacity of the developed silver image. The curve is obtained by plotting the logarithm of the exposure against the logarithm of the opacity or density produced by the exposure. Opacity is the ratio of the incident to the transmitted light, and is thus the reciprocal of the transmission. As stated previously in equation form

$$O = \frac{Ii}{It}$$

this is defined as the logarithm[2] (to the base 10) of the reciprocal of the transmission, which could also be the logarithm (to the base 10) of the opacity. Thus $D = \log_{10}\frac{I}{T} = \log_{10}{}^0$. The reciprocal of a number is found by dividing one by the number, e.g. the reciprocal of 5 is $\frac{I}{5}$. It is remembered that a logarithm is a number indicating the power to which

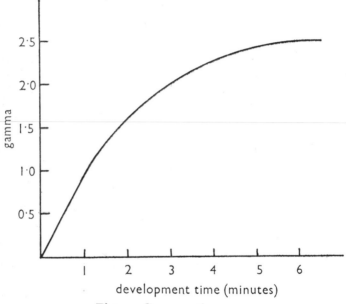

Fig. 43 Gamma – time curve

a 'base' number is raised to produce a given positive number, e.g. 2 is the logarithm of the positive number 100 to the base 10 ($\log_{10} 100 = 2$).

 The information for producing the characteristic curve is obtained by exposing the photographic material to a graded step wedge, such as the 'Kodak' Colour Separation Guide step wedge, and developing and processing under controlled conditions. The various densities in the wedge are measured on a densitometer and plotted on a sheet of graph

paper against the densities of the steps on the wedge from which they
were made. The resulting curve shows certain characteristics, which
may be sub-divided into three parts, the toe, straight-line portion and
the shoulder. The toe of the curve commences when the exposure has
been sufficient to create a measurable density (ideally 0·35/0·40 above
fog level). The curve $(A - B)$ gradually bends in proportion to the densities formed by light, until the straight-line portion is reached. Thus

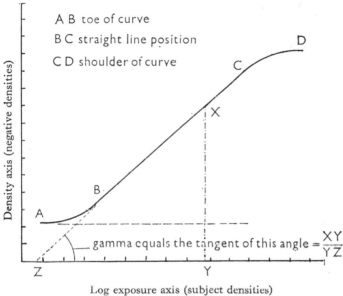

Fig. 44 A characteristic curve

$(B - C)$ defines the range when density increases proportionally to the
logarithm of the exposure.

In the section of the characteristic curve, the density of the negative is
proportional to the logarithm of the brightness of the subject, equal
exposure ratios being reproduced as equal density differences in the
negative. In colour work, to give the necessary colour balance, all the
separation negatives should be exposed to come within this section of
the characteristic curve. The shoulder of the curve begins at C. Here
the curve bends over and eventually becomes horizontal and exposure
differences are no longer recorded as corresponding density differences.
Absence of detail in the high-light areas of the negative result from over
exposure forcing the image on to the shoulder of the characteristic curve.

GAMMA

ANOTHER FACTOR found from the $D \log E$ curve is the contrast produced by a given development. This is ascertained from the slope of the curve or the angle that the straight-line portion of the curve makes with the base line. The steeper the slope (the larger the angle), the greater the contrast, and vice versa. The contrast increases with prolonged development and decreases with less development. Contrast is thus dependent upon development and the term *gamma*, symbolised by the Greek letter γ, is defined as 'a numerical designation for the contrast of a photographic material as represented by the slope of the straight line portion of the characteristic curve. Gamma is numerically equal to the tangent of the angle which the straight-line portion makes with the base line.'

This means that the slope of the straight-line portion of the characteristic curve, that is the tangent of the angle it forms with the horizontal, is termed 'gamma' and is a measure of the contrast produced in the negative by the degree of development. Gamma increases as development is prolonged, until a limiting value (gamma infinity) is reached. Thus gamma may be plotted against development time and the resulting time – gamma curve subsequently used to determine the development time necessary to give any required development contrast. Total contrast, it is observed, is due to numerous factors, including subject contrast, flare in the optical system, as well as development contrast. Gamma also increases with more vigorous agitation during development, higher development temperature and increased developer strength. The graph shows how gamma is determined. Vertical and horizontal lines intersect each other and the straight-line portion of the curve; and it follows that the numerical value of gamma is equal to:

$$\frac{\text{vertical distance}}{\text{horizontal distance}} = \frac{\text{density range of negative}}{\text{density range of copy}}$$

For example, assuming the copy range to be 1·70 and the resulting negative from this copy is found to have a density range of 1·40 (0·5–1·9) when measured on the same two points which were read on the copy, the gamma of the negative would be $\frac{1\cdot40}{1\cdot70} = 0\cdot82$.

Making a Time – Gamma Curve. A group or family of curves should be prepared all having received the same amount of exposure with development time as the only variable factor. When this is completed a chart is obtained similar to the one shown giving the various gammas obtainable with a certain emulsion and developer with different times of development. The density values on the horizontal axis should read from right to left and the same units must be used on each axis, for instance, if a density of 1 is represented on one axis by 10 squares of the

graph paper, the same should apply on the other axis. Otherwise a
false gamma reading will be obtained.

The gamma of each curve is measured by placing a ruler against the
straight-line portion of the curve and extending the line downwards
until it cuts the log exposure axis (at Z as shown). A perpendicular line is
dropped from a suitable point (X) near the top of the straight-line
portion so as to cut the horizontal axis (Y). Gamma is the ratio between
the lengths of the vertical and horizontal sides of the triangle produced

$$\left(\text{gamma} = \frac{XY}{YZ}\right). \quad \text{(Fig. 44)}$$

If, for example, there are 23 vertical spaces on the graph paper ($XY =$
23) and 30 horizontal spaces on the graph paper ($YZ = $ 30) then

$$\text{gamma} = \frac{\text{vertical distance}}{\text{horizontal distance}} = \frac{23}{30} = 0 \cdot 766$$

Alternatively a protractor and a set of trigonometric tables may be used
to measure the angle which the straight-line portion of each curve
makes with the horizontal. The tangent of this angle is the gamma value.

The graph clearly shows the different possible contrasts obtainable
with changes in development time. This can be simplified by plotting a

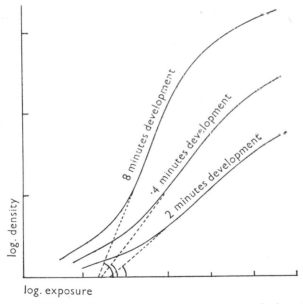

Fig. 45 Characteristic curves of negative material plotted
from different development times

time gamma curve, which plots all the information ascertained from a family of curves into a single curve. It is done by plotting the gamma obtained on the vertical axis against the time of development on the horizontal axis. This type of curve constructed from a series of curves is appended.

This simplifies and expedites procedure. The density range of the copy for reproduction is measured, and if we assume that, based on experience, the desired density range should be 1·40, we have the relevant data required, that is, the density range of the copy and the density range required in the negative.

$$\text{Gamma} = \frac{\text{density range of negative}}{\text{density range of copy}}$$

From this the gamma value necessary to produce the required density range is ascertained. Consulting the time – gamma graph, a horizontal line is taken from the value of the copy density range to where it intersects the time – gamma curve. From this point a vertical line is drawn until it intersects the time axis. This indicates the required development time to produce the desired gamma on the continuous tone negative.

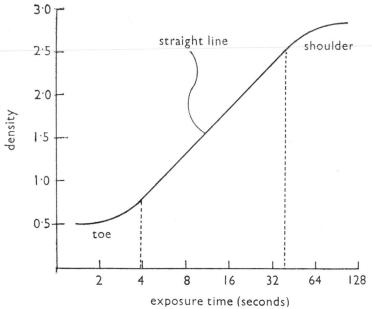

Fig. 46 Areas of a characteristic curve

Density Range. This should not be confused, in a negative or print, with its gamma. Gamma is purely a measure of the contrast obtained in a photographic material with a given set of development conditions. Whereas density range is a measure of the density difference between the lowest density in a negative and the highest density, which are subtracted from each other to obtain the density range. If the negative has a lower density of 0·40 and a highest density of 1·70, then the density range 1·70 — 0·40 = 1·30.

In the negative the various tones – corresponding to the tonal gradation of the copy – have different densities. The areas of the negative which receive a large exposure (highlights of the copy) show a high density, because a large amount of metallic silver was formed during development in these areas. The areas receiving little exposure (shadows of the copy) only form small amounts of metallic silver, resulting in a lower density. Thus a given exposure will always correspond to a given density on the photographic emulsion. The law of reciprocity (Bunsen–Roscoe Law), which does not take into account the reciprocity failure, states that 'if a given density is produced by a certain illumination over a given time, the same density will be produced by any values of illumination and time, provided that their product equals the product of the original illumination and time'. This law means that the same density will be obtained by exposing for 30 seconds using an illumination of 1 lux, as by exposing the same emulsion for 1 second using an illumination of 30 lux, providing that light angle and distance and processing conditions are constant.

In general exposure produces density and development time contrast in the resultant negative. It is recommended that the length of exposure is sufficient to give a minimum density in the shadow areas of 0·3–0·4. It can be assumed that a negative is correctly exposed when both the smallest exposure (corresponding to the shadow areas in the original) and the largest exposure (corresponding to the brightest areas of the original) produce negative densities which lie on the straight-line portion of the characteristic curve. In fact, when the densities which together constitute the negative image are located on the straight-line portion of the curve, a variation in the exposure time will not cause any change in the gamma value or in the density range. Development time will, however, affect both the gamma value and the density range. Within acceptable tolerances of exposure and development it can be accepted that without changing development time an alteration in exposure time causes a change in minimum density and a change in density range is brought about by varying development. This is not affected by exposure, provided the densities measured are located on the straight-line portion of the curve. It follows that (a) if the minimum density is too low, expose longer; (b) if the minimum density is too high, expose shorter; (c) if the density range is too small, develop longer; (d) if the density range is too great, develop shorter.

Reciprocity Failure (Schwarzschild Effect)

THE BUNSEN–ROSCOE Law of Photochemical Equivalence states that the same density will always be obtained when the product of illumination (I) and exposure time (t) remains constant. This does not always apply, because it is found that if the illumination is greatly decreased and the exposure time correspondingly increased to maintain the value of the product $I \times t$, density will become lower with decreasing I. Again when I is very great and t extremely short, as with flash illumination, it is also found that density decreases with increasing I and shorter t. Thus, if great changes are made in intensity and time, e.g. one-tenth or one-hundredth of the intensity acting for ten or a hundred times as long, the density produced will be much different, even though the product of intensity and time remain constant. This is known as 'reciprocity failure'. An explanation is that with a short high intensity exposure, the electrons are released too rapidly to be handled by the relatively slow second stage. The exposure is over so quickly that only a section of the electrons are neutralised by the slower moving silver ions. The surplus electrons recombine with bromine atoms to reform silver bromide. The electrons forming the latent image produce a high proportion of internal and sub-latent image, which are wasted for image formation. On the other hand the incidence of low intensity with increased exposure results in electrons being released at a very low rate so that they are trapped and neutralised, remaining isolated silver atoms for much longer than in normal latent image formation. This sub-latent image is unstable and a weak image results from many isolated atoms of silver losing their acquired electrons during the period of instability. Schwarzschild has stated that the exposure effect on a photographic emulsion is not proportional to $I \times t$ but to $I \times tP$, where the exponent P depends on the emulsion, light intensity, wavelength of the light, temperature and type of developer.

Latensification. A uniform, overall exposure, to medium or high intensity light, which would produce only a low density on development, provides sufficient latent and sub-latent image to act as a basis on which a weak low intensity latent image will be intensified and strengthened by this pre-exposure. This technique is used when the exposure time extends over a long period to record the subject matter. A uniform small pre-exposure to normal lighting removes low intensity failure and thus improves the quality of result to low intensity light. It is also effective when the emulsion is greatly under-exposed and would normally result in a thin negative. A subsequent uniform exposure to low intensity light shows no reciprocity failure where there is already latent or sub-latent image, thus building-up the latent image, particularly in the highlights and middle-tone areas. The original faint latent image is intensified. A darkroom lamp using a 15 watt bulb and a dark green panchromatic safelight is suitable. Expose before development for between 30–120 minutes at about 15 feet from the lamp.

Intermittency Effect. This is another phenomenon in which it is found that a large number of short exposures do not produce the same effect on the sensitive material as the theoretically equivalent single exposure. For example, when a given exposure time of, say, 45 seconds is divided up into a series of 45 separate exposures of 1 second each, the exposures will not produce the same effect as a single exposure of 45 seconds. It is also a fact that with very high intensities, as in flash illumination, the effect of intermittent exposure is not less than that of continuous exposure, but greater. The general explanation of intermittency is that exposure of a grain to light releases electrons from bromide ions which exist in a free state for a little time before being trapped. The concentration of electrons during exposure will increase with added intensity. During intermittent exposure, the light is shut off after each exposure increment before the concentration can reach the value appropriate to that intensity. Thus the total effect is similar to one of lower intensity and longer time.

Callier Effect. Enlargers equipped with point light sources and condensers produce more contrasty prints than those operating with diffuse light. This also applies on the camera when the negative is illuminated either by reflection from white paper, or through an opal glass. With a negative in the carrier, the light coming through the condenser, which normally comes to a focus, is partly scattered by the silver grains forming the image, so that some of it does not reach the lens. The highlights of the negative, corresponding to the heaviest deposit of silver, scatter and lose more light, the less dense parts, corresponding to the shadows, scatter least. This accentuates the difference between the highlights and the shadows, giving a print or a positive of higher contrast than if printed by contact. Both specular and diffuse (surface) densities would be the same if the image did not scatter any light at all and they most closely approximate to each other in dye images rather than in negatives or positives which are metallic silver images. Dye images scatter less light than silver grain images. André Callier first established a relationship between specular and diffuse densities, adopting the symbols DII to represent specular density and DH to represent diffuse density. The ratio of these two quantities is known as the Q factor. Thus $Q = \dfrac{DII}{DH}$.

The higher the grain of the emulsion, the higher the factor. Slow emulsions, which have little grain, have a value of 1·00, whilst fast emulsions, which have considerable grain, have factors in the region of 1·90.

The Clayden Effect. This is the term used when partial reversal of a negative occurs when exposing the emulsion to a short exposure using an intense light, followed by an exposure using normal lighting intensity. For example, a flash of lightning occurring during a daylight exposure may produce less density on the negative than the surrounding sky (black lightning effect). The phenomenon, it is suggested, is caused by the initial high intensity exposure forming an internal latent image which is an efficient electron trap for the following exposure. Much of the latent image is wasted in the interior of the grain. The effect is that the surface latent image, the product of both exposures, is less than that of the normal intensity exposure so that density is lower where there has been initial high intensity exposure.

The Herschel Effect. Sir John Herschell, in 1840, observed that red light appeared to have a bleaching effect on a silver chloride printout image. From this it was discovered that the latent image on a non-red sensitive emulsion is apparently destroyed when exposed to red or infrared radiations. It is believed that the image is not destroyed, but redistributed throughout the grain. The wavelengths of maximum absorption produced by latent silver and the Herschel effect are identical and it would appear that the absorption of energy by the latent image speck caused the silver to emit an electron and revert to a silver ion. The electrons moving to other areas are trapped and neutralised by a silver ion so that groups of silver atoms, which normally form the latent image, are dispersed in the grain as ineffective internal and sub-latent image. The positive-positive and negative-negative actions of reversal emulsions are based on the Herschel effect. (Autopositive and Auto-reversal emulsions.) When an exposed, undeveloped emulsion is exposed for a second time to light with a wavelength to which the emulsion is insensitive, the latent image formed in the emulsion by the first exposure fades or is destroyed. Thus, it follows that orthochromatic emulsion should not be exposed to the red safelight illumination of the darkroom before development. With the special reversal materials, during manufacture a latent density is formed on the entire surface. If development takes place without exposure the film would develop completely black. But if the blue-green sensitive emulsion is exposed before development to light with a colour for which it is not sensitised, the latent image will be bleached out in the areas where the light has exposed the emulsion and thus a direct positive is obtained from a positive original and a direct negative from a negative original.

Solarisation. Excessive over-exposure often results, not in higher, but in lower densities on development. The longer the exposure the more free bromine formed. This moves in the crystal by the transference of an electron from a nearby bromide ion to a bromine atom, when the roles are reversed, the ion becoming the atom and the atom the ion. The theory is that the bromine atom reacts with a reducing agent – probably gelatin, which is a halogen acceptor for small amounts of bromine.

The gelatin accepts the usual amounts of bromine liberated in normal latent image formation but is unable to absorb the large amounts liberated during excessive exposure which is a feature of solarisation. The free bromine, surplus to that which saturates the gelatin, builds up in the spaces between the grains, reacts with the latent image specks to produce a layer of silver bromide, isolating it from the developer and making the grain undevelopable. The action from acute over-exposure results in excess bromine coating the latent image specks with silver bromide, lowering the developed density. If the halogen-absorbing capacity of the gelatin is increased with the addition of some organic dye stuffs, or a halogen acceptor such as sodium nitrate, solarisation is eradicated. A small amount of hypo in the developer or the use of a developer containing a silver halide solvent, e.g. sulphite, minimises the effect.

Nowadays the term solarisation usually refers, not to the effect of complete reversal by absolute over-exposure (1000 times), which is the correct meaning of the term, but to the technique for producing a partly reversed image by exposing the negative to unsafe light during development (Sabattier effect). The already developed image acts as a negative through which the remainder of the silver bromide is exposed, so that some reversal of the image occurs, the result being part negative and part positive.

NEWTON RINGS

THE PHENOMENON known as Newton rings appears when a high gloss bromide print or a negative or transparency is mounted either between two sheets of glass in an enlarger or printing frame or in intimate contact with a sheet of glass. It is caused by an interference of certain wavelengths of light which is produced in areas where there remains a very thin layer of air between the film or surface and the glass. A method introduced to suppress this mottling effect and also to overcome scratch trouble is to use a cement made from acryl glass (polymethacrylate ester) which is soluble in toluene, ethyl acetate or methyl ethyl acetone. Such proprietary solutions are marketed as 'Plexiglas', 'Perspex', etc. The acryl glass is broken up into small pieces and dissolved in the toluene. This takes several hours and results in syrupy liquid which soon thickens, due to evaporation of the highly volatile solvent, unless kept in a well-stoppered bottle. When reproducing from a negative or transparency the technique is to seal the subject between two sheets of glass. First pour a thin layer on one glass and lay the film on it; then coat the back of the negative with the solution and lay the second glass on top of it. Using gentle pressure, spread the solution out uniformly on both sides of the negative which is now sandwiched between the two glasses in an airtight condition. After photographing remove from between the two sheets of glass by placing in toluene. This dissolves the cement and has no effect on the negative or the transparency. This also applies to colour prints and normal bromide prints.

AUTOMATIC MASKING FOR MONOCHROME WORK

THE GEVAERT Correctone Co23 film was the first of the two-layer type films for graphic reproduction. To reproduce black-and-white photographs containing scintillating highlights with a wealth of fine detail has always been difficult, requiring, in the past, a great deal of hand retouching on the negatives, or the use of a normal negative and a separate correcting mask – the correcting mask being a negative made on very high contrast material recording only the highlights of the original. This mask was superimposed on the normal negative giving a combined negative in which all the brilliance and detail of the copy were present. The procedure involved making two negatives with the possibility of register problems and the risk of scratches and dust between the two films.

Correctone film has a built-in correcting mask system. It consists of a thin transparent anti-stress layer, under which is an orthochromatic masking layer, of high contrast and low sensitivity. Below this is a blue-sensitive image layer of normal gradation and sensitivity positioned on an 0·008 in. base backed with an anti-halation layer. On exposure a normal image is formed in the blue-sensitive layer whereas a correcting mask is produced in the orthochromatic layer resulting in exact or improved reproduction in the highlights of continuous tone negatives and the shadows of continuous tone positives. Also highlights and shadows are improved if both positives and negatives are made on Correctone film.

In principle, the film is exposed twice. The main exposure is given in the normal manner and the auxiliary exposure given through a relatively deep yellow filter (R488c). The length of the auxiliary exposure depends upon the copy, the light source and the result required. The main exposure produces an image in the blue sensitive layer, thus light sources emitting considerable blue and ultra-violet, such as arc lamps or mercury vapour lamps, are highly suitable. Copying same size lens aperture $f/45$ with four open arc lamps of 30 amp. approximately 3 feet from the original average exposure would be: main exposure 10 seconds, auxiliary exposure 15 seconds with yellow filter, using G5p universal developer for 4 minutes at 68° F. The introduction of a blue filter (B488) for the main exposure could be used to lengthen and thus control the time of the first exposure. This also reduces contrast.

VIII

The Camera Department and Equipment

LAYOUT AND EQUIPMENT

THE LAYOUT of plant and equipment has been discussed in detail previously* and the recommendations apply to all photomechanical processes. From the planning standpoint a single storey building is preferable as it is conducive to a better layout of plant, and allows for a smoother work sequence with easier supervision and rationalised handling of materials. With multi-storey buildings heavy machinery and equipment are sited in the basement or on the lower floors and the cameras as far away as possible from the vibration caused by moving machinery. Narrow waste pipes with right-angled bends should be avoided and pipes, valves and flanges should be stainless steel, glazed earthenware or glass-lined channels and pipes. Floors must be waterproof and acid-resistant and several compounds are available to satisfy these needs. Ceramic vitreous tiling, or composition tiles of plastic, hard rubber, asphalt and synthetic material, which can be overlaid on wood floors, are quite satisfactory. Normal tap water is generally satisfactory, but if the water is very hard, calcium grit may be deposited on the negatives, causing spots and bad contact, so that a water-softening plant may be necessary. It is preferred, so as to avoid blockages, that all expended solutions from the sinks should drain into open glazed earthenware gutters and then flow into the waste pipes.

Temperature and humidity are critical factors, with a temperature of 65° F and a relative humidity of about 60% considered very suitable for all workshop conditions. Relative humidity (moistness) is the ratio of the amount of water vapour present in the air to the amount that would saturate the air at the same temperature. Good ventilation is essential, and incoming air should be filtered to remove dust particles with the flow of sufficient volume to change the air, in the darkroom, six to ten times each hour. Excessive humidity causes body perspiration, with moist fingers leaving marks on coatings and emulsion; a dry atmosphere increases static accumulation. Also, high temperature and humidity,

* *Camera and Process Work*, Chs. 2, 4, 5, 6, Ernest Benn, 1964.

when printing down, accelerate the hardening reaction of a coating. To produce predictable and standardised results, processing solutions in the darkroom must be maintained at a constant temperature and a dependable temperature control system is a necessity.

Thermostatically-controlled darkroom sinks are available in two basic types. One type has a built-in refrigeration unit with cooling coils under the sink and maintains a shallow level of water at a constant temperature. The other kind continuously circulates the water through a built-in mechanical cooler at the right temperature. Automatic, thermostatically controlled mixing valves are a cheaper proposition and are compact and efficient. The valves operate by mixing warm and cold water to give the required temperature. Where, during summer, the

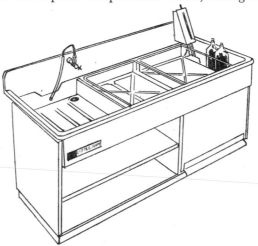

Fig. 47 Temperature-controlled sink unit

cold water is itself warmer than the required temperature, an auxiliary cooling system would be necessary.

Walls should be painted a light colour, the exception being the camera room where, to avoid light scatter and flare in the lens system, they should be dark, for example, a matt grey. It is necessary to be able to enter and leave the darkroom without admitting any light. The open-passage type of light trap with walls of a dark matt finish is recommended because it provides easy access and good ventilation. Where space is limited, a double-door light lock is suitable, with one door (or both) replaced, if necessary, by heavy curtains. The switch operating the white light should be situated in the darkroom and the safelights in the darkroom should provide as high a degree of illumination as possible, consistent with the safety of the type of material being processed. The walls should be light coloured to assist in realising this objective. With 'lith' material, which is sensitive only to blue and green, a relatively high illumination of red light can be used, without any danger of fogging. A deeper red light would be used for faster ordinary and orthochromatic emulsions and panchromatic emulsions should preferably be processed in complete darkness, or alternatively under controlled conditions using a dark green safelight with a 15 watt lamp and indirect lighting.

WATER

TAP WATER cannot be considered 'pure' water because it always contains certain substances which, whilst not injurious to health, can have adverse effects photographically. Thus the term 'distilled' water appearing in a photographic formula infers that the formula contains chemicals which would react with the substances found in tap water and could change the composition of the solution, resulting either in inferior results or complications in processing the light-sensitive emulsion. Sand, dirt and rust from the pipes result in spots and pinholes, whilst substances like copper, iron, magnesium and calcium also produce spots and streaks and sometimes fog. Chloride and bicarbonate reduce the effectiveness of the developer and the latter forms a streaky deposit. Sulphide and hydrogen sulphide will produce a heavy fogging effect, and air or oxygen in the water slows down development, causing spots and unevenness. Elimination of water impurities is done by divers means, depending upon the nature of the impurities. This includes filtration, boiling and distillation, demineralising and various chemical methods.

Tap water always includes some dissolved organic salts which are ionised, and most water contains sodium, calcium, magnesium and iron positive ions and carbonate, bicarbonate, chloride, sulphate and silicate negative ions. Hard water contains calcium, magnesium and iron ions and one method of recording 'hard' water is when it contains 100 parts or more of calcium carbonate in a million parts of water. ('Soft' water – up to 55 parts per million of calcium carbonate.) Water may be softened by using ion exchange tank apparatus to remove the calcium, magnesium and iron ions from the water with an organic resinous ion-exchange material (cation exchanger). Another method uses two tanks and removes almost all the positive and negative ions from the water. The negative ions, when removed, demineralise and purify the water comparable to distilled water, by means of an 'anion exchange resin'. This process of electrolysis causes the negative ions to travel towards the positive pole (anode) and also removes the hydrogen ions.

THE PROCESS CAMERA

THE WORD camera covers a vast field of instrumentation. It may be small and compact to give a maximum film size of 16 in. × 20 in., or large

enough to accommodate 48 in. × 72 in. work. For monochrome line
or halftone work the design may be simple, whilst for colour separation,
photocomposition and multiple exposure work high precision and auto-
mated equipment is necessary. Basically it must consist of two parallel
planes at right angles to the optical axis of the lens which is in between.
The focal plane is contained in a frame, mounted on a suspended
chassis to counteract vibration, to which are attached the focusing
screen, the holder for the sensitive emulsion, the screen gear and the
copy holder. The lens is maintained independently in ratio to the other
two planes, with a mechanism for adjusting the relationship between the
lens, image (film) and copy for reducing or enlarging the image. Parallelism is required between the three essential planes and the camera
bellows eliminate all extraneous light.

Modern cameras are precision instruments with critical tolerances
and the post-war years have brought about a revolution in sleek styling,
anti-vibration precautions, short focus wide-angle lenses to save floor
space, electro-magnetic shutter, integrating light meters, spot-on
registration devices and re-set location controls using dial micrometer
gauges which measure to within 1/1000 of an inch accuracy the physical
location of lens mount and copyboard. The need for high-speed working
has seen the almost complete elimination of the gallery camera which
operated away from the darkroom and required a bulky darkslide which
had to be transported between camera and darkroom for loading, exposing, and unloading. The loading and unloading procedure could interfere – if only minutely – with the size, sharpness and register of the
image or images, and the advent of films and contact screens made the
use of vacuum backs essential. These cannot be satisfactorily fitted to
gallery cameras.

THE DARKROOM CAMERA

DARKROOM CAMERAS, because they are fixtures, are more rigid
and sturdy and therefore more accurate. The discarding of darkslides,
turn-tables, manually operated prisms and the like, and their substitu-
tion by vacuum film holders, pin bar and plate holders with three point
lays and punch-register systems, ensures that the image falls in the
same plane, permitting precise planning and registration of work.
Straight-line reversal, which avoids swivelling the camera body and
therefore eliminates the risk of out of alignment plus the attached
'built-in' darkroom, lightens the work of the operator, leading to
increased speed and efficiency of output.

Darkroom cameras are of the horizontal (overhead and floor type)
or vertical kind, the advantage of the latter being the conservation of
space. A screen removal mechanism, which prevents handling of the

glass ruled screen, is usually an optional extra. This mechanism is available in either of two types – the elevating principle in which the screen is raised out of position, and the sliding method in which the screen is moved to the left or right out of the image plane. Rotating filter holders, a flashing lamp, for the flash (shadow dot) exposure, and a screen compensator (clear glass disc the same thickness as the glass screen) sited behind the lens to ensure registration in size and sharpness of line and halftone images, are necessary accessories.

Because the distances separating the sensitive emulsion, lens and copy are not determined arbitrarily by the camera operator, but by precise optical laws, the exact position of the camera in relation to the copy-

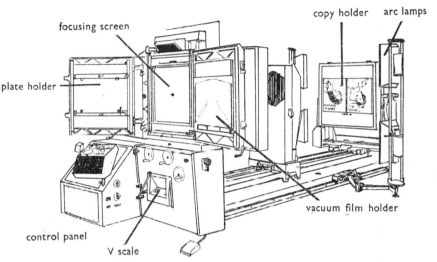

Fig. 48 Horizontal darkroom camera

board for each degree of reduction and enlargement can be predetermined. This is based on the optical formulae governing the minor and major conjugate foci and the focal length of the lens. Thus it is possible to compute mathematically the required settings which are correlated and mechanically applied in different ways. For example, a sliding tape of flexible metal attached to the lens board and copyboard going to the back of the camera and passing under indicators in a panel, or by using a rev-counter and vernier dials attached and synchronised with the movements of the lens board and copyboard carriages. The systems operate in conjunction with some method of proportional slide rule or dial and master chart. Once the relationship between image and copy size has been determined, using the control device, the camera settings are adjusted according to the indicated distance, percentage, or number. Lens aperture settings can also be controlled from the darkroom by the use of a graduated dial attached to the lens mount and a pointer or vernier scale attached to the lens diaphragm. Thus the operator has no need to leave the darkroom to alter the lens aperture during multiple-stop exposures, etc.

OPTICAL REVERSAL

LATERAL (left to right) reversal is effected on the gallery camera by the use of the right-angled prism. For deep etch offset plate making, negatives should be so reversed. Offset printing from surface plates requires non-reversed negatives. With the darkroom camera the single mirror or prism reverser is useless because the copy is not at right angles to the lens. Multiple-mirror reversers are made to operate in a straight line and therefore are used, usually in conjunction with a lens of longer focal length to avoid distortion of marginal rays, with darkroom type cameras. Double, multiple-mirror reversers are used to give both laterally reversed images and 'lens only' (non-reversed) images. Two

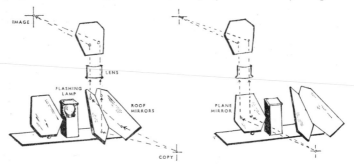

Fig. 49 Klimsch reversal system: (*left*) Roof mirror in use, giving reversed images; (*right*) Plane mirror in position – two reflections giving none-reversed images

flat mirrors, or a prism and a mirror in conjunction, cancel out each other's reversal, producing a 'lens only' image. Three flat mirrors or one flat mirror and one split mirror produce lateral straight-line reversal. For double reversal the changeover is usually done electronically and both images coincide, that is, they are same size and in exact register at the focal plane. Furthermore, some double-reversing mirror system cameras are designed to provide 'lens only' images. It is obvious that with, for instance, three reflecting surfaces, a considerable amount of light intensity is lost. Assuming that each reflecting surface has a maximum reflection factor of 80%, the combined effective light intensity will be only about 50%.

HIGH PRODUCTIVITY CAMERAS

THERE ARE two main sources of camera equipment in this country, Pictorial Machinery Ltd and Hunter-Penrose-Littlejohn Ltd. The former market the Rotadon camera, designed by R. Guppy. It is a compact unit, containing copyholder, lamps, lens, bellows and filmholder, suspended on trunnions, so that it can be rotated through 180 degrees, the complete assembly occupying very little floor space, with working procedure confined entirely to the darkroom. Focusing is effected by means of easily readable scales calibrated on a percentage basis. For loading purposes the camera can be turned over on its axis by push-button control to bring either the copyholder or filmholder uppermost. Twenty

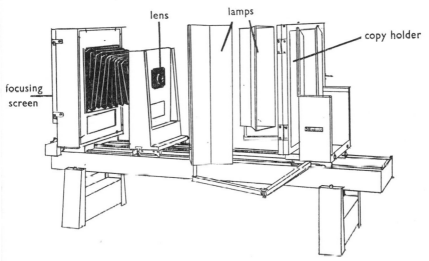

Fig. 50A HPL Reprospeed small offset camera (plate size 16 in. × 20 in.)

seconds suffice for positioning the copy and focusing to size. The unique action of the camera enables the operator to manipulate the controls, centralised on a panel, simply by stretching out a hand, and all operations including processing can be effected within a working radius of a few feet.

The Pictorial 'Chemco' camera is a high-speed darkroom camera using the roll film principle, which eliminates the need for the changing of plates and films between each exposure. Strip-film is used and the camera specialises in monochrome line and halftone work. The image is stripped and 'turned over' for lateral reversal or 'Diaback' roll film is used which allows exposure to be made through the extremely thin base. A three-roll film magazine accommodates five standard widths of film –

6, 10, 16, 20 and 24 in. Focusing is automatic, the carriage being adjusted to scales calibrated on a percentage basis. For halftone work, a screen can be unrolled automatically into vacuum contact with the film and retracts after exposure. For colour reproduction Pictorial market the Multi-chrom two-in-one camera in four models. These cameras can be used in conjunction with all the established masking processes and have facilities for the exact siting of films, plates, transparencies and masks with three-point lay and location pins for accurate re-siting and register of copy. Vacuum filmholders permit the use of contact screens.

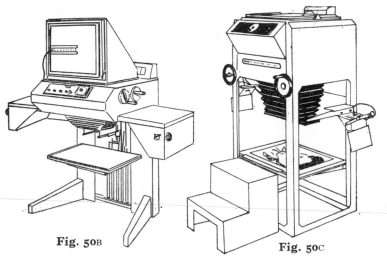

Fig. 50B

Fig. 50C

Fig. 50B Robertson-Eurograph Meteorite Camera. M.T.U. prismatic head, percentage focusing system, 14 in. × 17 in. vacuum filmholder. Argophoto lamps. Reproduction and Printing Equipment Ltd. (The Mole-Richardson Organisation)

Fig. 50C Algraphy-'Lithotex' Vertical Camera. Type 24. 14 in. × 18 in. plate size × 4 enlargements and × 4 reductions with 2–800 watt quartz iodine lamps. Algraphy Ltd and Pictorial Machinery Ltd.

Exact positioning in the dark is assured by a punch register system operating in conjunction with retractable studs. The equipment can be used for both transparency and reflection copy. The Lithotex Precision Darkroom Camera has a 'lathe-bed' track and the degree of accuracy is such that when copying a 12 in. square same size the deviation in parallelism and squareness will not exceed 0·002 in.

With the development of small offset printing and office duplicating systems versatile, compact cameras and equipment have been specifically designed for the production of lithographic plates, applicable to small offset printing machines. Such firms as J. J. Huber, Pictorial

(Lithotex Repro Unit) and S. R. Littlejohn (Copyspeed) have marketed cameras, whirlers, printing-down frames in well-designed, highly efficient units to cater for this expanding field of work.

The firm of S. R. Littlejohn has introduced many types of darkroom cameras, such as the Auto-focus Type 24C for 20 in. × 16 in. image size with two lenses allowing a magnification range of 2 times enlargement to 5 times reduction with reflection copy and $3\frac{1}{2}$ times enlargement to $\frac{1}{2}$ reduction with transparent copy. The camera protrudes little more than three feet each side of the darkroom wall. The Littlejohn Graphicolor is a 20 in. × 24 in. horizontal darkroom camera which, with an additional lens, can give 5 times enlargement and 10 times reduction. A special back-projection lighting unit and a 40 in. × 60 in. vacuum copy baseboard, fitted over the copy holder, project halftone screened negatives to give dot positives for poster work.

ENLARGER PROJECTION CAMERAS

THE ENLARGER as a photographic reproduction instrument is a recent innovation in graphic reproduction, but it has steadily gained in popularity, since the introduction of the Swiss-made Pawo Colorep in 1954. The increasing use of colour transparencies for reproduction, including the miniature 35 mm. up to $2\frac{1}{4}$ in. × $2\frac{1}{4}$ in., has been a deciding factor plus the fact that it is a more economical proposition, being much cheaper than the conventional equipment, and occupies little floor space. The equipment is simple to operate, is situated in the darkroom, making for ease of working with a minimum of movement, which encourages speed and efficiency in production.

Most types incorporate a vacuum baseboard which can be used either to hold film or contact screen, when employed as an enlarger, for making continuous tone or screen separation sets or again for projecting screen negatives or positives. Lens turrets containing two or more lenses to accommodate size changes, with filter bands, are standard equipment and back and front focusing controls are available in some models. Punch register systems are incorporated at the baseboard end and three-point location in the transparency image plane. Lighting units are interchangeable and include tungsten, cold cathode and electronic flash. This combination makes it a complete self-contained camera reproduction unit, easy to operate and able to function as an alternative to the process camera, provided that rigidity and squareness of construction are essential features. A precision process colour camera embodying many features common to most of this type of equipment is the Model 167, Caesar Saltzman camera enlarger, made in New York. This is a combination copying, enlarging and reducing camera, taking copy from 35 mm. to 8 in. × 10 in. transparencies up to 40 in. × 50 in.

reflection copy. The column is a 6 in. diameter chromeplated seamless steel tube and the camera travels this column on ball bearing rollers. To prevent lateral movement of the camera lens double guide tubes are fitted and movement can be registered to 0·010 in. The base board measures 36 in. × 40 in. with a magnetic chuck to lock the base in any position and includes pin register, vacuum hold and accommodates contact screens up to 31 in. × 31 in. A 12 in. Goerz Artar process lens is fitted giving 5 times enlargement. A secondary camera can be fitted on the camera to deal with transparencies from 35 mm. up to 4 in. × 5 in. size. With a 4 in. lens, 35 mm. work can be enlarged 16 times; and with a 6 in. lens 4 in. × 5 in. transparencies can be enlarged 10 times. Light sources can include cold cathode, mercury vapour, high intensity mercury vapour, incandescent lights, quartz light source, and pulsed xenon arc lamps (Ascorlux). The mercury vapour cold cathode source and the incandescent lamps, which are in a unit of 29 bulbs, are fitted with a blower. The 1000-watt Ascorlux pulsed xenon light source is used with condensers for projection. The control panel includes a Microflex timer, a circuit stabiliser and a time delay circuit to be used in conjunction with a shutter. The condenser lamp houses are fitted with 500-watt enlarging lamps or 1000-watt point source lamps for use when direct screening through transparency, mask, filter and contact screen.

The Durst process enlarger, the Laborator 304, handles 5 in. × 7 in. to 12 in. × 16 in. transparencies and is fitted with cold cathode lighting. Alternatively, for work up to 10 in. × 12 in., condenser or electronic flash lighting may be used. The enlarger head is brought from the vertical to the horizontal position by electric motor as is the vertical adjustment with the lens panel and vacuum plate. The negative carrier and vacuum plate are fitted with punch register and the former held by a centring frame with double-locking mechanism for accuracy in re-registering. A suction carrier is also fitted. The lens carrier incorporates three filter turntables with three lenses in the turret giving up to 5 times magnification when the camera operates vertically, and from 11 to 26 times when operating horizontally. Total height is 8 ft. 3 in., with a 3 ft. × 4 ft. table.

The Pawo Colotron 112 is an automatic universal camera which, when used with the automatic developing unit (G.T. 56), provides a technically first-class working system from exposure to processed negative. Point light source, cold cathode grid or Pawolux electronic exposure control are available with automatic adjustment for six lenses giving a magnification range from 0·3 to 19 times enlargement and automatic control of filters, diaphragm and colour temperature. Vacuum film holder, with punch register and automatic precision locking, also attachments for reflection copy work, are some of the first-rate features of this equipment.

The Langham colour separation enlarger type 1215 produces colour separation negatives up to 12 in. × 15 in. in size with carriers to accommodate all sizes of transparencies down to 35 mm. A 42 in. × 32 in. baseboard with reflectors means that the camera can be used for reflection copy work. Cold-cathode assembly is provided and Reproflash 4000 or Repro Xenon makes it possible for direct screening to be done, using pan 'lith' material, from colour transparencies. The three moving carriages are carefully counterbalanced to allow smooth and positive focusing and the register system with pin bars and vacuum hold accommodates all known masking systems, both at baseboard and transparency

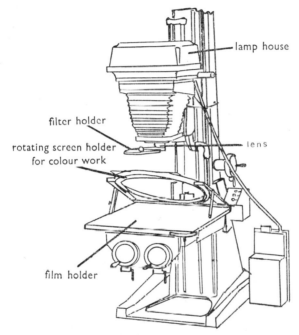

lamp house

filter holder

rotating screen holder
for colour work

lens

film holder

Fig. 51 Enlarger type camera

stages. A re-set system guarantees precise re-register. The baseboard is mounted on a fully counterbalanced carriage having a rise and fall movement of 24 inches. The vacuum base can be clamped in any position on the table. A point source tungsten light can be placed in a central position in front of the lens for screen flashing or for making masks at transparency level by reversing the position on the housing. Glass bound filters of any make are provided.

The Littlejohn Magnacolor is one of the latest of these precision-built colour separation cameras. The negative carriage holds 12 in. × 15 in. transparencies and the vacuum baseboard takes a maximum film size of 22 in. × 32 in. Lighting is either high intensity fluorescent tubes or electronic flash. Five lenses accommodate a magnification range of 20 times enlargement to 4 times reduction. Very high intensity tungsten filament lamps mounted on articulated arms can be fitted to the baseboard for reflection copy reproduction work.

THE DENSITOMETER

FOR MEASURING densities in a photographic emulsion a densitometer is used. This instrument may be visual or photo-electric. The visual densitometer is the cheaper instrument, but is slower and tiring in use and sometimes not sufficiently accurate. The photo-electric type balances the two light intensities by means of a photo-electric cell instead of the eye. The light transmitted by the test density can fall on a self-generating barrier layer cell and the current generated, proportional to the light intensity, is then passed to a micro-ammeter calibrated in densities. Another type uses a photo-emissive cell coupled to a valve amplifier for the same purpose, and a further type employs a photo-multiplier tube. This is more sensitive than a photocell, measuring densities over 4.

The Kodak visual instrument measures the tone area by placing it in the path of a beam of light that passes through an eyepiece to one-half of a split viewing area. A second beam of light passes into the other half of the split viewing field, by-passing the tone area. This control beam is dimmed by a change in position until its visual appearance in the split field of the eyepiece seems to match the light intensity that is being transmitted through the area being measured. A calibrated scale is attached to the control beam adjustment and when the visual appearances of both halves of the split field are the same, the density can be read from the scale.

Visual and photo-electric densitometers are made to read transmission density, reflection density, or both. For transmission work the range should cover 0·00 to 3·00 density units and for reflection density a range of 0·00 to 2·00 density units is necessary. The densitometer can also be used to calculate filter factors, as an exposure calculating device, and also as a means to calculate the evenness of illumination on the copyboard as well as on the ground glass of the camera, to measure the amount of light coming through the lens. In this country, two densitometers of British manufacture are in general use. Both are satisfactory and are photo-electric instruments. One illuminates the negative at 45 degrees and is viewed normally by a photo-electric vacuum cell. The other illuminates the negative normally and views by an annular barrier-layer type photo-cell at about 35 degrees (Fig. 52).

The latter instrument, the EEL densitometer, has as basic components a lamp, condenser system, barrier cell and microammeter. Densities up to 3·0 can be measured in three ranges of one density unit each. The lamp light is focused by condensers and an iris diaphragm is used to set the zero. Two gauzes, inserted in the light beam, each correspond to a density of one (with 10% transmission). The light through the mirror is reflected vertically through another lens system which focuses the beam at the aperture. The sample to be read is placed over the 1, 2 or 4 mm. aperture and the photocell, on a hinged arm, is brought into position. Densities are read directly on the log scale microammeter. This is directly coupled to the photocell so that variation is

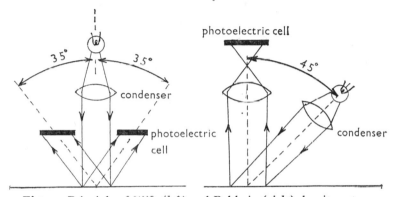

Fig. 52 Principle of EEL (*left*) and Baldwin (*right*) densitometers

only possible in the lamp, which is stabilised by using a constant voltage transformer.

The former instrument, the Baldwin densitometer, is more complex, using a vacuum tube photometer with a densitometer attachment. A photoemissive Cintel photocell is used, coupled to the galvanometer by a D.C. amplifier. Measuring apertures are $\frac{1}{16}$ in. and $\frac{3}{16}$ in. and the accuracy is +0·02. Density readings 4·5 and over can be taken. An integrating bar of high refractive index material is incorporated for measuring diffuse densities. The light traverses this bar longitudinally and the integrating action on the emerging (incident) light is due to total internal reflection from the sides of the bar. The photometer and the densitometer are separate units with, as also applies in the case of the EEL, a reflection densitometer available for use with the photometer unit.

COLOUR TEMPERATURE

LIGHT RAYS falling on an object are part reflected, part absorbed and part transmitted. When the object is very dense, no radiations will be transmitted and all non-reflected rays will be absorbed. A body reflecting no light and completely absorbing all radiations falling on it would be a 'black body'. This does not in actuality occur in nature and if it did this hypothetical black body would re-emit maximum radiations when heated. This explains the concept of 'colour temperature' in which the temperature in degrees Kelvin is the temperature in Centigrade plus 273. The definition being 'The colour temperature of a light source is the temperature on the "absolute" scale which is expressed in degrees Kelvin to which a black body must be heated to emit light of the same colour as that of the light source in question'.

TEMPERATURE OF HEATED BODIES

Colour	Temperature, °C	Temperature, °K
Heavy dense red	480	753 (480 + 273)
Dark red	750	1023 (750 + 273)
Orange red	990	1263 (990 + 273)
Yellow	1150	1423 (1150 + 273)

COLOUR TEMPERATURE OF VARIOUS LIGHT SOURCES

Light source	Approx. colour temperature, °K.
Candle	1900
Half-watt tungsten lamp (below 100 watts)	2600
Carbon filament lamp	2800
Half-watt lamp (tungsten) 1500 watt	3020
Over-run lamps 500 watt (2-6 hour life, photoflood)	3400
Fluorescent daylight tubes	4800
White flame arc	5000

TYPES OF ILLUMINANT

Incandescent Lamps

USUALLY TUNGSTEN filament suspended in an evacuated glass envelope filled with an inert gas continuous spectrum, average colour, temperature 2800° K. They generate a large amount of heat and emit more red than blue light. Used mainly for illumination, contact printing frames and enlargers. Actinism factor 0·8; average luminous efficiency in lumens per watt: 100 watt (14), 500 watt (17), 1500-watt lamp (18), with corresponding actinic luminous efficiency about 11, 14, 18, respectively. The lighting is very deficient in blue.

Over-run Lamps

THESE ARE incandescent lamps which burn at a higher voltage curtailing the life considerably from 1000 hours to between 2–100 according to how much they are over-run. Continuous spectrum, average colour temperature, 3,100° K (100 hrs. type), 3,400° K (2 hrs. type). Great heat is generated, the colour is good with some excess in red. Have a general application for process cameras, enlargers and studio photography. Actinism factor 1, luminous efficiency 100 hrs. lamp (20), 2 hrs. lamp (30), with corresponding actinic luminous efficiency about 20 and 30 respectively. Lamp life can be lengthened by the use of a variable resistance to regulate the voltage.

Fluorescent Lamps

GAS-DISCHARGE lamps with the tube filled with an inert gas and some mercury vapour and the envelope coated internally with a fluorescent substance. An electrode is fitted at each end of the tube. When the lamp is switched on the negative electrode emits a stream of electrons which impinge on the free electrons present in the gas, forming more electrons until the number increases to make the gas conductive. The circuit is now closed and an electric current flows from one electrode to the other. The coating on the inside of the tube fluoresces by the absorption of the u.v. radiations, thus emitting visible light. Line plus continuous spectrum, average colour temperature 3000 (warm), 4200 (white), 6500° K (daylight). Little heat is generated and the colour depends on the fluorescing substance. Used for illumination, printing frames, process cameras and cold-light enlargers. Actinism factor 1·5; average luminous efficiency 40; actinic luminous efficiency 60.

High-pressure Mercury-vapour Lamps

THESE ARE gas-discharge lamps with high gas pressure so that a second protective envelope is used. The lamp is connected to the mains via a transformer or inductance coil. Line or band spectrum with peaks in the ultra-violet region. No red light present, with average green and excess blue. Thus unsuitable for colour separation work and mainly used for printing frame and black and white camera work (monochrome). Must cool down before being switched on again and a time lapse occurs before reaching maximum efficiency after switching on. Actinism factor 1·6; average luminous efficiency 40; actinic luminous efficiency 64.

High-pressure Xenon Lamps

THE MERCURY vapour in high-pressure mercury vapour lamp is replaced by the rare gas xenon, whose spectral composition approaches very close to that of daylight. Thus xenon lamps are very suitable for colour separation work. Great heat is generated in the larger type of lamp and water or air cooling is necessary, plus a transformer as well as a rectifier. The spectrum is continuous, plus a few lines, and the colour temperature approximates 6300° K, giving a white light. Suitable for printing frames, process cameras and enlargers. Actinism factor 1·5; average luminous efficiency 3·5 and actinic luminous efficiency 52. Alternating current oscillations produce a flash every half-cycle giving, with a 50-cycle source, 100 flashes per second without any apparent intermittency.

Open-type Carbon Arc Lamps

ALTHOUGH NOT emitting as much ultraviolet as the enclosed arc lamps the light is much richer in the visual rays, so that they are suitable for all kinds of photographic material. They are costly to operate, current and carbon consumption being very high, yet it is still the most widely used light source. The arc-shaped electric discharge occurring between two carbon rods (negative and positive electrodes) produces the light, which is partly from the arc itself and partly from the arc crater. With the ordinary carbon arc, the electrodes are pure carbon and almost all the light comes from the arc crater in the positive electrode. With mineral (cored) carbons the arc flame itself emits about 80% of the light giving much higher luminous efficiency. The length of arc helps to determine colour temperature and intensity increases with added amperage. A great deal of dust and smoke is produced and the spectral composition of arc light lacks stability because of impurities present in the carbons, whilst the distance separating the carbons has to be continually adjusted. The spectrum is continuous, plus a few lines, and the colour temperature is about 5000° K with cored carbons and about 3700° K normal. A great deal of heat is given off. They are widely used for process cameras and printing frames. With cored carbons actinism factor 1·5; average luminous efficiency 35 lumen per watt (no resistor), actinic luminous efficiency being about 52.

Electronic Flash Lamps

THE CHARACTERISTICS and importance of electronic flash units are considered on pages 45 and 49 in *Camera and Process Work*. The spectrum is continuous, having few lines with a balanced lighting and a colour temperature of about 6300° K. The units are suitable for process cameras and enlargers and for studio photography. Again, for contact work from masked or unmasked transparencies or for direct screening on 'lith' Pan. material, an instrument like the Langham Monotron shows the advantages of electronic flash in reproducing shadow detail without highlight loss. The power unit operates at 200 watt-seconds with xenon-filled flash tube and 50-watt tungsten lamp.

On account of reciprocity failure there is less density produced by electronic flash compared, for instance, with carbon arc lamps. The result is a characteristic curve with a shorter toe, a longer and less-steep straight-line portion, and a smaller shoulder curve. This gives a better rendering of detail in the shadow areas and the lengthening of the straight-line portion into the shoulder area indicates that the highlight detail will be better reproduced. In practice, the largest possible lens aperture should be used consistent with the knowledge that a lens gives optimum sharpness at certain openings (process lens between $f/16$ and $f/32$; enlarger lens between $f/5\cdot6$ and $f/8$). Also the light intensity of the flash should be adjusted so that the exposure consists of as few flashes as possible. An increase in the number of flashes progressively results in a loss of detail.

Iodine-quartz (Tungsten Iodine) Lamps

THE STANDING of open-arc lamps for camera work illumination has been further challenged by the introduction of the tungsten iodine lamp. Pulsed xenon lamps are very good and most suitable, but are expensive to install with high cost of lamp replacement. Tungsten melts at about 3650° K, thus the running temperature is a compromise with low temperature giving long life and low efficiency. Increased voltage across the bulb raises the temperature giving a whiter light and increased efficiency. The compromise is at 2800° K, with a rated life of 1000 hours. Photoflood lamps operating at 3200° K have a 2–6 hour life. Basically a tungsten iodine lamp is a tungsten filament lamp plus a little iodine vapour in the bulb which combines with tungsten at a temperature over 250° C. The compound dissociates into tungsten and iodine again at 2000° C. This 'iodine cycle' requires special material to withstand temperature over 250° C and the lamps are comparatively small, with quartz envelopes (tubes) and metal caps. They are run hotter, are more efficient with less falling off of intensity during the life of the lamp. When the current is on, the iodine vaporises and prevents the tungsten vaporising and blackening the tube despite the short distance and high temperature. The rated life varies from 100 hours to 2000 hours according to the colour temperature (2900–3200° K). Lamp replacement cost is between £3 and £6.

FLARE

WHEN DIFFICULTY is encountered in obtaining sufficient contrast in screen and continuous tone negatives when photographing through a process camera, using sensitive emulsions and developers of known contrast and gradation, it is advisable to check for the amount of flare present. The Kodak Graphic Arts Leaflet GA/18 is most helpful in this connection. Lens flare in its widest interpretation refers to the unwanted light which is spread over the image by multiple reflections and inter-reflections from the lens surface and also to the scattered light in the camera, owing to, amongst other causes, reflections from the lens barrel, the camera bellows and the light scattered by dirt or scratches. All these sources of flare are intensified by any reflections from the copy-board, light coloured walls and uncovered windows. Smoke from arc lamps settles on the lens, which should be regularly cleaned. Copy-boards should be painted matt black, unused areas of the coverglass should be covered with black paper to prevent indirect reflections of light entering the lens. Other lamps should be screened and possible reflections from all bright objects should be avoided. The lens should be coated, a lens hood fitted and, if necessary, a baffle placed inside the camera bellows to prevent reflection from the bellows on to the sensitised surface. If the camera gives 2% flare, an original with a density range of 2·0* will be recorded as if the range was only 1·53.*

EFFECT OF FLARE ON DENSITY OF ORIGINAL

Density of original	Percentage flare			
	1%	2%	4%	8%
0·0	0	0	0	0
0·5	0·49	0·48	0·47	0·44
1·0	0·96	0·93	0·87	0·78
1·5	1·38	1·29	1·16	0·99
2·0*	1·70	1·53*	1·32	1·09
2·5	1·88	1·65	1·39	1·11
3·0	1·96	1·69	1·41	1·13

IX

Photographic Materials and Processing

THE LIGHT-SENSITIVE MATERIAL

THE SILVER emulsion consists of a colloid such as gelatin, silver nitrate, alkali halides and water. By mixing a solution of silver nitrate with a halide solution of one of the alkali metals (potassium bromide, sodium chloride or potassium iodide), an almost insoluble silver halide results and separates out as silver bromide, silver chloride or silver iodide respectively. This silver halide is the light-sensitive element of the emulsion; a halide being a compound of one of the halogen elements – fluorine, chlorine, bromine or iodine – and is a salt of the hydride of one of these. Silver fluoride is rarely used because of its fogging action when combined with other halides. Silver bromide (AgBr) forms the major portion of the halide salts giving speed and low fog action. Silver iodide (AgI) has a speed of about one-third of silver bromide and silver chloride (AgCI), used mainly for paper-type emulsions, has a speed of about one-eighth that of silver bromide. Gelatin has unique properties; during the first ripening process it acts as a protective colloid surrounding the newly formed silver halide crystals and preventing them clogging together, and during the second ripening process the sulphur compounds in the gelatin effect the speed of the film. One part of sulphur compound to one million parts of gelatin produces a big increase in sensitivity, an excess produces emulsion fog. It is a protein obtained from the tissues, hides, cartilage and bones of animals. Main specifications for photographic use are jelly strength, pH, moisture content, metal contents (iron, lead, copper, etc.) plus ash and sulphur dioxide. The procedure of emulsion making is soaking and dissolving some gelatin, adding bromides and iodides, precipitating of the silver halide (emulsification), recrystallisating the emulsion by heating (first ripening), adding the balance of the gelatin and chilling, forcing the chilled gelatin through a wire mesh (noodles formation), washing to clear away unwanted salts, re-heating to crystallise the silver salts (second ripening) and finally adding the colour sensitising dyes, preservatives, stabilisers, anti-fogging and hardening agents.

In the making of high-speed emulsions, ammonia content is important. When present, minute silver halide crystals dissolve forming complex compounds to increase the size of the larger crystals. High-speed emulsions have large silver halide crystals, normally prepared in the presence of ammonia. They are added either to the silver nitrate solution or to the emulsion just after crystallising out of the silver halide. In the process of precipitation of the silver halide (emulsification) the silver nitrate can be added rapidly or slowly. Slow addition makes the size of the silver halide crystals larger, resulting in a higher speed emulsion, which is softer working. A rapid addition of the silver nitrate solution results in a slower speed emulsion which has a higher contrast. The grain size is increased in ripening by the rate of stirring, an increase in temperature, the duration of the ripening process and the pH value of the emulsion. As stated, ammonia accelerates the rate of ripening, whilst the presence of acids slows down the rate of ripening, resulting in a smaller grain and a more contrasty emulsion. Silver bromide is more soluble in a solution of ammonium bromide than in a solution of potassium bromide and the rate of ripening is faster in the presence of the former. When the physical ripening is completed, that is when the silver halide grains have reached the required size and distribution, the emulsion is allowed to set by placing the container in ice water. Washing, second ripening, etc., follow.

Dimensional Stability of Photographic Film

CHANGES IN the dimensions of photographic film are mainly caused by fluctuation in temperature and variations in the relative humidity of the atmosphere. Gelatin, which is the basis of the emulsion layer, readily absorbs and relinquishes moisture and causes tensions to the base material when it stretches or shrinks due to the above-mentioned changes. Triacetate is much more water absorbing than polyester and thus polyester has a greater dimensional stability than triacetate base. Many sheet films are made on cellulose acetate butyrate or cellulose triacetate safety base. In manufacture it is cast from solvent solutions, a small amount of the solvent remains in the base and its gradual escape during ageing is a cause of shrinkage. On heavy bases, when stored at a relative humidity not exceeding 60%, low shrinkage is apparent, particularly with triacetate bases. Polystyrene (PB) is made by melt extrusion and has a low moisture absorption giving a humidity expansion coefficient only about one-third that of similar film on acetate base. Permanent shrinkage is also less because polystyrene contains no solvent or plasticiser.

The more recent introduction of the thermoplastic material polyethylene terephthalate, which belongs to the class of plastics termed polyesters, as a support for photographic emulsions has increased considerably the dimensional stability of films. For colour work and close register work this base is preferred, but it must be realised that there is no such thing as absolute dimensional stability for photographic film.

A relative humidity of 30 to 50% (average 40) and a temperature of 65 to 70° F are the most satisfactory working conditions. For many years the film base in general use was cellulose nitrate film. This was strong and reasonably dimensionally stable, but highly inflammable. Thus it was replaced by cellulose acetate and polyacetate compounds and also by various polymerised compounds. Cellulose tri-acetate is the general film base in use today for commercial films. It is possibly not as strong or as dimensionally stable as the older nitrate base and is made in thicknesses from 0·003 in. to 0·009 in. Most colour film, miniature, sheet, roll and cine, use it as a film base. For graphic arts work more stable bases using polymerised compounds are employed. These are polystyrene, polycarbonate and polyester films. The latter is far tougher and more stable than nitrate film and almost equals glass in dimensional stability. A further advantage is its higher resistance to creasing and cockling plus reduced absorption of moisture, with a consequently more rapid natural drying action after processing.

Colour Sensitivity of Photographic Emulsions

ALL PHOTOGRAPHIC emulsions are sensitive to blue, violet and ultra-violet light. This range of sensitivity has to be extended for colour reproduction to include green, yellow, orange and red. This is done by the addition of dye during emulsion manufacture. Blue sensitive emulsions record high negative densities for blue areas of a coloured copy and in reproduction render blues very light, and reds, yellows and greens very dark. They are used for black and white copy. Orthochromatic materials are not sensitive to red light, therefore red reproduces as black. Because they are sensitive to a wider range of colours they are normally faster than blue-sensitive (colour blind) materials. Panchromatic emulsions are sensitive to all visual colours plus ultra-violet, thus giving satisfactory monochromatic rendering of full coloured originals. Infra-red materials are very sensitive to infra-red radiations and in photomechanical work are used mainly in conjunction with an infra-red filter (deep red) for making the black printer negative.

FILTERS

LIGHT FILTERS, usually in the form of dyed gelatin sheets, allow a portion of some colours to pass through and stop other colours. A 'red' filter appears red because it transmits red light to the eye and absorbs most other colours. The selective absorption of light increases exposure time and the *filter factor* indicates the number of times the exposure must be increased using the filter, compared to the exposure under the same conditions without a filter. The *filter ratio* in colour reproduction is based on the ascertained correct exposure for the red filter. This is used as a basis for obtaining the correct exposures through the other filters, which are calculated directly by multiplying the red filter exposure by the appropriate filter information supplied by the manufacturers for each of the other filters. The factors obviously apply to a particular type of light source and cannot apply to other light sources.

	FILTERS			
	Red	Green	Blue	Yellow
Factor	1	1·4	0·5	0·3
Exposure (secs)	40	40 × 1·4 = 56	40 × 0·5 = 20	40 × 0·3 = 12

Contrast Filters

WHEN, FOR a particular reason, a colour has to be reproduced as a black or dark grey on the finished result, the colour of the filter used must be complementary to the colour being reproduced, and should certainly be of a different colour from that on the copy. Alternatively, when a colour is required to appear as a white or a light grey on the final result the colour of the filter must be similar to the colour being reproduced, or at least approximate to this colour as closely as possible.

Neutral Density Filters

THESE ARE photographically produced and are various densities of grey. They are used when it is necessary to increase the exposure time without affecting colour rendering and apply when a powerful light source is used. Without such filters the exposure time would be too short to be efficiently controlled.

DEVELOPERS AND DEVELOPING

THE EFFECT of light action upon a photographic emulsion is the formation of a latent image. The action of the developer is to convert to metallic silver the silver halide grains which have been exposed to light. The developer is thus a mixture of compounds which have the ability to convert a silver salt into metallic silver. Substances which form a metal from its salt or oxide are known as reducing agents and whilst there are many reducing agents capable of reducing silver bromide to metallic silver, very few are satisfactory as developers because they will not selectively differentiate between exposed and unexposed silver bromide. The most successful developing agents for general use are found to be derivatives of benzene, in which two or more hydrogens have been replaced by hydroxy, amino, or substituted amino groups. The hydroxyl (OH) and amino (NH_2) radicals are present in varying amounts with paradihydroxy benzene (Hydroquinone $C_6H_4(OH)^2$) and methylpara-aminophenol (Metol or Elon $CH_3NH . C_6H_4OH$) the most important.

Some reducing agents are more vigorous than others in urging electrons on to the silver ions and are known to have a high reduction or redox potential. When this is too negative, all silver grains, exposed and unexposed, are reduced; when it is too positive, there is difficulty in reducing even the exposed grains. Hydroquinone is a slow, powerful developer, taking longer to show a visible image but gaining density rapidly over an extended period of time. Metol is a more energetic reducing agent, the image appears quickly but builds up density slowly. A combination of the two, hydroquinone and metol, makes an excellent compromise, and varying mixtures of them are found in many developers. Hydroquinone is normally used with metol in varying proportions. On its own it is used for very high contrast solutions. Metol with alkaline substances alone gives very low contrast and is generally used with hydroquinone. Glycin can be used without an alkali. Pyrocatechin is in the hydroquinone group but gives a softer result, and Phenidone also gives soft results with a tendency to fog and is best employed in combination with hydroquinone.

Developers contain, apart from the developing agent, other components which have specific purposes. Water is the normal solvent, and it should be of a good standard of purity and reasonably free from calcium, magnesium and chloride salts. Hard water contains calcium bicarbonate, calcium sulphate and magnesium chloride which, when washing, can leave a sediment on the film. On the other hand, it toughens the emulsion, which may hold in warm weather to prevent frilling, softening and swelling. Distilled water should be used when it is indicated in the formula. Demineralising equipment is commercially available, using an 'ion exchanger' through which the water flows to remove the unwanted ions.

Accelerators

BORAX, SODIUM carbonate, potassium carbonate, sodium hydroxide (caustic soda), potassium hydroxide (caustic potash) are the *alkali*, *activator* or *accelerator*. It increases the pH of the solution thus increasing the ionisation of the developing agent and also absorbs the bromine ions formed by the action of the reducing agent on the silver salts. Paraformaldehyde is used in 'lith' developers because of its ability to produce great contrast. It fills the same role as the alkali in that it activates the developer.

Preservatives

SODIUM SULPHITE, potassium metabisulphite and sodium bisulphite are the antioxidant agents. An alkaline developer is soon oxidised by the oxygen in the air. The preservative also acts as a silver solvent and prevents staining.

Restrainers

THE MOST widely used restrainer, or antifoggant, is potassium bromide, which reduces the ionisation of the silver salt. In developing, it is known that unexposed crystals are also reduced a little, giving a 'chemical fog'. The restrainer retards the development of this fog to a much greater extent than that of the photographic image, so that with normal development the fog does not reach an objectionable level of density.

Development

THE CHEMICAL action of development is most complex and is still being evaluated. In general terms the reducing agent is gradually assimilated and during this process it forms complex developing agent salts, which also act, to a degree, on the image. When the developing agent has completed its work a point of exhaustion will be reached and the bromine ions formed by the silver bromide prevent further action, so that no more density is produced. At that stage of development there is very little contrast. This increases gradually and reaches its limit at gamma infinity, when all the silver grains which have received the minimum quantity of exposure necessary for development, are reduced to the metallic state. Then the various densities of the image will be formed in crystals which have been completely developed and density variations will depend on the differing number of developed crystals. The normal temperature for developing is 68° F (20° C). The higher the temperature of the developer, the more rapid development will take place. The longer the development period (within limits), the more the contrast attained. Also an increase in the agitation of the developer increases contrast. The contrast of the image can be decreased by diluting the developer with 1, 2 or more parts of water. Too much dilution flattens the middle tones and causes an increase in fog.

Each time development takes place the developer is reduced in volume and is also weakened. This is because some of the developing agents are used up in converting the exposed silver halide into silver and the liberated bromine ions retard the action of the developer. Also the liberated hydrogen ions lessen the solution's alkalinity. Oxidation is also continually taking place – the larger the area of contact between the developer and the atmosphere, the greater the rate of oxidation, so that the solution loses its efficiency and power of development. With tray or dish development the only practical solution is to frequently discard the developer and replace by a fresh solution. With tank development, re-generation of the solution, by the addition of an ascertained quantity of replenisher at regular intervals, is essential. The tank should be pro-vided with a close-fitting lid, when not in use, to prevent exhaustion of the solution through oxidation from the air. Replenishment is calculated in proportion to the number of films processed and should at least replace the amount of developer transferred from the tank by the films. Suppliers recommend a standard technique for tank replenishment using a solution of the same composition as the original developer, only more concentrated, or a special, separate replenisher solution, adapted to both the developer and the type of film. Compared with the normal developer, the replenisher solution contains a much higher concentra-tion of developing agents, with more alkaline components and less bromine ions.

Hydroquinone-Paraformaldehyde Developer

A 'LITH' film must have a gamma above 10 which is necessary to build up screen dots having an extremely steep density gradient. The required dot on a halftone negative should have an acute density gradient profile with density above 3·0 surrounded by a transparent area and free from halo. A characteristic feature separating 'lith' developer from other de-velopers is that in every phase of its bath life it contains a clearly defined quantity of free sodium sulphite. This excess amount of sodium sulphite in solution is attached to formaldehyde with which it forms a chemical combination preventing a reaction. When free sodium sulphite is used up it is replaced by an equal amount of sodium sulphite freed instantly from this combination, resulting in a continuous perfect balance of the developer. According to Dr Rebner the quantity of free sodium sulphite in the 'lith' developer is just sufficient to protect the developer from oxidation by air, yet it is too small to influence the developing process itself. Thus the oxidation products of hydroquinone, stemming from the developing process, are not eliminated but wander freely from the area where they originated in all directions, reducing the neighbour-ing silver halide grain although it does not carry a developable image. This, it is stated, is the reason for the sudden appearance of the elements of the image during 'lith' development. The discoloration effect of the oxidation products reaches a maximum and gradually is reduced until it clears with the gamma value of the film reduced to about 5·0, which would be maximum gamma for any other type of developer. With normal development technique the blackening of the image areas begins simultaneously over the whole scale of tonal values and gradually increases till gamma infinity is reached. With 'lith' developer blackening starts in the areas of maximum action of light, spreading gradually until the areas of minimum light action are developed. Thus the density threshold is held back and its effect only apparent in the last phase of full development. The period between the beginning of blackening and complete development of the density threshold is the period of extreme steep or 'lith' gradation. The gamma value at the beginning of blackening should be above 10. The processing latitude of 'lith' gradation depends on the structure of the 'lith' film and developer. This large processing latitude is compensated by an increase of developing time, with maximum sensitivity only reached if full development is carried through to the limits of the latitude of 'lith' gradation. Dr Rebner of Agfa has shown that there is a direct interrelation between screen dot definition and 'lith' gradation, with the 'lith' gradation providing for the required steep density gradient for screen dots through the combined efforts of hydroquinoneformaldehyde developer and 'lith' sensitivity of the emulsion. In conjunction they are capable of tackling the problem of dot definition. Gevaert have also published a great deal of information on the subject of Litholine developer and Litholine emulsions. Their observations confirm the findings published by Dr E. Zund in *The Process Engraver's Monthly*, 1953, vol. 60, page 179.

HIGH-CONTRAST DEVELOPER FOR LITH EMULSIONS – 82 (AGFA FORMULA)

(A)			(B)		
Sodium Sulphite (anhyd.)	120 g		Sodium Sulphite (anhyd.)	1 g	
Boric Acid (cryst.)	30 g		Paraformaldehyde	30 g	
Hydroquinone	90 g		Potassium Metabisul-		
Water	2000 cc.		phite	10 g	
			Sodium Bromide	6 g	
			Water	2000 cc.	

Mix equal parts of A and B before use.

HIGH CONTRAST DEVELOPER (NON-LITH EMULSIONS) – GP220 (GEVAERT FORMULA)

(A)			(B)		
Water (105°F, 40°C) 64 oz	800 cc.		Water (105°F, 40°C) 64 oz	800 cc.	
Potassium Metabisulphite			Potassium hydroxide		
2 oz.	25 g		4 oz	50 g	
Hydroquinone 2 oz	25 g		Water to make up to		
Potassium Bromide 2 oz	25 g		80 oz	1000 cc.	
Water to make up to 80 oz					
	1000 cc.				

Just before use mix equal parts of A and B. The developer oxidises rapidly. Mix enough for a single development and discard after use.

Developers for Continuous Tone Work

I.D.2. (ILFORD)	Avoir.	Metric	DK 50 (KODAK)	Avoir.	Metric
Metol	70 gr	2 gm	'Elon' (Metol)	88 gr	2·5 gm
Sodium Sulphite (anhyd.)	6 oz	75 gm	Sodium Sulphite (anhyd.)	2 oz 175 gr	30 gm
Hydroquinone	280 gr	8 gm	Hydroquinone	88 gr	2·5 gm
Sodium Carbonate (anhyd.)	3 oz	37·5 gm	'Kodalk'	350 gr	10 gm
Potassium Bromide	70 gr	2 gm	Potassium Bromide	18 gr	0·5 gm
Water	80 oz	1000 cc	Water	80 oz	1000 cc.
Dish	1 part with 2 water		Dish	No dilution.	
Tank	1 part with 5 water		Tank	1 part with 1 water.	

AUTOMATIC PROCESSING

IN FILM processing there are four main factors to consider – temperature control, agitation, replenishment and drying conditions. To integrate these four factors into one processing unit means an expensive piece of equipment. Such equipment is available, there now being a selection of between twenty and thirty automatic processors on the market. As a cheaper substitute mechanical tray rockers and tanks fitted with nitrogen burst are useful aids to assist in standardising procedure. Reasonable temperature control can be effected quite cheaply and the next most important processing variable is agitation. Tray rockers, operated by a small motor, ensure far better control and uniformity than manual tray rocking. For tank development of continuous tone negatives and positives nitrogen burst agitation is very successful. The gas, which is inert and therefore does not affect the chemical solutions, is forced through tubes which have small holes in them and are located at the bottom of the tank. Timing of the short bursts at specified intervals controls the rate of agitation. With both a mechanical tray rocking and nitrogen burst non automatic tank methods, the replenishment of the developer and control of its chemical activity are left to the discretion of the operator, based on the square inches of film processed. Fully automatic machines control all the variables of temperature agitation and replenishment, some also drying the films automatically. A number of machines are continuous flow type and employ a powered conveyer system which transports the exposed film through developer-fix-wash tanks by means of pin bars, rollers, belts or combinations of them plus an integral dryer. Other machines are batch processors using an overhead carriage and an elevator-type film basket which automatically immerses the film in successive steps into processing tanks, following a pre-set time schedule. This is useful when more than one type of film is to be developed, requiring different developers. The different developer tanks can be optionally selected, to suit the particular film, then operating a switch so that the carriage by-passes the tanks not required by the selected process. The Crosfield Gammatron and the Nottaris and Wagner Devlomat are designed for colour separation films and incorporate control patches exposed alongside the film. During development the patches are scanned by infra-red light and the density measured by photocell. When the control patches have reached the pre-determined density, a relay is operated by the photocell which activates a motor to lift the film out of the developing tank into the stop bath and finally to the fixer and wash. The required density is scale indicated and selected by turning a knob.

Nitrogen Burst Agitation

USING GASEOUS burst agitation, Gevaert conducted many tests using an experimental tank and finding the following optimum values. Duration of each impulse of nitrogen gas $\frac{1}{2}$–1 sec., time between two impulses approximately 3 secs., gas pressure from nitrogen supply 1·4 lb/sq. in. to 2·8 lb/sq. in. Too high pressure resulted in uneven development, so that for even development low gas pressure, short impulse duration, short interval periods and not too great distances between film and film and the walls of the tank (maximum, 5 cm.) were essential.

To develop to a given gamma under specified conditions requires a shorter development time with nitrogen burst than with dish development using hand agitation. To equate the result the tank developer solution would have to be diluted. By constant development time and timing schedule, an increase of the gas pressure produces an increase in contrast, but over a certain pressure, unevenness results. Constant intervals between bursts and constant development time plus longer agitation periods give a higher gamma – again tending to unevenness. Longer intervals between bursts will decrease the contrast. Thus gamma can be influenced, within limits, by varying the gas pressure, the agitation period and the interval between bursts, but this is not recommended on account of resulting unevenness in development. The preferred method is to first regulate the agitation to give maximum evenness of development and obtain the desired gamma by reducing or increasing the development time. Also to ensure evenness the pipe system and the bottom of the tank must be mounted in a perfectly horizontal position, the nitrogen supply tank must be absolutely airtight and the apertures of the pipe system must be checked to see that they are unobstructed and fully open.

Machine Processors

MACHINE PROCESSING of graphic films, whilst initially involving a large
outlay of capital, is in the long run a time and money saver. One machine
can process the work of five or six camera operators and contact workers,
eliminating darkroom bottlenecks and cutting chemical cost by 50%
since the chemistry is changed every 45–60 days or more, when the
machine is emptied for complete cleaning. Valuable floor space formerly
occupied by sinks, traps, washers, clothes lines and drying cabinets is
saved. The Logeflo Processor LD24 has a dial-in replenishment method
which considers both the amount of exposed film and its length and
width. A switch allows fully automatic metering of replenisher in direct
proportion to length of film. A positive roller-belt transport system is
provided accepting any film base from 0·002 to 0·075 in. thick without

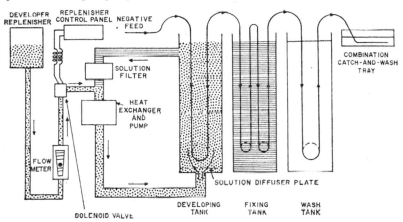

Fig. 53 Logeflo Processor

the use of leaders, hangers, clips, etc. Temperature range is controllable
from 65° F to 86° F with an accuracy of plus or minus 0·2° F at any
setting. It accommodates any film and any chemistry and the machine
has a unique roller-jet agitation using stainless steel tubes located between the rollers, allowing for the developer to be recirculated, filtered,
temperature controlled and sprayed against the rollers to assure absolute
uniformity of agitation and development.

The Pakoral G24 machine (Gevaert) proves statistically and in practice that the cost of the machine can be paid for in less than two years
in an average size firm with a daily output of over 100 films. The exposed film is conveyed through the developer, fixer, wash water and
drying cabinet in a single continuous movement, taking 6 minutes for
large-size film, by means of a transport system of pairs of rubber rollers
rotating in opposite directions. As each film passes through the machine,

automatically the required quantities of replenisher solutions are added to the tanks, and agitation is so uniform that on every square inch of film exactly the same amount of solution agitation is obtained. Development time depends on the rate at which the film passes through the machine – 65 of 20 in. × 24 in. (3 mins.) and 97 of 20 in. × 24 in. films per hour for 2 minutes' development, or 460 of 8 in. × 10 in. films.

The Kodalith Film Processor Model 324L employs a torque-driven roller clusters system with temperatures controlled by a thermostat and heat exchanger system; developer 80° F ± 0·15° F; fixer 77–78° F; wash 75° F. The exposed film enters the processor at the film feeding station, the film activating a microswitch that starts a metering pump which, in turn, draws the replenishment solutions from the developer and fixer storage tanks. The film is advanced by roller transport racks through a 12-gallon developer tank. From the developer it passes through a $5\frac{1}{2}$-gallon fix tank and then through a $5\frac{1}{2}$-gallon wash tank. The film is prepared for drying by passing through a water-subtractor at the entrance of the film-drying section. Thermostatically controlled warm, filtered air exits through drying tubes to ensure uniform drying. When dry, the film descends into a film-receiving bin – all in less than 6 minutes!

Replenishment of Solutions

DEVELOPER EXHAUSTION is due to two causes: exhaustion through use in development and exhaustion through standing – oxidation of the solution on exposure to air. Every film developed diminishes the developing power of the solution, because a certain quantity of developing agent is spent by reducing exposed silver halide to metallic silver. Also the bromide ions liberated during the reaction have a retarding effect on the developer activity, and the acid hydrogen ions reduce the alkalinity of the solution, thus also diminishing the developing power. Again each film taken out of the tank carries a certain amount of developer solution with it, depending on the size and thickness of the emulsion and the time during which the developer is allowed to drain back from the film into the tank. The developing agents are soon oxidised through contact with air, losing their developing power. The larger the area of contact with air, the faster the oxidation, hence a narrow, deep tank (which should be covered with a floating lid when not in use) is better than a large, shallow tray or dish.

The relation between exhaustion through use and exhaustion through standing depends on the working conditions and volume. Normally, replenishment takes place according to the number of films developed and is done by keeping the developer at a constant level by addition of replenisher solution. This solution must have a higher concentration of developing agents, more alkaline components and less bromide ions. With nitrogen burst agitation replenishment can be with a solution similar to the original developer but more concentrated, or by using a replenisher specially adapted to the developer and film being processed. This latter is the better method. As the replenisher is added, in general, in relation to the area of developed film, aerial oxidation is not accounted for, which makes it impossible to provide a replenisher to give ideal compensation for both factors of exhaustion and replenishers are therefore adapted to meet 'average' circumstances. The quantity of replenisher required depends upon the volume of work and the nature of the processing installation and, within certain limits, an average quantity of one litre of replenisher is required per square metre of processed film.

Replenishment of the fixing bath is a simpler problem because aerial oxidation does not occur in practice and exhaustion depends solely on the amount of films processed, another factor being the use or otherwise of a stop bath or rinse between developing and fixing.

Roebuck and Staehle have thoroughly investigated the reactions which occur during development using a hydroquinone developer. The reactions are most complex with the alkali producing dissociation of the hydroquinone and liberating ions of the developing agent in the solution; this reacts with the silver bromide to yield quinone plus ions of silver and bromine. The quinone reacts with sodium sulphite to form sodium hydroquinone monosulphonate and sodium hydroxide. Oxidation converts the sodium hydroquinone monosulphonate to quinone monosulphonate which reacts with sulphite to form sodium hydroquinone disulphonate. This is more or less inert as a developer and, as the development proceeds, hydroquinone ionises, whilst at the same time hydrogen ions are formed. The hydroquinone is used up and replaced by the weaker hydroquinone monosulphonate. Finally bromide ions are released into the solution – which is equivalent to adding potassium bromide to the developer.

FIXATION

HERSCHEL IN 1819 discovered a compound now known as sodium thiosulphate or 'hypo' which had the ability to dissolve silver halides. The Rev. J. B. Reade in 1837 was the first to use it for the fixation of photographic images although the credit for the discovery of its use is usually given to Fox-Talbot (1839). More recently, the more rapidly working ammonium thiosulphate fixers have largely replaced sodium thiosulphate, because of their greater rate of reaction, longer life and superior solubility which permits the production of liquid concentrates such as Amfix, one of the first proprietary ammonium thiosulphate fixers to be marketed.

The function of the fixing solution in photography is to facilitate the removal of the unexposed and undeveloped silver halide from the emulsion and render the image permanent. Two kinds of fixers are used, an acid fixer containing two or three constituents, and an acid hardening fixer, which is more complex. In addition to the main task of dissolving the unexposed and undeveloped silver salts the purpose of the fixing bath is also to neutralise developer alkali thus stopping the developer action and eliminating oxidation staining, and to harden the emulsion sufficiently to prevent scratches and the washing away of the gelatin image. For process work the bath would consist of a *solvent* (water) with a *silver halide solvent* – sodium thiosulphate – to dissolve the silver halides. Emulsions with large grain size clear more quickly with ammonium thiosulphate. The speed of fixing and the life of the bath depend, to a large extent, upon the emulsion being fixed – the amount of the different halides present, the grain size, the distribution and thickness of the emulsion layer, all have an influence. A fine-grain emulsion fixes more rapidly than a coarse-grain emulsion because it is thinner, thus allowing more rapid penetration. Slow films often contain less silver halide which assists speedy fixation. Hardening of the film does not really affect fixing time, although the subsequent washing out of the products of fixation may be considerably affected.

Also in the fixing bath is an *acid* which is needed to neutralise any alkaline developer solution carried in to the bath by the film. It also brings the bath to the required pH for neutralising the film's alkalinity. The acid has to be chosen carefully otherwise it will decompose the thiosulphate and precipitate sulphur. Potassium or sodium metabisulphite can be used providing they are pure. If acetic acid is used sodium sulphite should be added as a *stabiliser*, preventing the decomposition of the hypo by forming a complex sulphite salt with the ionised sulphur of the sodium thiosulphite and stopping the formation of a sulphur precipitate.

Potassium alum is recommended as a *hardener* in preference to chrome alum which, although more potent, loses its hardening power after short use and forms a sludge. The effect of hardening is to toughen the emulsion to withstand normal washing and handling when dry. Boric acid is employed as a *buffer* to restrict alteration of pH. Its use assists the bath to tolerate a fair amount of developer with little pH change and prevents the sludge formation of precipitates. In general the pH should be maintained at between 4·2 and 5·0 with acetic acid where hardener is used and between 4·6 and 5·4 where no hardener is used. The temperature should be about the same as the developer to prevent reticulation of the film. This should be about 18° to 24° C (65° to 75° F); higher temperatures cause the film to swell and lower temperatures slow down the clearing action.

Stop Bath

NORMALLY, DEVELOPERS are only active in an alkaline medium and the alkalinity must be neutralised if development is to be terminated at a certain point. This is done by rinsing the film, for preference in water to which acid has been added. This action also protects the fixer, because if alkaline developer is continually carried into the fixer, a rise in pH will occur which will eventually cause a breakdown of the fixer. Where a hardener is present in the fixer, precipitation will take place if a quantity of films are fixed without being rinsed in a stop bath or well washed. A satisfactory stop bath is a 3% acetic acid solution. Too strong a stop bath has a pH so low that there is a risk of film reticulation. This is on account of the inherent tendency of alkalis to swell the emulsion and acids to reduce swelling.

After fixing, the film must be washed in running water for a certain definite period to remove the residues of the fixing salt and other soluble salts from the emulsion. If these are not removed before the film is dried and stored, it will eventually break down and result in yellow-brown stains or fading of the image. Thiosulphate eliminators, such as 'Thiolim' and 'Thiodet', are available to speed up and shorten the washing process and to counteract the effect of an exhausted fixer.

CHEMICAL REDUCTION AND INTENSIFICATION

Reduction

A REDUCER, used to lower the density of the image, acts by converting some of the silver forming the image into a soluble or a complex salt. It is essentially an oxidising agent, oxidising the metallic silver to form a soluble salt. If this is insoluble in water another chemical must be added to convert the silver salt into a soluble silver compound. *Surface reducers* act uniformly overall, thus having a relatively stronger effect on the lighter areas of the negative image than on the deep metallic blocks, with a slight increase in contrast. *Proportional reducers* act proportionally to the quantity of silver present, thus acting more strongly on the deep blacks than on the clearer areas of the image, thereby decreasing contrast. *Super-proportional reducers*, in which one of the reaction products is a catalyst which acts where formed, means that the denser areas are attacked first and the lighter deposits of silver, the shadows, are almost unaffected. This flattens the tonal range and is used to correct over-developed negatives made from contrasty originals.

Farmer's Reducer (surface)

    (A) Potassium ferricyanide 4 oz; water 80 oz
    (B) Sodium thiosulphate 20 oz; water 80 oz

Mix just prior to use 1 part each of A and B with 8 parts water. The more hypo used, the more uniform the reduction; an increase in ferricyanide has a greater effect on the middle tones. The potassium ferricyanide is reduced by silver to potassium ferrocyanide, silver is converted to silver ferrocyanide which dissolves in hypo solution. The potassium ferrocyanide dissolves in the washing water with the surplus potassium ferricyanide.

$$4Ag + 4K_3Fe(CN)_6 = Ag_4Fe(CN)_6 + 3K_4Fe(CN)_6$$

(Silver + potassium ferricyanide = silver ferrocyanide + potassium ferrocyanide.)

Cerium Sulphate Reducer (surface)

Cerisulphate 8 oz
Sulphuric acid 140 gr
Water to make 80 oz

Reduction is proportional to the concentration of the solution, thus it will act more slowly with increased dilution. It is stable and does not react at all with the gelatin of the emulsion and gives even uniform reduction. The silver sulphate formed is soluble and after reduction the film is washed and the creosulphate, silver sulphate and excess cerisulphate are dissolved.

$$Ag + Ce(SO_4)_3 = 2CeSO_4 + AgSO_4.$$

(Silver + cerisulphate = cerosulphate + silver sulphate (soluble).)

Ammonium Persulphate Reducer (proportional)

Ammonium persulphate $3\frac{1}{2}$ oz
Water to make 80 oz

Stop the action by immersion in a solution of sodium sulphite (8 oz sodium sulphite, 80 oz water). The ammonium persulphate reacts with the silver forming silver sulphate and ammonium sulphate.

$$2A + (NH_4)_2S_2O_8 = Ag_2SO_4 + (NH_4)_2SO_4.$$

(Silver + ammonium persulphate = silver sulphate + ammonium sulphate.)

Ammonium persulphate with sulphuric acid and water (6 oz ammonium persulphate, 2 drams sulphuric acid, water to 80 oz) is used as a super-proportional reducer. Similar to a proportional reducer, it acts in the opposite way to a surface reducer, attacking the denser areas first. For use dilute with an equal quantity of water and after reduction pass the film through an acid fixing bath before washing.

Intensification

INTENSIFIERS INCLUDE mercury, mercuric iodide, chromium, silver, uranium and lead. The process involves adding the elements of metals, apart from silver, such as mercury, chromium, lead and uranium to increase the opacity of the silver deposit. Alternatively, it consists of adding dense insoluble salts to the silver image. The operation is necessary when the negative lacks opacity or contrast for the printing process. It increases the density of the negative image or alters its colour so as to render it more actinic. Intensifiers can be divided into two classes – those which operate in single solution and those which entail a preliminary 'bleaching'. Emulsions should only have to be intensified as a last resort. The best line, screen and continuous-tone negatives and positives are obtained with correct exposure and development. The main value and use both in chemical reduction and intensification are in obtaining reproducible results when circumstances make it necessary to use unsuitable or inferior photographic materials or when reproducing poor quality originals.

Chromium Intensifier. This gives a permanent result with minimum staining effect and is suitable for continuous tone work. Bleach in a bath made from a stock solution of potassium bichromate (3 oz), hydrochloric acid (2 oz) and water made up to 1 litre (32 oz). Wash for 5 minutes and redevelop in a metol-hydroquinone developer. Reintensify if added contrast is required. Eliminate any discoloration in a 5% solution of sodium sulphite followed by washing. After blackening the negative should be passed through the fixing bath. The effect of bleaching the negative is to form silver chloride, silver chromate and chromic oxide and re-development converts these salts to silver, chromium and chromic chromate.

Monckhoven's Intensifier. This is the preferred intensifier for line and half-tone dot work. Solution (*a*) potassium bromide ($\frac{3}{4}$ oz), mercuric chloride ($\frac{3}{4}$ oz), water to 1 litre (32 oz); solution (*b*) water (32 oz), potassium cyanide ($\frac{3}{4}$ oz), silver nitrate ($\frac{3}{4}$ oz). (Dissolve separately before mixing, each in 16 oz water.) Bleach in (*a*), wash and blacken in (*b*). The cyanide is deadly poisonous and ammonia can be substituted as a blackening agent.

The silver nitrate and the potassium cyanide are dissolved separately and the silver added to the cyanide slowly and carefully until a permanent precipitate is produced.

$$KAg(CN)_2 + HgCl = HgAg(CN)_2 + KCl.$$

(Potassium silver cyanide + mercurous chloride = mercury silver cyanide + potassium chloride.)

WEIGHTS AND MEASURES

WEIGHTS AND measures used in formulae are English (avoirdupois and apothecaries') or metric systems.

Weight (Mass) Avoirdupois

27·355 gr = 1 dram = 1·78 gm (metric)
16 drams = 1 oz (437½ gr) = 28·35 gm
16 oz = 1 lb (7000 gr) = 453·6 gm
28 lb = 1 quarter = 12·7 kilos

Weight (Mass) Apothecaries'

20 gr = 1 scruple = 1·3 gm (metric)
3 scruples = 1 drachm (60 gr) = 3·9 gm
8 drams = 1 oz (480 gr) = 31·1 gm
12 oz = 1 lb = 373·3 gm

Fluid Measure (Volume) Apothecaries' (Imperial)

60 minims = 1 dram = 3·55 c.c. (metric)
8 drams = 1 oz (480 minims) = 28·4 c.c.
20 oz = 1 pint = 568 c.c.
2 pints = 1 quart (40 oz) = 1·136 litre
4 quarts = 1 gallon (160 oz) = 4·544 litres (4544 c.c.) (1280 drams)

The avoirdupois system is used in America for weights but the fluid measure differs as follows:

60 minims = 1 dram
8 drams = 1 oz
16 oz = 1 pint
2 pints = 1 quart (32 oz)
4 quarts = 1 gallon (128 oz)

The ounce, weighing 456 gr, is larger than the English equivalent (437½ gr). Thus the American pint equals about 16¾ English oz.

Metric Weights and Measures

1 gr. = 15·43 gr (1000 milligrams = 1 gram)
1000 gm = 1 kilo = 2 lb 3 oz 120 grains (1000 grains = 1 kilogram)
1000 c.c. = 1 litre = 35 oz 101 minims
(1000 cubic centimetres (c.c.) = 1 litre; 1000 millilitres (ml.) = 1 litre)

Conversion

Grammes to grains	multiply by 108 and divide by 7
gm to oz (avoirdupois)	multiply by 20 and divide by 567
Litres to gallons	multiply by 22 and divide by 100
Litres to pints	multiply by 88 and divide by 50
Millimetres to inches	multiply by 10 and divide by 254
Metres to yards	multiply by 70 and divide by 64
Kilogrammes to tons	multiply by 0·0009842
Centigrade to Fahrenheit	multiply by 9, divide by 5 and add 32 to the result

X

Line Negative Making

ESSENTIAL FACTORS

THE QUANTITY of light admitted to the camera is controlled by the diaphragm which consists of a number of overlapping blades leaving a central aperture which can be adjusted from the 'maximum aperture' to an opening of any desired diameter. This is known as an iris diaphragm. The usual aperture numbers are 8, 11, 16, 22, 32, 45, 64, 90, 128. These numbers indicate that the diameter (D) of the marked apertures are respectively $\frac{1}{8}$, $\frac{1}{11}$, $\frac{1}{16}$, etc., of the focal length of the lens. Thus:

$$\text{Diameter diaphragm aperture} = \frac{\text{focal length of the lens}}{\text{aperture number}}$$

$D = \dfrac{f}{d}$ when $D =$ diameter of the diaphragm aperture,

$\qquad f =$ focal length of the lens,
$\qquad d =$ aperture number.

$D = f/8, f/11, f/16,$ etc.

For line work the normal openings used at same size are $f/16$, $f/22$, $f/32$, or between $f/16$ and $f/32$, because process lenses have their best definition and resolution between these apertures. By using the V/ratio system (V/32, V/45, V/64), e.g. $\dfrac{64}{1 + M}$ (size ratio), the aperture for

same size working would be $\dfrac{64}{1 + 1} = f/32$.

Using this method the aperture is varied according to the enlargement or reduction whilst the exposure time remains constant. A pointer connected to the lens collar extending to a diaphragm chart would give the following approximate readings.

REPRODUCTION	V/32 RATIO	V/45 RATIO	V/64 RATIO
Percentage	f/16 (same size)	f/22·5 (same size)	f/32 (same size)
25	f/26	f/36	f/51
33	24	34	48
50	21	30	42
75	19	26	36
same size	16	22	32
150	13	18	25
200	11	15	21
300	8	11	16

The exposure would be twice as long using the V/45 ratio, compared with using the V/32 ratio, and four times the amount of exposure would be required if the V/64 ratio were employed, compared with the V/32 ratio. Thus, if an exposure of 1 minute were satisfactory when copying same size at f/32 (V/64 ratio) the same exposure would be given copying half-size using the V/64 ratio, when the aperture would be reduced to f/42, but if it was desired to utilise an aperture between f/16 and f/32 in order to obtain the maximum definition from the lens then f/30 (V/45 ratio) would be a suitable aperture for half-size copying and the exposure time would be reduced by half to 30 sec. If the aperture used was f/21 (V/32 ratio) the exposure required would be 15 sec.

An alternative procedure is to maintain a fixed lens aperture, such as f/22 or f/32, and vary the exposure in relation to alterations in the scale of reproduction. The exposure is based upon the camera extension (V^2) and assuming the exposure when copying to the same scale as the original object to be unity, for other sizes the exposure would be as follows: 3 times scale (4), equal scale (1), ¾-scale (0·76), ½-scale (0·56).

The equation for calculating exposure multiplication factors is as follows:

$$F = \frac{(M + 1)^2}{4}$$

Based upon the exposure given at same size (S/S) multiply by the factor (F) corresponding to the magnification (M) required.

Same size $\dfrac{(M + 1)^2}{4} = \dfrac{(1 + 1)^2}{4} = \dfrac{2^2}{4} = \dfrac{4}{4} = 1$

Half size $\dfrac{(M + 1)^2}{4} = \dfrac{(\frac{1}{2} + 1)^2}{4} = \dfrac{1\frac{1}{2}^2}{4} = \dfrac{\frac{3}{2} \times \frac{3}{2}}{4} = \dfrac{\frac{9}{4}}{\frac{4}{1}} = \dfrac{9}{16} = 0·56$

Twice size $\dfrac{(M + 1)^2}{4} = \dfrac{(2 + 1)^2}{4} = \dfrac{9}{4} = 2·25$

Thus if the exposure for S/S is 1 minute, the exposure for ½ scale would be $\dfrac{56}{100} \times 60 = 33·6$ sec. and for twice size $\dfrac{9}{4} \times 60 = 135$ sec. (2¼ min.).

Magnification (M)	Exposure Factor (F)
$\frac{1}{4}$ (25%)	0·39
$\frac{1}{3}$ (33%)	0·44
$\frac{1}{2}$ (50%)	0·56
$\frac{3}{4}$ (75%)	0·76
same size (100%)	1·0
$1\frac{1}{2}$ (150%)	1·56
2 (200%)	2·25
3 (300%)	4·0

The illumination is normally set at an angle of 45 degrees at a distance of three feet from the centre of the copyboard. Reducing the angle gives flatter lighting with a reduction of light intensity. This is sometimes necessary to increase the coverage of a large copy. Increasing the light angle with a more frontal lighting gives greater intensity of light on the copyboard but can increase the flare factor.

During exposure the film receives the action of the light reflected from the copy, forming a latent image. Exposure is defined as the product of the intensity of light times the period of action.

$$E = I \times t \text{ (Exposure = Intensity} \times \text{Time)}$$

The use of a light integrator measures intensity and time. When set to a certain light value it registers on a condenser the required amount of electrical energy to be generated by the action of the light on a photo-electric cell. The integrator measures not the time of exposure, but the product of exposure, which is the light intensity times the exposure time.

A factor to be considered in ascertaining exposure, apart from variation of aperture and camera extension, is the required alteration in exposure time caused by varying the light distance and light angle. This can be determined from the following formula which simplifies the finding of the new exposure required when these changes have been made. The inverse square laws are involved which state that (*a*) the intensity of light varies inversely as the square of the distance from the source and (*b*) intensity of illumination of a surface varies directly as the cosine of the angle of incidence.

$$\text{New exposure} = \left(\frac{\text{new distance}}{\text{old distance}}\right)^2 \times \text{old exposure} \times \frac{\text{sine of old angle}}{\text{sine of new angle}}$$

If filters have to be employed they will also increase, according to the filter factor, the required exposure. For monochrome reproduction they serve two purposes, either to increase the contrast of the copy, and to reproduce certain colours monochromatic thus holding them or dropping them out on the negative. For poor and faded copy – yellowish and grey backgrounds, etc. – contrast filters in yellow and pale orange which increase blue absorption on orthochromatic and panchromatic materials are most useful.

RESULT REQUIRED	EMULSION-FILTER COMBINATION EMULSION AND FILTER		
	Ordinary	Orthochromatic	Panchromatic
Lime green as black	none or blue	blue	blue
Lime green as white		green or yellow	green
Yellow as black	none or blue	none or blue	blue
Yellow as white		yellow or orange	red or orange
Violet as black		deep yellow	green
Violet as white	none or blue	none or blue	blue
Red as black	none	none or green	green
Red as white			red or orange
Orange as black	none	blue	green or blue
Orange as white			red or orange
Green as black			red
Green as white		green or yellow	green
Turquoise as black			red
Turquoise as white		blue or green	blue or green
Blue as black		yellow or orange	red or orange
Blue as white	none or blue	none or blue	blue

DEVELOPMENT

IN LINE work 'lith' type of emulsion should, for preference, be used. Two controlling factors of developing are agitation and temperature. The developer, containing an alkali of extreme contrast, is affected considerably by agitation. The technique of 'fine-line' or 'non-agitation' development in the paraformaldehyde developer is often used. The bath is agitated for the first thirty seconds and left without agitation for around about two minutes. The result can be further improved if the developing solution is changed from equal parts of A and B solutions to one part of A and two parts of B and retaining the 'still-bath' procedure. Kodak also market a special Kodalith Fine Line Developer. During normal development with agitation, the products of development are continually removed from the rapidly developing image areas by the movement of the solution, and are replaced by fresh developer of full strength. During still development with fine line developer these development products accumulate around the dense areas of the negative and restrain the development action in these regions. When copying halftone proofs 'dot for dot' these areas represent the highlights, and the accumulation of weakened developer slows down the development so that the dots do not become filled-in. The shadow areas have low density and little development occurs initially. These areas are in contact with full-strength developer which develops the small dots fully. In fine line work, the filling-in of fine clear lines in the negative is prevented by this restraining action of development products from the adjacent dark areas. It is recommended that 10–15% more exposure should be given than for conventional development. Agitate for the first 20–30 sec. and still-bath for 2–2½ min. at a temperature of 68° F (20° C). In general, still development reduces contrast whilst agitation increases contrast. A cold developer will reduce density and contrast and a warm developer will increase it.

Positives

A LARGE percentage of photolitho work is printed to metal from line and halftone positives. These are made either by contact, projection or chemical reversal.

CONTACT AND PROJECTION WORK

Contact

THE WORK is undertaken in a darkroom using a contact cabinet fitted with a manual or motorised vacuum pump and point source light. The

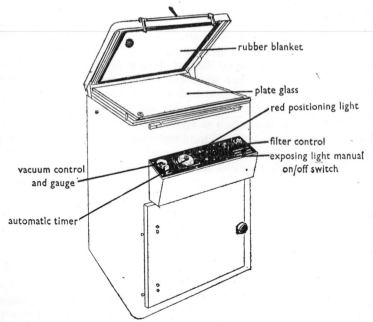

Fig. 54 Vacuum contact cabinet

negative should be right reading as the original, i.e. laterally reversed by means of the right-angled prism or mirror system. The film side of the negative is placed emulsion to emulsion with the sensitive plate or film, and exposed to the low wattage filament lamp. The printing cabinet should incorporate a safe light to facilitate easy register of the two surfaces on the glass top. The exposure should permit a developing time of at least two minutes so that the silver is fully reduced to the metallic state to produce hard dots and images for any subsequent dot correction and reduction. The negative is positioned image-side-up on the plate glass frame and the sensitive film for exposing the positive placed face-down in contact with it.

Halftone positives can be made from continuous tone negatives using the grey or magenta contact screen. The emulsion side of the negative is placed face-up on the frame in contact with the base (celluloid side) of the screen, which is sandwiched between the negative and the 'lith' type orthochromatic film. The unexposed film is placed face-down on the frame with its sensitive coating in contact with the emulsion (face-up) side of the contact screen. Contrast can be controlled with the magenta screen using, if required, yellow and red contrasting, controlling filters.

Projection

AN ENLARGER-TYPE projection camera is made for this purpose complete with vacuum baseboard, various sizes of negative holders, three-point locations, point source lights, etc. A description of this type of equipment has already been given (page 107).

The normal process camera can be used for this purpose by either projecting the image out of the camera, or projecting it into the camera, with the obvious advantage that by projection the resultant position can be enlarged or reduced in size. Firstly the prism is removed and the camera rotated on the turntable to be at right angles to the copyboard and the negative is sited in the normal negative image plane or in the screen gear of the camera. The illuminant is fitted on to the rear of the camera and the image projected on to the copyboard or a wall. Cold cathode lighting, or other forms of incandescent lighting placed behind a diffusing glass, occupy the position usually taken by the darkslide and the camera becomes virtually a horizontal enlarger, which is quite versatile in its capabilities.

Alternatively the negatives are projected into the camera by placing them in a transparency holder which is positioned on the rails between the copyboard and the lens. White paper covers the copyboard and the lamps are arranged so that light is reflected from the paper through the negative on to the sensitive emulsion held in the darkslide. Thus the film is loaded into the camera in the normal manner and the exposure determined and calculated as usual with the proviso that an increase in exposure time of about 25% will be necessary using transmitted light. A lighting unit can be fitted behind the transparency holder so that the illumination can be transmitted directly through the negative. Using this method screen positives can be made from continuous tone negatives. The glass-ruled half-tone screen is used in the screen gear in the normal way, the screen distance determined and the exposure made using the V/64 (detail) and V/45 (highlight) ratios. Flashing, to give the small dots in the highlights of the positive a hard core, is done using a small stop and exposing to a light of 15 watts flashed into the lens, or by removing the negative from the transparency holder so that the light reflected from the white paper covering the copyboard reflects into the lens. Extraneous areas surrounding the work should be masked out with lead foil or opaque prior to exposure.

CHEMICAL REVERSAL

THE ADVANTAGE of this method is that a positive image is obtained from a positive copy without an intermediate negative being made. It is chiefly used for line subject reproduction. The camera-exposure, which is a 20% increase on normal exposure, is made on 'lith' emulsion and developed out fully using normal procedure. When viewed at the termination of development the image should appear to have high density when inspected from both sides of the emulsion. The image is not fixed, but transferred to a stop bath for 15 sec. with continuous agitation and then placed in a bleach bath which dissolves out of the film the exposed developed silver, leaving intact and unaffected the residual unexposed silver halides. After 30 sec. immersion in the etch-bleach bath, the room light (white light) is switched on permanently. This fogs the remaining silver salts. Gentle swabbing with cotton wool will assist in the removal of the silver image, and when all the original image has been dissolved (bleached) away, wash and redevelop in a high contrast developer until the image is completely blackened. The Kodak etch-bleach formula consists of: (A) water (80 oz), copper sulphate (9 oz), citric acid (12 oz), potassium bromide (260 gr); (B) hydrogen peroxide – 3% solution. For use, mix equal parts of (A) and (B). Use a fresh mixture for each positive.

Contact positive making is obviously restricted to same size working and for printing down to metal has the advantage of giving sharp, firm, hard lines and dots because there is a minimum of light spread. Retouchers find this type of dot difficult for dot reduction work. Because of its uniform density it tends to lose opacity before reducing in size, especially with 'lith' emulsion. On the other hand, positives made by projection are suitable for dot correction work, due to the fact that they have a hard core with a soft edge which lends itself to chemical correction in that the periphery of the dots is quickly reduced, leaving the hard small centre intact.

AUTOPOSITIVE AND AUTOREVERSAL METHODS

TRANSPOSITION OF tone from black to white can also be effected using Gevaert Autoreversal or Kodak Autopositive materials. Herschel was the first to realise the possibility of reproducing a positive as a positive and a negative as a negative. Latent images can be reduced by radiation to which the emulsion itself is sensitive. The resulting effect is known as 'solarisation'. This will never destroy a latent blackening completely as the exposure used in fact gives rise to a further latent blackening. With the Herschel effect, however, the image can be completely eliminated and this involves the reduction of latent images by radiations to which the emulsion is not sensitive. This is the principle of the positive-to-positive and negative-to-negative systems used by Gevaert and Kodak. With Autoreversal, for instance, the emulsion is non-colour sensitive (blue sensitive only) and during the manufacture of the sensitive material a uniform latent blackening is produced over the whole surface. On development without any preliminary exposure the emulsion accordingly turns black all over. By exposing before development to green, yellow, orange or red light – to which it is not sensitive – the latent blackening is destroyed in the areas where these rays reach the emulsion, yielding a positive image from a positive original, and a negative image from a negative original.

In the areas affected by light – where the latent blackening has therefore been destroyed – the emulsion regains the characteristic of a normal non-colour-sensitive material in that the emulsion can react again to blue, violet or ultra-violet rays. Printing a negative on to such an area produces a positive and vice versa. Thus the process goes on, in areas affected by blue light there is once more a latent blackening which in turn can be destroyed by an appropriate 'yellow' exposure. The basic principle is that yellow light destroys the latent blackening, and white light (blue rays) produces a new blackening. The material, which is high contrast and developed with a 'lith' developer, may be handled safely in moderate room lighting (15-watt tungsten lamp) and a bright light source emitting as few blue rays as possible, such as tungsten and sodium lamps, warm fluorescent lamps and photofloods, should be used in conjunction with the yellow filter exposure. When mercury vapour and carbon arc lamps are used it is necessary to employ a dark yellow or an orange filter. Tints, combination effects, drop-out masks, outlines, partial and complete reversal, step-and-repeat and intermediates for positive blue-key plates are some of the results that can be obtained.

PLO—L

Auto-reversal methods are explained in *Reprorama*, no. 9 (1959), and in Gevaert Technical Information literature.

Kodak Autopositive Film is fully discussed in Graphic Arts Leaflet GA13. Using Autopositive Film with Kodak Flexible Screen S58/2 and using a no. 2 photoflood 18 in. from the printing frame the yellow light exposure averages 120 sec. The white light exposure is some 7 sec. (ratio 20:1). Unexposed Autopositive film would develop out 'black' but, if exposed to strong yellow light before development, clear film would result. If, after yellow light exposure, a white light exposure is given, development will again produce solid black metallic silver and this process of 'bleaching' with yellow light and re-exposing with white light can be continued indefinitely, before development. Thus, if unexposed film is exposed to yellow light in contact with a negative, a negative image will result, but if the film is first exposed to yellow light and then exposed to white light in contact with the negative a positive image will result. Hence the basic rule – 'yellow light removes density, white light adds density'.

THE KODAK TONE-LINE PROCESS

THIS IS a method of converting a continuous-tone image to a line drawing by photographic means, producing an effect similar to a pen-and-ink drawing. It involves combining a negative with a positive of almost equal contrast, the positive being used as a mask. It has nothing in common with solarisation methods of producing outlines or pseudo-relief principles of combining together a slightly out-of-register negative and positive.

The negative and positive images match each other in contrast and are taped together back to back, in register. The two images cancel out each other's tone values, excepting on the extreme edges where a little light is transmitted. Thus a contact print made on Kodalith Ortho Film will produce a line positive from which a line negative can be produced by contact, and from this, if required, a bromide print for further retouching can be made. The original continuous tone negative must be critically sharp, with a highlight density of about 1·4 and fully exposed so as to have plenty of shadow detail. The final result must have thicker outlines in the shadows than in the highlights, thus the first negative should be overexposed by normal negative standards, but certainly not overdeveloped. The positive mask is made on Kodak Super XX Panchromatic Film, using a point source light, and for preference, the Kodak punch register system. Develop in darkness, using full strength D-11 developer to give a minimum density of 0·5 to 0·7 with a density range similar to that of the negative. If the film positive is correct, there should be almost complete cancellation when it is superimposed on the negative and this 100% positive mask should give a print made from the combination, which will be a true outline copy of the original. An 80% mask would give heavier shadow areas in the reproduction, an effect which is sometimes required. The line positive is made on 'lith' film from the negative-positive combination. The width of the outline is controlled by the angle of the light source plus the thickness of the supports of the emulsions and on the exposure and development of the line positive and negative. A 100-watt pearl lamp, 3 ft. from the printing frame, at an angle of 45 degrees, is suitable. The printing frame should be rotated during exposure at a minimum rate of one revolution per second to enable the light to pass through the openings from all sides. A ball-bearing turntable or an ordinary record player turntable is suitable. The positive mask and the continuous tone negative are registered back-to-back and the combined highlight density of the two images will be about 2·0. An exposure time of about 30 seconds will be required. Still development, after agitating vigorously until the image appears, gives greater detail and total development time should be $2\frac{1}{4}$–$2\frac{1}{2}$ min. at 68° F. The result is a positive line image of the continuous tone original. This can be printed to metal for deep etch plate making or a contact negative made for bromide printing or for surface plate making.

Duotones

A DUOTONE can be defined as a two-colour set of plates made from a monochrome (usually black and white) continuous-tone original in which both images record the approximate tonal range of the copy. One of the plates is printed using a dark ink to record the shadow detail and the other plate printed in a light colour ink to record the highlight detail. Two negatives or positives are made through the glass or contact screen, both at different screen angles. The primary negative or positive for printing in the darkest colour is made at 45 degree angle, and has approximately 90% tonal range with a firm shadow dot. The secondary image for printing in the lighter colour is made at the 75 degree angle and is flatter and much more open in the highlights, with a small shadow dot which can print solid if required. The overall tonal range of this image approximates to 50% of the original. In practice a black may be used for overprinting on to yellow or red. Sometimes the desired effect is obtained by printing the primary image in a dark green or blue ink with the secondary colour, printed first, in a pastel shade.

XI

Halftone Negative Making

THE MACHINE-RULED CROSSLINE SCREEN

A GLASS screen is made by diamond ruling lines on two optically flat pieces of plate glass coated with an etching resist. The lines are etched with hydrofluoric acid and filled with an opaque pigment. The two pieces of glass are then cemented together, using Canada balsam, with the lines crossing at right angles. When assembled the cross-line pattern resembles a wire mesh in which the width of the opaque element equals

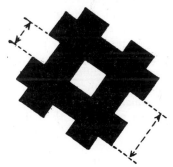

Fig. 55

Sections of a glass ruled halftone screen. Ratio of transparent to opaque area is 1:3 with only 25% of the screen transparent. Screen aperture is equal to one half of the screen ruling

the width of the clear opening. When this type of screen is interposed between the lens of the camera and the sensitive emulsion, each tiny screen opening acts as a pinhole lens photographing a specific part of the copy in terms of its relative brightness. It breaks the continuous tone image up into a series of dots of equal density and gradient, but of different sizes. Many factors enter into the optimum use of glass screens and there is no complete agreement on all the details of either theory or shop practice. These have been discussed in greater detail in *Camera and Process Work* (ch. 8), to which the student reader is referred.

Historical Background

TWO SCREEN processes are applied in practice today, the glass screen process and the contact screen process. Many opinions are advanced in favour of the latter in respect of superior rendition of detail. These are discussed later. It has long been realised that better results can be obtained in the camera by the use of a screen composed of vignetted lines or dots, conveniently described as an optical V screen, used in contact with the sensitive film instead of under the geometrical conditions required in the case of the opaque ruled screen. Horgan's original process was based on this idea and F. E. Ives also suggested it. A. J. Berchtold (1855), Ronald Trist in the 1920's and A. Murray (Kodak) introduced methods for producing screens utilising this principle in which the diameter of the lens aperture had no control over the dot formation in the negative.

The Albert process was an interesting experiment in halftone reproduction, in which a halftone print on metal was produced from a continuous tone negative by placing the crossline screen with the negative and the sensitised metal together in the printing frame. The frame was rotated in a plane perpendicular to the rays from the illuminant and, although too involved commercially, examples produced by A. G. Symmons were first-rate in their reproduction of highlight detail. The Bassani process of the 1920's used a similar idea, the screen being rotated in a minute radius in the camera, independently of the sensitive plate, during the exposure. The dot formation was effectually controlled by relating the amplitude of the oscillation with the lens aperture. About the same time Alexander Tallent sponsored an ingenious method whereby halftone negatives or positives could be made from continuous tone transparencies without the use of a lens.

Single Line Screens

FOR ADVERTISING purposes, silk screen printing and, for tint plates, screens with a single ruling only are often used. The normal ratio is 1:1. The rendering of detail is inferior to the results obtained with the crossline screen. A slit stop is used in the lens with its longer dimension parallel to the screen ruling and the width of the slit approximates to the V/64 ratio. If the effect is obtained using the slit stop with a crossline screen focused to give a single line, the result is often inferior, with ragged edged lines.

Schulze Screens

THESE ARE often called rhomboid screens, and are now rarely used. The sets of lines cross each other at an angle of 60 degrees instead of 90 degrees, so that the number of dots per unit area is increased, giving, it is claimed, better rendering of detail. A special shaped lens stop is required for coarse screen rulings.

Hedopra Screen

THIS SCREEN is obsolete. The screen assembly consisted of one set of coarse lines crossing at right-angles with a set of finer lines. The finer lines could be eliminated, if required, by lighting arrangement, so that only the coarse lines provided the image formation.

Wavy-line Screens

THIS TYPE of screen is used to imitate the structure of wood engravings. Screens formed of a pattern of concentric circles or a spiral pattern are made for publicity effects. Also wire mesh screens, fabric (silk) and linen screens are employed to produce unusual results.

Grained Screens

THESE INCLUDE the Metzograph Screen invented by James Wheeler, the Erwin Screen and the Hausleiter Screen with irregular shaped elements repeated in a regular manner over the total screen surface and used at one time in photogravure. The Metzograph Screen was made by depositing pyrobetulin as a resinous resist on glass and etching with hydrofluoric acid to produce an irregular series of lenticular cavities. With a grained screen the surface of the glass, whilst remaining almost transparent, is granulated and the tonal gradation is due to refraction of the light at the surface of the glass.

Respi Screen

THIS IS made by Policrom, based on the principle evolved by Jacobi. The screen consists of a double-line screen and is designed for printing on rough or poor quality paper. It has two sets of lines, one thin and the other thick. These are superimposed so that the thin mesh divides the transparent opening of the thick mesh into four equal parts. During exposure the fine line crossing enables the formation of the central core of the dot, formed by the thick lines, to be slowed down, and helps the formation of a bond between the various dots of equal strength and intensity forming the central core. The result, it is claimed, is an improvement in brilliancy and detail. The normal round aperture can be used, but improved tonal rendering is obtained with a leg stop (square stop with elongated corners).

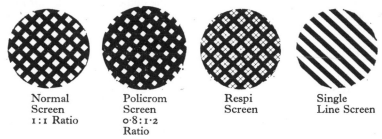

Normal	Policrom	Respi	Single
Screen	Screen	Screen	Line Screen
1:1 Ratio	0·8:1·2		
	Ratio		

Fig. 56A Normal screen ratio enables a copy with a contrast range of 1·4 to be correctly screened. The policrom S.O. screen enables originals with a density range of 1·8 to be correctly reproduced

Fig. 56B Klimsch Allton gradar screen

Optical screen for direct highlight or powderless etch type negatives. Screen lines not opaque consist of different densities of magenta dye. Dyed lines penetrated by intense light emanating from light areas of copy, with light reflected from darker areas retained by the crosslines. Screen elements of greatest density located in the line crossings, protecting the core of the highlight dots. Screen separation is calculated, based on V/32 ratio. Two short exposures required – flash exposure at f/32, followed by main exposure two stops up (f/16, same size copying).

Rotogravure Screens

THE ORIGINAL screen for rotogravure does not, like the screens for photolithography, have the mesh between the two glass plates, but on a single, perfectly smooth flat plate glass, 6–8 mm. thick, employing a screen ruling of 150, 175, 200 lines per inch. The ratio between transparent lines and black squares is usually 1:3 – the side of a black square being three times the width of a transparent line. Screens with a ratio of 1:2·5 are recommended. These make for greater ease of engraving and allow greater depth of etch, giving the cylinder longer life. The screen is not used for the purpose of conveying tone values in dot formation, but solely to retain the inks in the etched cells or hollows and to provide a support for the doctor blade.

New Halftone Screen

NORMAL GLASS screens consist of two sheets of plate glass, each of which is ruled with equally spaced parallel lines filled-in with a black medium and having the spacings between the lines equal to the width of the lines themselves. The glasses are cemented together with their rulings facing each other and arranged in such a manner that they both cross at right angles. Klimsch have made a new glass screen known as the Allton Gradar halftone screen, which is a thinner screen, thus minimising diffraction effect, and requires shorter exposures with improved tonal rendering. This is effected by employing the new principle in screen ruling which uses two distinct densities of magenta. The transparent crosslines let through more light than the lines of an orthodox glass screen, so that exposure times are shorter and separate highlight exposures are not necessary. The dense magenta crossline ruling is keyed with a pale magenta edging to give a vignetted line effect. The only screen of a comparable nature is a flexible line contact screen made by Policrom, in which the dot is replaced by a micrometrical succession of shaded lines in magenta colour which vignette as a soft edge from the red–black lines, producing a halo effect which increases the variability in the tonal rendering of the image or in the formation of lines, the ratio of which changes according to the changes of the grey densities of the original. The screen has a contrast of 1·5 and is used for offset, letterpress, silk screen and textile work. The Policrom Negative Rototipo screen for gravure printing, which again is a flexible screen on a cellulose acetate base, also utilises the principle of a black mesh having perpendicular crossing lines at 45 degrees with a magenta shade behind the black crossing lines which radiates from the line edges to a clear central transparent core in the centre of the mesh. Screened positives are obtained from continuous tone negatives for invert or intaglio dot printing.

Screen Angle

FOR MONOCHROME reproduction the angle of the lines of the screen is set at 45 degrees to the perpendicular. This angle simulates better the illusion of a continuity of tone, that is the dot formation is the least discernible to the eye when positioned at this angle. For colour work, to avoid superimposition of the dots, different angles are used as follows: two-colour – 45 degrees (heavy colour) and 75 degrees for the lighter colour; three-colour – cyan 45 degrees, magenta 75 degrees, yellow 15 degrees; four-colour – black 45 degrees, magenta 75 degrees, cyan 15 degrees, yellow 90 degrees. Similar angles are used for six-colour work with pink normally at 15 degrees (cyan angle) and light blue at 75 degrees (magenta angle). This is varied, according to the nature of the work, and sometimes the more open (flatter) negatives for the pink and the light blue are reproduced at the same screen angles as the heavier colours – that is, magenta and pink (75 degrees), cyan and light blue (15 degrees). The filters used to obtain the required printing records are as follows:

Blue filter	yellow printing record.
Green filter	magenta and pink printing record.
Red filter	cyan and light blue printing record.
Yellow (or gamma filter)	black printing record.

Screen Ruling

HALFTONE SCREENS are classified according to the number of opaque lines ruled to the linear inch. Thus when there are 120 ruled lines to the linear inch, the screen is known as a 120-line screen. They are available in standard rulings from 50 to 400 lines per inch, with the 120 , 133- and 150-line screens generally used for photolitho work. The lines of the screen are normally the same width as the space between them (1:1 ratio). This means that a 120-line screen has 120 lines and 120 open spaces to each inch. The openings between the lines are therefore $\frac{1}{240}$ of an inch wide. This width is an important factor in determining the distance that should be allowed between the screen and the sensitive emulsion. A screen ratio of 1:1 has the fundamental disadvantage that the proportion of transparent to opaque areas on the screen is 1:3, so that only 25% of the screen is transparent, resulting in a loss of detail of the halftone as compared with the copy. Nevertheless a ratio of 1:2 would result in light bending at over-thin lines, giving premature closing of tones. A normal screen ratio of 1:1 enables copy with a contrast range of 1·4 to be satisfactorily screened. Policromi supply a screen with a ratio of 0·8:1·2 which enables copy with a density range of 1·8 to be correctly reproduced.

Light Action

LIGHT IS a form of radiant energy acting upon the eye to produce vision. Newton, in the Corpuscular Theory, assumed light to be propagated as a stream of corpuscles emitted by a luminous body. This theory does not provide a complete explanation. The Quantum Theory states that light consists of packets of light termed quanta or photons, the energy of which depends upon the frequency of the radiation. The wave theory considers light as radiant energy propagated in waves that vary from 400 mu in the violet to about 700 mu in the red area of the spectrum. This latter theory does help to explain many of the complexities of light phenomena.

THEORY OF THE HALFTONE SCREEN

THE HALFTONE screen is always positioned in the camera a short distance in front of the sensitive emulsion in such a way that the light projected from the lens must pass through the opening in the screen before it reaches the film. Ives (pinhole theory, 1888) believed that each opening in the screen acted as a tiny pinhole lens and that every lens projected its image on the film according to the amount of light striking it. He reasoned that only a pinpoint of light was projected through the dark areas, whilst the brighter areas of the copy reflected enough light to produce a large, solid dot. Max Levy (supported by F. E. Ives) advanced another theory, which was investigated thoroughly by Fruwirth, Mertle and Yule. He believed that the size of the dot was influenced by deflected light, for when light passes through a grating, such as the halftone screen, it produces a central bright spot on the negative. This spot is surrounded by a series of concentric light rings of diminishing intensity and if the light from one ring overlaps the bright spot of another it adds to its intensity (diffraction theory).

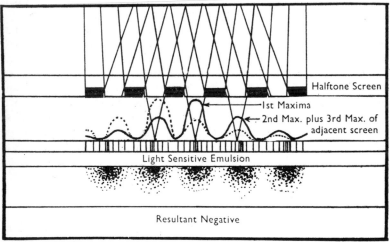

Fig. 57 Dot formation diffraction theory.

$$\text{Screen distance} = \frac{d^2}{3\lambda}$$

where d = side of screen aperture, λ = wavelength of light used. This gives a smaller screen distance than applies with the penumbral theory (V/64 ratio).

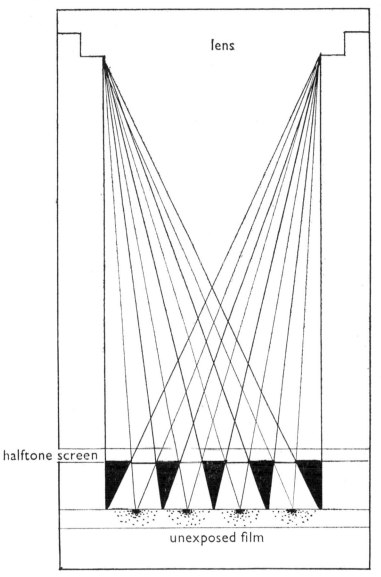

Fig. 58 Dot formation penumbral theory

A different theory, known as the penumbral theory of dot formation, was furthered by Clerc and Calmels (1908) following the work of Tallent, Dolland and Deville. It assumes that the screen casts a shadow on the film which is large or small according to the intensity of the light. If a large amount of light reaches the film, the light spreads and there is little shadow, but broader shadows are produced by parts of the copy which reflect little light. Portions reflecting light are reduced to metallic silver on development, with shadow areas clear or transparent.

The main criticism of the pinhole theory is that no study is given to the relationship of the lens aperture to the screen distance. With the penumbral theory the term umbra refers to the sharp edge shadow behind the opaque screen lines and the penumbra (partial shadow) is formed around the umbra from light falling in areas from which other rays of light have been cut off. It consists of a continuous shadow varying in light and shade with the dot formation caused by the vignetted effect of the halftone screen. Geometrical optics are used to illustrate the depth of shadow produced at any point to give the dot effect. It is based on the straight line propagation of light and its weakness is that it takes no account of the diffraction caused by the halftone screen, although diffraction has little effect when using coarse screens.

Diffraction refers to the bending of light rays from a straight course when cut off by an opaque medium such as the halftone screen. It acts as a double diffraction grating in that the light waves are separated and then recombined. The light emerging from a small aperture fans out so that diffraction plays a major role with fine screen rulings. Fruwirth studied the theory very thoroughly and arrived at the following conclusions which are now generally accepted: (a) each screen has a definite focal length and its distance from the sensitive plate varies according to the screen ruling; (b) every individual screen has a speed ratio, the finer the ruling the faster the ratio; (c) the lack of colour correction of the screen calls for an adjustment in screen separation when various filters are used.

W. B. Hislop has suggested, in *Camera Work for Process Engravers* (part 2), that the screen distance should be found by observation, with a strong light in front of the lens and a very small stop, where the diffraction maxima from the four edges of the screen aperture coincide to form a tiny, very bright dot. This was to be done for each individual screen and avoided the necessity for calculations but nevertheless included all the relevant factors – line-to-space ratio, thickness of cover-glass, refractive index of the glass, etc.

The distance between the sensitive emulsion and the screen may be calculated with sufficiently accurate approximation by means of the following formula (penumbral hypothesis) based on the triangles ABE and CDE as indicated.

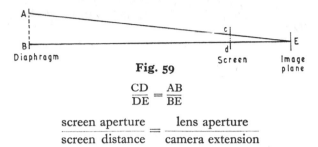

Fig. 59

Diaphragm Screen Image plane

$$\frac{CD}{DE} = \frac{AB}{BE}$$

$$\frac{\text{screen aperture}}{\text{screen distance}} = \frac{\text{lens aperture}}{\text{camera extension}}$$

thus

$$\text{screen distance} = \frac{\text{camera extension} \times \text{screen aperture}}{\text{lens aperture}}$$

Agfa-Screen Key

screen aperture width 0·208 mm

(= approx. 60 line screen, ratio 1:1)

position valid for Camera No............

ascertained correction 2·5 mm

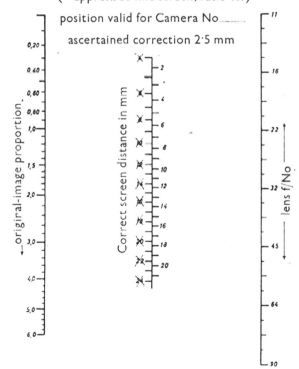

Fig. 60

An accurate method of determining screen distance has been devised by Dr W. Rebner and is known as the 'Agfa Screen Key'. With this method the distances are not calculated from theory, but are taken from a statistical experimental summary adapted to a simple calculator. The Screen Key takes account of both the penumbral effect and the modification caused by diffraction, which has the effect of reducing or shortening the screen distance as calculated on the penumbral theory. It consists of three vertical scales, the left-hand scale being the size scale – 0·20 ($\frac{1}{5}$), 0·40 ($\frac{2}{5}$), 1·0 (same size), 2·0 (twice size). On the right is the lens aperture scale – $f/11$, $f/16$, $f/22$, $f/32$, etc. – whilst the centre scale shows screen distances found by observation. The distance is measured from the actual screen lines to the sensitive plate or film, thus corrections have to be made for the thickness of the cover glass of the screen and for any error in the camera screen indicator. The centre scale is then corrected and the screen distance found by placing a ruler across the three vertical lines (scales). The left side is placed on the size scale and the right end on the stop scale to be used ($f/16$, $f/22$, etc.). Where the ruler cuts the centre scale denotes the correct screen setting. The screen distance alters with the size of stop. In practice, if negative contrast is altered by using a larger stop to increase contrast and a smaller stop to decrease contrast, without altering the screen distance, the shape of the dots becomes unsatisfactory – especially in fine screen rulings, owing to the greater effect of diffraction.

The formula given previously, which ignores diffraction, indicates that the correct dot formation is the result of adjusting the lens aperture and the screen distance so that their ratios are balanced. The camera extension and the screen aperture are known predetermined factors and the screen distance and lens aperture are variable factors to be determined. The ratio 1:64 (or 1:45 or 1:32) is applied in general for this equation.

$$\frac{\text{diameter of lens aperture}}{\text{camera extension}} = \frac{\text{screen aperture}}{\text{screen distance}}$$

To calculate the required data using the V/64 ratio copying same size with an 18-inch focal length lens the procedure is as follows:

Lens Aperture

$$\frac{64}{1 + m} = \frac{64}{1 + 1} = f/32$$

or

$$\frac{\text{diameter of lens aperture}}{\text{camera extension}} = \frac{1}{64}$$

$$\frac{x}{18 \times 2} = \frac{1}{64}$$

$$x = \frac{1}{64} \times 18 \times 2 = \frac{9}{16} \text{ in.}$$

$$= \frac{9}{16} \times 25 = 18 \text{ mm. approx.}$$

Alternatively the f opening $= \dfrac{\text{focal length of lens}}{\text{diameter of lens aperture}}$

$$= \frac{18}{\frac{9}{16}} = \frac{18 \times 16}{9} = f/32$$

or the f opening $\qquad = \dfrac{\text{camera extension}}{\text{focal length of lens}} \times \dfrac{1}{64}$

$$= \frac{18 \times 2}{18} \times \frac{1}{64} \times \frac{1}{32} = f/32$$

For half-size working
the aperture would be $\qquad = \dfrac{64}{1 + \frac{1}{2}} = \dfrac{64 \times 2}{3} = f/43$

Screen Distance (screen ruling to sensitised material)

THE LENS aperture has been calculated as $\frac{1}{64}$ of the camera extension. Thus the screen distance will be 64 × the screen aperture – which is twice the screen ruling. For a 150 screen the screen distance would therefore be:

$$\frac{\text{screen aperture}}{\text{screen distance}} = \frac{1}{64}$$

$$\frac{\frac{1}{150 \times 2}}{x} = \frac{1}{64}$$

$$x = \frac{64}{300} = \frac{7}{32} \text{ in. approx.} = \frac{64}{300} \times 25 = 5\cdot3 \text{ mm.}$$

The calculated distance is measured from the actual ruling of the glass screen, that is from the centre of the screen, and not from the cover glass of the screen. In general the screen separation is measured from the outer edge of the cover glass to the sensitive emulsion, so that the thickness of the cover glass should be subtracted from the calculated screen distance.

Highlight Stops

METAL STOPS, used in addition to the iris diaphragm, fit into a slot in the lens mount. Contrary to general belief they were not invented by Major-General Waterhouse, but by John Waterhouse, and they are used not only to control the amount of light reaching the plate, but also to influence the dot formation. Using the V/64 ratio the diameter of the stop is $\frac{1}{64}$ of the camera extension, and the screen distance must be sixty-four times the screen aperture. This means that the desired effect is attained when the distance from the sensitive plate to the screen aperture is in the same ratio as the camera extension is to the lens aperture. Conditions then assure that a portion of the light rays passing through the lens aperture are limited by the opaque line of the screen to form a cone, the apex of which just falls on the sensitive plate.

The famous trio of halftone pioneers, Levy, Deville and Turati, invented and used metal stops of many shapes and sizes, the majority of which are now obsolete, due to the perfecting of the iris diaphragm systems, the improved standard and quality of lenses, lighting units and photographic materials. The function of these stops is to increase contrast by joining-up to pinpoints the high-light dots and eliminating or dropping out the exaggerated or pure high-lights. The Penray Hilite Lens (Laws) is an ingenious device built into the lens system in the form of two transparent crosses with the centres cut away and crossing each other, the width of the cross and the central opening being controlled by a lever in the same way as an ordinary lens diaphragm. The central opening has three apertures corresponding to $f/32$, $f/45$ and $f/64$ with the width of the crosses controlled by the central opening so that the widest cross or shaft opening is at $f/32$. When used in conjunction with the iris diaphragm the length of the shafts could also be controlled. The illustration shows a selection of contrast stops, some of which are still used for special effects where accentuation of contrast is important.

Fig. 61 Selection of metal stops used to increase contrast

For high-key work, such as pencil sketches where delicate high-light detail has to be retained in offset printing, the Sear's method of making a continuous tone negative (range 1·3) is used. After hand-retouching a screen positive is made with joined shadows and fine high-lights. This is dot-etched and corrected before making a final contact negative for printing down to metal.

Factors to be considered in screen negative making are the copy to lens – lens to image distance (conjugate foci), stop size as a ratio of the camera extension, screen aperture and screen distance, exposure, speed and contrast of the sensitive emulsion. In general a single round stop exposure using the V/ratio system plus a flash exposure, is satisfactory. Alternatively the middletone and shadow detail is obtained using the V/64 ratio and the high-light detail obtained with the same screen setting but with the lens opening increased to V/45 ratio and a supplementary exposure given equal to one quarter or one half of the V/64 ratio exposure.

Flash Exposure

THE PURPOSE of the flash exposure, made to a sheet of white paper or an evenly diffused light from a small opal electric bulb held in front of the lens, is to increase the opacity of each shadow dot at its core without increasing the dot size or shape and affecting gradation. It overcomes the lack of sensitivity (inertia) of the slow process or lith emulsion and

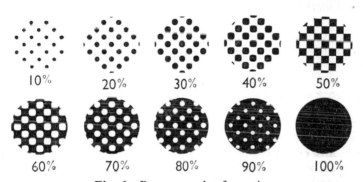

Fig. 62 Percentage dot formation

approximates to $1\frac{1}{2}$–3% of the main detail exposure. For preference it should precede the main exposure.

Faulty dot and tonal rendering when the screen setting is correct is due to under-exposure if the dots lack join-up in the high-lights and have thin shadow dots. Over-exposure would result in completely joined-up or obliterated high-lights with too large shadow dots. Correctly exposed negatives which have filled-in high-lights, full middle tones and diffused woolly shadow dots indicate excessive screen distance. Dots lacking join-up in the high-lights with large cone-shaped or square shadow dots denote that the screen distance is too small. Assuming

correct exposure and screen separation, a negative having excessive contrast in the high-lights has been made using too large a lens aperture,
whereas under these conditions a negative made with too small a stop
would be flat and screeny, having large shadow dots and open, insuf-
ficiently joined-up high-lights.

MOIRÉ PATTERN

THIS IS produced by interference between the image lines or dots and
the screen ruling in halftone reproduction. The effect is minimised
when the lines or dots of the copy form an angle of 30, 45 or 60 degrees
with the screen ruling, with 30 degrees (75 degrees screen angle) being
generally the most satisfactory. Slight out-of-focus and gentle vibration
of the front of the camera during exposure are 'dodges' also used. A sheet
of fine ground glass, treated with glycerine to assist transparency, placed
over the copy minimises moiré, which is best eliminated by air-brush
retouching on the copy. Optical equipment includes the Klimsch Vario-
mat; this fits over the lens using a rotating glass plate which, during
exposure, causes a sequence of deflections of light rays to overlap the
dot formation of the copy to reduce pattern in reproduction. Optical
Tone Filters made by Dainippon Screen Manufacturing Co. Ltd,
Tokyo, consist of a random arrangement of dots on a plain glass disc,
so arranged that the total dot area and the total clear area are equal.
The dot areas are optical coating on glass with a thickness corresponding to one-quarter the wavelength of the light with which they are used.
Monochromatic light is required at about 150 millimicrons. The complete range covers dot sizes from 1 to 11 mm. A computer included
helps to select the correct filter based on size, screen, copy and focal
length of the lens. These Canon optical tone filters are mounted behind
the lens and eliminate moiré by diffusing the screen pattern through
interference effects during rescreening.

A continuous tone photograph taken from the halftone proof, that is
without any screen in the camera, and made slightly out of focus, can
produce a satisfactory result. The bromide print, made from the continuous tone negative will scarcely show the dots and the general flattening of tone values can, if necessary, be rectified by some retouching
using the air-brush or applying body colour here and there in the high-
lights and the shadows. Alternatively the camera operator can brighten
the result in the halftone negative making stage.

The Agfa-Gevaert Diffusing Diaphragm is also a most useful asset in
eliminating undesirable moiré and avoiding the need for excessive retouching. The original to be rescreened is first copied by making a continuous tone negative through the diffusing diaphragm. The central
opening of the stop corresponds to $f/45$ and the sixteen surrounding

small apertures each correspond to $f/90$. The outer edge of the circle containing the sixteen small apertures corresponds to $f/16$. Normal action of the diffusing stop, when all the small apertures are clear, results in a moderate degree of unsharpness. If four of the small holes are covered with matt translucent film arranged in a symmetrical pattern more unsharpness is obtained and if these four holes are completely filled in or obscured less unsharpness results. A bromide print made from the negative shows an almost complete absence of dot formation. The print can be retouched if required.

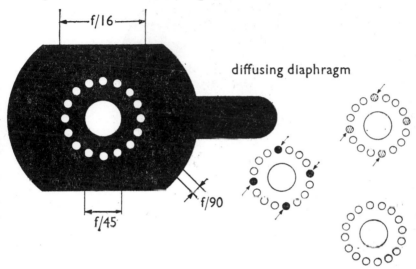

Fig. 63 Agfa-Gevaert stop

VIGNETTED CONTACT SCREENS

Invention and Claims

BERCHTOLD IN the last century (1855), Trist, Murray and Dittman (1905) in the early part of this century, were pioneers in the use of contact screens. Trist made a contact screen in 1927 for use with his Pantone Process but it was the work of Murray, Yule and others in the Eastman Kodak Company of America in finally producing the Kodagraph Contact Screen process in 1941 which provided the first commercially applied process for lithography. The method utilised two screens, an orange screen for positive making in conjunction with a magenta dye coupled continuous tone negative, and a magenta one for negative making. Both the magenta and grey contact screens in use today form halftone dots on sensitised film through the modulation of light by the optical action of the vignetted dot pattern of the screen acting on the film emulsion. The screen elements are graded in density, or vignetted, on a flexible film base. The dot formation is produced as a magenta dye image in magenta screens, and a developed silver pattern in grey screens. In use, the emulsion or image side of the screen is held in intimate contact with the sensitised 'lith' film emulsion during the dot forming exposure. Advantages claimed for contact screens are: better resolution,

Fig 64. Vignetted contact screen

easier and quicker to use, no screen separation or screen gear mechanism required – thus a cheaper camera fitted with vacuum hold can be used, contrast control simple to achieve, giving wide latitude, initial screen cost is low. Disadvantages: dot formation lacks evenness over large flat areas of tone, screen is fragile – easily kink-marks – stains and scratches, dye density of magenta screen fades owing to age, density ranges and exposure factors may vary considerably from screen to screen and from maker to maker.

Manufacture and Structure

THE CONTACT screen consists of 50% white and 50% black, as opposed to the glass crossline screen which comprises 25% transparent and 75% opaque elements. There is also no abrupt transition between black and white, but a gradual build-up in formation of the dots. These factors, with the feature of direct contact, obviously increase the resolving power with better reproduction of the tone values of the original, especially in higher middle tone and light grey areas. Each dot of the screen consists of an intermediate zone which gradually passes from transparency to a determined density, so that the light reflected from the original passes through the screen in a controlled manner, giving rise to dots of determined size.

In general, the contact screen is made from an engraved glass screen. They are made by other means, for example the Patra I.G.T. Negative Screen is added dot for dot by means of an exposure system, and Harrison's view is that contact screens obtained from engraved glass screens inherit the faults of the master screen. This is a matter of opinion as it would appear that the key to screen reproduction, to give correct tonal values, is found solely in the density structure of the contact screen dot.

It is essential in manufacture from an engraved glass screen that the correct screen distance is maintained, so that the cone of light formed behind each of the screen apertures strikes the surface of the sensitive material with its tip. The reader is familiar with the way the light is distributed behind the screen aperture, in which the intensity of the light is greatest at the tip of the light cone. It decreases on all sides because the image of the diaphragm opening is covered to an increasing extent by the screen aperture the further away the point of vision lies from the tip of the light cone. Thus when photographed on a film of medium gradation a vignetted dot results, in which the maximum density is at the core. Each individual dot in the contact screen is characterised by its density structure, variation in density, colour and shape of base – with the density structure *only* exerting an influence on the tonal reproduction. The density structure follows a course rising from the minimum density to the maximum density, which then falls again in the same rhythm. The laws of geometric optics would, under the circumstances, provide a density structure in the form of a cone – but it must be realised that other factors are involved in the dot formation, such as light refraction, contrast range of the sensitive material, light scatter, etc. Nevertheless the shape of the base of the dot and the colour of the dot does not influence tonal reproduction. The colour of the magenta screen helps to change the reproducible density range by means of red and yellow filters, with the grey screen having a reproducible density range which is predetermined. The differences between the maximum and minimum densities of the dot condition the reproducible density range of the contact screen, but it does not influence tonal reproduction which, as stated, is really influenced by the density structure of the dot.

The problem of the density structure of a contact screen to produce correct tonal values when screening has been studied by Dr Rebner at the Agfa laboratories at Leverkusen, who arrived at the conclusion that two different halftone dot profiles are necessary, each with a special density structure. The result has been the production of positive contact screens and separate negative contact screens. This principle is also followed by Kodak and others. Curves plotted from the density structure of a positive contact screen show a different slope (more gradual at the beginning) than applies with a negative contact screen, which begins with a steeper slope and declines uniformly to end much more gradually. Under the influence of the different dot profiles, different results are obtained when screening, the growth of the dots on the 'lith' film proceeding more rapidly in the case of the positive contact screen and more slowly with the negative contact screen than with the standard contact screen.

There is no basic difference between the formation of halftone dots behind a glass-ruled crossline screen and a flexible vignetted contact screen. With the glass screen the unit dots grow by exposure to a graded pattern formed by diffraction effects and, as indicated by Yule, their contour shapes follow the isolux lines of equal intensity. With the contact screen the dots grow in relation to the graded pattern of the unit dot elements built into the screen during manufacture, following the

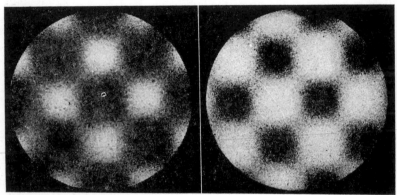

Fig. 65 Dot formation – positive and negative contact screens

isolux contours based on ideal reproduction curves. Maximum resolution is obtained because with the transparent dye images no scattering occurs during the passage of light to the sensitive emulsion.

Tritton and Wilson, as recorded in the *Photographic Journal* of June 1939 and March 1940, used various types of apertures when following the generally accepted method of preparing contact screens from crossline screens. A. R. Trist (1933) employed a rotating aperture in the lens and Deville used a star-shaped aperture with a chessboard type screen. Most workers in this field have used multiple apertures in an effort to eliminate the inherent defects in the crossline screen; Yule and Johnston, for example, employed twelve apertures placed at the corners of a Geneva Cross. Paul W. Dorst has described, in GATF Research Bulletin No. 16, equipment for the superimposition of tint exposures, one method used consisting of exposing a high-contrast emulsion at a predetermined distance behind a crossline screen and using selected lens apertures. A number of tint negatives are then made which are printed in register on to a sensitised film, the length of the individual exposures being carefully controlled to give the correct gradation in the final vignetted contact screen. A fine-grain, low-contrast developer is used in conjunction with a lith-type emulsion.

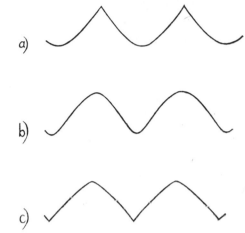

Fig. 66 (*a*) Density profile of positive screen dots; (*b*) density profile of normal contact screen dots; (*c*) density profile of negative screen dots

Practical Considerations

Dr V. G. W. Harrison is of the opinion that a universal screen is a misnomer, in that a contact screen which will give good screen negatives will not be suitable for making screen positives and any screen which claims to do both will do neither properly. It is generally agreed that it is more difficult to make a contact screen positive than it is to make a contact screen negative and many camera operators are of the opinion that, given a suitable range of continuous tone negative, a crossline screen positive compares in contrast and gradation with a contact screen positive. The loss in both instances is found in the shadow detail. Using the glass crossline screen, a fairly low contrast continuous tone negative combined with a high-light mask produces a good screen positive. In general, when the density range of the original is in the region of 1·4 little difficulty is experienced in reproduction. The difficulties usually arise in compressing a density range of 1·8 or above into a range of 1·4 or thereabouts. An original with a range of 1·4 which requires screening to a gamma of 1·0 (range 1·4) is preferred.

The contact screen can be used in the process camera, in an enlarger or with a contact printer, provided that the equipment is fitted with a vacuum back to ensure close even contact between surfaces. Excessive under-pressure is not necessary because it can give rise to the formation of air bubbles between the screen and the emulsion, causing spots to appear on the image especially if the atmosphere is fairly damp. A vacuum of not more than 40 to 50% is satisfactory and spots and uneven markings can be eliminated by diminishing the suction power of the pump ascertained by a vacuum meter or by inserting small strips of adhesive tape under the top corners of the screen, so that a small amount of air can leak in to reduce the degree of vacuum. When a contact printer is used the point light source must not be too sharp or strong because every minute dust particle will be copied and the screen dots will have a serrated edge. A tungsten lamp or diffuse light source is, on the other hand, not recommended, as it tends to give rise to spots. The solution is to use a point light source with a diffuser or a soft-working condenser. The light source should be positioned so as to illuminate evenly the whole of the frame, which means placing the lamp at a distance at least equal to twice the diagonal of the largest size of image to be copied. The exposure should be long enough to be controllable and if necessary the light intensity can be reduced, without altering the colour temperature, by using a neutral density filter to reduce the intensity of light in a definite ratio.

Temperature control is important in developing because all the characteristics which contribute to good quality control are adversely affected by temperature variations. The norm should be 68° F (20° C). Higher temperatures increase contrast, lower temperatures result in flattening and loss of shadow detail. Developer exhaustion through use and through oxidation results in loss of quality and weakness of dot formation and contrast. 'Lith' developers, in dish work, are highly unstable once the two solutions are combined and fresh developer should be used at frequent intervals to maintain quality and uniformity of result. Agitation increases contrast and 'still-bath' development flattens and in line work prevents fine detail 'filling-in'. Sometimes in halftone work '*bromide drag*' is apparent. This is caused by insufficient agitation during development, resulting in streaks. It is realised that the function of the developer is to convert the exposed silver salts to metallic silver which releases soluble halides into the developer. These halides are an effective restrainer to the development process and must be removed by agitation, otherwise streaks may occur. Another restraining effect of released halides during development is called '*adjacency effect*' in which the shadow dots disappear next to an area of very fine high-light dots. This occurs most often during 'still-bath' development when the film is given little or no agitation in the developer. The cure is to agitate the solution and in some situations to use a cotton swab to sweep away the spent developer and halides very rapidly and thoroughly. The dilution of the developer – one part A, one part B and one part water – also helps to eliminate this effect.

Camera screening (optical screening) yields a greater density range than occurs when contact screening. The difference is caused by the effect of scattered light. An anti-static cloth should be used to make the screen and sensitive emulsion dust-free before use. Carbon tetrachloride will remove finger-marks, etc., and will not damage the surface of the screen. Exposing through the back of the screen increases contrast.

Magenta and yellow filter coefficients obviously depend on the quality of the light source used. They approximate as follows: no filter (1), yellow filter (3), magenta filter (8).

Agfa-Gevaert Contact Screens

BECAUSE THE required profile structure cannot be built up entirely by optical means, Agfa-Gevaert have evolved films having a special grada-tion for the production of positive and negative contact screens. Each type of screen gives the correct tonal values with a single exposure – the positive contact screen producing correct halftone positives and the Agfa-Gevaert negative contact screen producing correct halftone nega-tives. The Agfa-Gevaert positive contact screen provides sufficient lati-tude to absorb fluctuations in the density structure of the continuous tone negative amounting to more than 0·3. Thus there is no necessity for a magenta positive contact screen. This applies also with the Agfa-Gevaert negative contact screen which is also grey in character. Copy for reproduction fluctuates in density range within wide limits. The main factor in reproduction is the printing conditions which, at best, can reproduce a possible range of 1·6 and the range of the contact screen has to take account of this limit. Agfa-Gevaert contact screens have a single density range – approximately 1·3 for the positive contact screen and approximately 1·45 for the negative contact screen. They are not produced in angled sets but are all ruled at 45 degrees. Contrast control is effected by variation in developer agitation. With the positive screen full agitation yields a range of 1·5, slight agitation a range of 1·1. Cor-respondingly with the Agfa-Gevaert negative contact screen the range is 1·6 and 1·3 with an average range of 1·45. The screens have a base of 0·2 mm. thickness and are provided with an anti-Newton coating on both sides. Screen rulings are 70, 100, 120, 133, 150 in the negative and positive range plus a 175 ruling positive screen.

Pawo-Nottaris and Wagner (Swiss) Contact Screens

THESE ARE grey contact screens with a range of screens each constructed for a special purpose. These are as follows: a screen for making negatives with a basic contrast of 1·35 and three screens for making positives, each having a basic contrast of 1·2, 1·5 or 1·8 respectively. This means that normal tone rendering can be obtained from originals having density ranges of 1·2, 1·5, or 1·8 when screened under standardised exposure and development conditions.

Efha (German) Neutral Grey and Magenta Contact Screens

THE RANGE of grey screen is 1·3 to 1·8 density; sizes 8 in. × 10 in. to 27 in. × 35 in. supplied as single screens or in pre-angled sets. Magenta screens are made in similar sizes to grey screens, in pre-angled sets or single screens at 45 degrees with contrast variation effected by filter control.

Policrom (Italian) Magenta and Neutral Grey Contact Screens

THESE SCREENS are supplied in conventional pattern and elliptical (chain) dot form, either rectangular or circular with matched pre-angled sets for three- and four-colour work. Single screens are available in sizes up to and including 40 in. × 40 in. and matched pre-angled sets in sizes up to and including 32 in. × 40 in. Rulings: 50, 65, 75, 85, 100, 120, 133, 150, 200 and also 250 and 300 lines per inch. All screens receive a special Anti-Newton Ring Coating which completely eliminates Newton Rings and humidity spots. Policrom contact screens are also available in a wide variety of forms – concentric circle, wavy line, irregular grain, and tint screens, plus 'Rototipo' negative and positive screens for invert dot photogravure.

Kodak Magenta Contact Screens – Negative and Positive

THE SCREENS are made by a special photographic process and developed in a magenta dye-coupling developer which gives a magenta coloured vignetted dot pattern after the developed silver is bleached out. The dye density varies gradually from a very light shade at the perimeter of of each vignetted area, becomes darker and darker as the centre of the dot-like structure is approached, and light again as the opposite side is reached. The formation of the halftone dot on the 'lith' film begins in the light area included between four adjacent vignetted magenta areas. When light is reflected from the shadow area of the copy, a relatively small amount of light is reflected, the light penetrating the screen only where the dye density is the lightest, thus forming the small black opaque pin dots or shadow dots on a transparent ground. Where the intensity of light increases (middle tones of copy) the magenta dye density gradient is penetrated to form the fifty per cent checkerboard pattern, and the heavy high-light dots (small clear openings on dense metallic silver) result from the amount of light reflected from the high-light area of the original which penetrates more of the dye density gradient of the screen.

Contrast control is governed by four standard methods – the use of colour compensating filters, controlled flash exposure, still development and supplementary high-light exposure. Irrespective of the copy contrast range accurate reproduction of it can be achieved. The Kodak Magenta Contact Screen Negative is available in rulings of 120 and 133 lines per inch, the Kodak Magenta Contact Screen Positive in rulings of 120, 133, 150 and 200 lines per inch.

Screen Negatives in the Camera

THE CONTACT screen is held in close contact with the 'lith' emulsion using a vacuum of at least 20 in. of mercury maintained during exposure. The base side of the sensitive film is placed on the vacuum back and the magenta contact screen (negative type) placed over the emulsion with the matt (coated) side of the screen in contact with the sensitive surface. The screen should overlap at least two inches all round to ensure good vacuum contact. A lens aperture of $f/22$ for exposure is satisfactory. A general exposure, without a filter, is followed by a flash exposure using Wratten filter No. 8 (yellow) or Wratten series safelight filter OO (yellow) or OB (lime yellow) followed, if necessary, by a high-light exposure made without the screen.

Exposure

THE GENERAL exposure reproduces the high-light and middle tones, being made to white light, and it should be long enough to give the correct dot formation in the high-lights. The flash exposure should produce the correct size of dot in the shadows, where there is a difference between the density range of the original and the range covered by the screen. The method is to cover the original with white paper and expose through the No. 8 filter, alternatively using a flashing lamp in place of the white paper. When the darkroom camera is used, the flash exposure can be given by exposing the opened vacuum back to light from a Kodak Beehive Safelamp, fitted with the series OO or OB safelight filter. When required, the contrast of the negative in the high-lights may be increased by removing the magenta screen, without altering the position of the film, and re-exposing the film to the copy. This exposure should not exceed 10% of the general exposure and can be controlled by the use of neutral density filters with the lens. With average range copy, reproducing same size, using four single 30-amp. open arcs at three feet distance (45 degree angle) at $f/16$ aperture, the exposure would be in the region of 40 sec., with 5–10 sec. flash to series OO Wratten safelight filter at five feet distance using a 25-watt bulb in the beehive safelamp. Continuous agitation at 68° F (20° C) for $2\frac{1}{2}$–$2\frac{3}{4}$ min. in 'lith' developer.

Screen Positives in the Camera

FILTERS ARE used in conjunction with the Kodak Magenta Contact Screen Positive to control contrast and variations found in the continuous tone negative compared with the copy. Yellow filters lower contrast and red filters increase contrast. Flash exposure technique used to control the contrast in screen negative making, if used, would tend to lose delicate tonal separation in the high-lights. Kodak Colour Compensating Filters (CC filters) are supplied in gelatin with a wide range of densities (0·05 to 0·50). For instance the designation CC20Y signifies colour compensating with a density of 0·20 (yellow). The density applies only for the light of the colour which the filter is designed to absorb – in this instance, blue light. Yellow CC filters reduce the contrast given by the screen thus permitting the use of continuous tone negatives of higher contrast. Magenta CC filters increase the contrast, and permit the use of negatives of lower contrast.

CC Filter Rules

THE TERM 'one half of the filter density' is the key to the method of control using white-flame arc lamps. The amount by which the CC filter compensates for lack or excess density range in a negative is equal to one half of the filter density. Thus if the range required is 1·3 a CC20Y filter permits the use of a negative with a density range of 1·4 and a CC20M corrects for the use of a negative with a density range of 1·2. If a continuous tone negative has a range of 1·30 and a screen positive of similar range is required (1·30) then no filter would be required during screening. On the other hand if the negative range is 1·30 and the screen positive range required is 1·15 the excess density range to be corrected is 1·30 — 1·15 = 0·15 which requires the use of a CC30Y filter when screening. Again if the continuous tone negative range is 1·10 and the screen positive range required is 1·15 the lack of density range (0·05) can be rectified by the use of a CC10M filter.

Assessing the Exposure

THE USE of a CC filter with white-flame arcs requires an exposure increase equal to that which would be needed if one half of the filter density were added to the high-light density of the negative. Here the Kodak Graphic Arts Exposure Computer provides a quick and easy calculator. For example, if the exposure for a negative with a high-light density of 1·70 is 120 sec. for white light, the exposure for a negative with a high-light density of 1·80 requiring a CC20Y filter (effective density 0·10) for correction is 190 sec. The total density read on the computer would be 1·9 which is the known high-light density (1·80) plus the effective filter density (0·10).

Screen Positives by Contact

THE POSITIVE contact screen is used in contact with a continuous tone negative in a vacuum printing frame. A point source light is preferred, which must be small in size, uniform over the printing area, with a lamp housing able to accommodate the Kodak CC Filters. Definition is very high and, if no form of diffuser is used, cleanliness, using an anti-static polish, must be observed, otherwise dust and marks will be recorded.

Screen Images using an Enlarger

A SUITABLE vacuum baseboard or vacuum printing frame is required in the image plane of the enlarger. Screen enlargements from continuous tone negatives or positives can then be made. The contrast of the screen image can be controlled using the CC filter technique for positives or controlled flash for negatives. The tungsten light source of an enlarger should be filtered using two Kodak Wratten filters No. 80B (light blue). The degree of agitation during development has a marked effect on the tonal contrast of the screen image. If agitation is decreased, a low contrast screen negative or positive results; if it is increased, the contrast will also increase. A transparent dish, with a safelight underneath the dish which is switched on after 1½ min. development to judge the dot growth, is most useful. The film should not be removed from the dish for inspection because this may cause streaks.

Grey Contact Screens with Elliptical (Chain) Dots

KODAK GREY Contact Screens are available in rulings of 65, 85, 100, 110, 120, 133, 150, and 200 lines per inch. They function in making halftone negatives from monochrome copy and direct halftone separations from coloured originals. Exposures are about 20% less than those required using magenta contact screens. The controlled flash procedure is recommended with the main exposure made to white light and the flash exposure made through the screen using white paper or the flash lamp. High-lighting, or no-screen exposure, prior to the main exposure through the screen to give additional high-light contrast should average

5 to 10% of the main exposure time. Improved middle tone gradation is obtained in screen rulings of 110, 120, 133 and 150 lines per inch by the use of an elliptical or chain dot formation which is apparent in the middle tones. This obviates the sudden jump in density encountered in vignetted areas of the reproduction caused by the fact that the four corners of the dots join up at the same place in the tonal scale. With the elliptical dots only the two diagonal corners join-up at any one place in the tonal scale so that a smoother reproduction is obtained. There is no valid reason why a square checkerboard pattern should appear in the middle tones (50% areas). The eye does not resolve individual dots in reproduction and the integrated reflection density read from a reproduction does not depend on dot shape, but on area and density of the dots in question. So that as long as the correct density distribution is built into a contact screen, overall tone reproduction should match that of conventional screens, regardless of dot shape. The experience of Kodak is that the chain dot effect reproduces better middle-tone detail with smooth vignettes and flesh tones without any harsh tone break in middle-tone areas. It also minimises faults in the original, such as graininess, blemishes or retouching marks.

Universal Contact Screen (Herbst u. Illig)

THIS FRANKFURT firm made the Hass-Kohinoor engraved glass screens at the beginning of the century and have manufactured vignetted contact screens since 1953. These screens were based on the then accepted chessboard pattern which produced different contrasts according to the different gradational densities of the screens. Thus the dots were made up of light and dark spots in an alternate pattern, with the proportion of light to dark area ranging from 50:50 to 40:60. This variation affects the contrast obtainable with the screen – a 50:50 ratio giving more contrast than a 40:60 ratio. The density of the dark dot also controlled the contrast factor so that not only the area, but the density of the dark dot was important for contrast control. This was realised to be a basic weakness in contact screens based on the chessboard dot arrangement, since the density characteristics of the screen itself influenced the screened result. For offset, a lighter screen of soft gradation would be required and for block work a hard gradation is needed. The hard gradation reproduced shadow detail well, flattening the middle tones and high-lights and making work for the etcher. A lighter screen for litho reproduced the middle tones and high-lights far better, whilst losing detail in the darker tones. Results were good or bad, depending on the specific density of the screen. The crosswise character of the screen, where the borders of the transparent areas themselves represent a certain amount of dark characteristics, resulted of necessity in the reproduction at this limit being inadequate. Also, because the transparent dot is bedded in a light spot of fairly large area, the density range of which is low, the flash exposure or shadow dot tends to flatten the result, and is difficult to control.

The New Universal contact screen is a single type screen, ruled from 50 to 250 lines per inch and angled at 15, 45, 75, 90, 30 or 60 degrees, in magenta or neutral grey which is interchangeable for both offset and letterpress printing. The density of the screen has no influence on the contrast obtained in the screened result – the contrast being controlled solely by the dot structure of the screen. A special method of ruling the original master screen was evolved, from which suitable vignetted dot structure screens were made by a photographic procedure. Contrast is varied solely by the control of exposure and of developing. The density of the screen is made to accommodate a density range of up to 1·8 in the negative when making screen positives. High vacuum pressure should be avoided, and a light sponge rubber sheet is helpful to avoid Newton Rings. Thirty per cent vacuum pressure is suitable, the use of 80% vacuum pressure, often advocated, can lead to contact difficulties. Relatively short main exposure and extended developing will yield crisp high-light and snappy shadow dots with correct middle-tone gradation. If the original has a density range of 1·7 or 1·8 a longer exposure with shorter development would be required to produce open high-lights for letterpress work. A short pre-exposure (flash) to yellow light may also be necessary. Still development would tend to flatten the result and agitated development increases the contrast. An intermediate clear foil (0·003 in. thick) between the film and the screen increases contrast, also non-direct contact, by exposing through the back of the contact screen (emulsion side away from the emulsion side of the film), will obtain a similar result. The 'Universal' contact screen will produce cushion dots or square dots. On the camera a slight cushion dot can be obtained by exposure; and using a pneumatic holder, or enlarger, and a point source light the effect can be further increased. Longer exposure on the camera, or the use of diffused light, opal plate between the point source light and the screen in the pneumatic copy frame, or enlarger, will produce square dots. The screens are made in a density range of 1·2, 1·6 or 1·8 and a feature is that the 50% dot in the screened result at the same tone value, is in true relationship to the copy. With many conventional contact screens of varying densities, the 50% dot is often at a different tone value altogether.

Jemseby Contact Screening Method

THIS SWEDISH system invented by Anton Jemseby is a combination of contact and orthodox screening plus the use of a multi-light source and increased sharpness and definition are claimed. Contact screening is restricted to same size and the negative is placed in emulsion contact on the sensitive film with the special screen over-positioned and, if required, a mask on top of this three-layer sandwich for correction in colour work.

The main feature of the system is a special light source consisting of thirteen lamps with a soft centre light surrounded by a series of three groups of four lamps each positioned to give normal, hard and extra-hard light (furthest away). Positioned near the centre light is a point light source. The centre lamp effects the high-light exposure and the banks of lamps control the middle tones and shadows with the outer lamp banks, being at a more acute angle, undercutting the screen to give larger dots. Thus by a combination of different lamp-angle exposures contrast is extended or compressed within any one of the four tone areas, without affecting other tone areas. A further screen is placed over the complete film-negative-contact screen sandwich at an angle of 30 degrees away from the angle of the actual contact screen. An additional exposure through this screen, using the point light source, strengthens some of the grey dots in the high-lights, producing more dots at greater distance instead of closely packed larger dots, resulting in a vignette effect and eliminating the sharp drop-out which could occur in the extreme high-lights.

PRESCREENED FILMS

IN THE photomechanical printing processes, with the exception of collotype and photogravure, intermediate tones between white and black are obtained by breaking the image up into dots of varying sizes according to the tone values required. This is done using the conventional glass crossline screen, which is positioned at a predetermined distance from the sensitive emulsion, or by the use of a contact (vignetted) screen which in general gives better results and is simpler to use, but requires a vacuum back or a vacuum printing frame. With a contact screen a weak exposure from the shadows of the copy penetrates the lightest areas of the screen with sufficient intensity to form a latent image on the emulsion producing a small shadow dot. A stronger exposure, that is light reflected from the middle tones, is sufficient to expose the film even after passing through some density in the screen, so that larger dots are formed. With the maximum exposure from the high-lights, the light penetrates high densities in the contact screen exposing the film almost completely.

With a prescreened film the contact screen is absent, and instead of absorption of light by the contact screen dots producing the dot pattern, the sensitivity of the film itself is varied in the form of a dot pattern. A weak exposure from the shadows produces a latent image only in the most sensitive areas of the emulsion. A stronger exposure from the middle tones exposes less sensitive areas also, thus producing larger dots. A maximum exposure reflected from the high-lights is strong enough to form a developable latent image in all but small areas, producing high-light dots. In every case, the edge of the halftone dot is found at the point where the sensitivity of the emulsion is just sufficient to produce a latent image. If the range of sensitivity of the film is equal to the range of brightness of the subject, then a full-scale negative – pin-point high-light to pin-point shadow dot – will be produced. With a film having a maximum sensitivity ten times that of the minimum sensitivity between the dots a full-scale halftone negative can be produced from a copy having a brightness range of 10 to 1. To accommodate originals of greater range, the scale is extended by a flash exposure.

The Kodak Autoscreen Ortho Film embodies a dot pattern which is primarily a variation of sensitivity, producing dots with sharpness comparable to that of Kodalith film. In continuous tone negative making the principle is to expose for the shadows and develop for the high-lights. With Autoscreen film the policy is to expose for the high-lights and flash for the shadows. The film produces a halftone negative direct with a screen ruling of 133 lines per inch. The exposure required is about 50% increase on ordinary Kodalith film for line work. Thus it is quite fast and the result is sharper than applies with any other medium. This is on account of the absence of any screen in the path of the image and to the technique of still development employed. If the film is developed without exposure to light minute shadow dots are produced, so that the film contains a pin-point latent image, which improves shadow-dot quality and extends the scale of the emulsion. With prolonged storage the shadow dots become inferior in quality and the pin-point latent image tends to fade after a year's storage. The high-light contrast is higher and the shadow contrast lower than with other screening methods and the dot quality somewhat inferior in that the high-lights are slightly veiled over and the shadows not perfectly sharp. Nevertheless, they print down exceptionally well and the prevailing brownish tinge causes no problems or difficulties. Dot etching is possible up to about 50% dot reduction. The material was designed for photolithography, the contrast of the negatives being too high for normal photoengraving work. Film sizes are 8 in. × 10 in. and 11 in. × 14 in., in one ruling 133 lines per inch. Positives made by a two times enlargement from Autoscreen negatives are widely used for silk-screen stencils.

The emulsion, which is sensitive to ultra-violet, blue and green, is coated on an acetate base of approximately 0·005 in. thickness. Kodak recommend a detail exposure at $f/22$ or $f/32$ – for example using arc lamp, same-size copying, 20 sec. at $f/32$ followed by a flash exposure (uniform fogging) to control contrast and the size of the shadow dot. This is done using a Kodak Beehive Safelamp with a 25-watt bulb and a Wratten OB amber-yellow safelight. Exposure approximately 10 sec. at 4 ft. from the film. Development takes place at 68° F (20° C) in fresh Kodalith Developer using 1 part of A, 1 part of B and 1 part of water. Agitate for up to 2 min., then still-bath for another minute before removing to the stop bath, followed by fixing and washing.

Method of Manufacture

THE PHOTOSENSITIVE silver halide emulsion layer carrying the halftone pattern is desensitised by localised pressure. Emulsions susceptible to kink desensitisation will remain desensitised in the areas where pressure has been applied. It is assumed that this is caused by shear stress as opposed to tension and compression stress. Tension refers to instances where the distance between molecules is increased at least in one direction. With compression the distance between molecules is decreased and shear refers to a transverse or sliding movement of one molecule relative to another and is almost always present when the other two occur. The halftone pattern is applied using a cylindrical printing plate which has a hard surface with a halftone pattern of raised dots. The pressure applied by the top of the dots desensitises the corresponding areas of the film forming the corner of the prescreened dot in the film. The 'centres' are the points of maximum sensitivity which have received the least amount of localised pressure and the 'corners' are the points of minimum sensitivity which have received the maximum desensitisation by pressure. Shear stress is greater when the surrounding emulsion is wet, thus the emulsion is subjected to localised pressure in the presence of moisture (water) and a chemical desensitising agent such as methylene blue which assists desensitisation. The top surfaces of the undulations have not been desensitised by pressure and have the maximum sensitivity so that they constitute the centres of the prescreened dots, whilst the dips of the undulations constitute the corners of the dots. These pressure-desensitised dots are in the valleys and the centres of the dots are the crests of the undulations, which are the areas most sensitive to light action thus recording middle tones and high-lights. The method employed is to feed the film between two rollers, one being a back pressure held against the base of the film, whilst a hard surfaced printing roller, embodying a 133 halftone pattern of raised dots, comes in contact with the emulsion side of the film. A dampening roller, revolving in a trough, moistens the surface of the printing roller.

XII

The Platemaking Department

DIRECT PRINTING

THE DIFFERENCE between 'direct' and 'offset' printing in lithography is fundamental. Direct printing implies that the impression is received from the printing surface by direct contact, in which the paper is pressed against the surface of the stone or plate. Thus the image on the printing medium must be wrong reading and therefore for printing-down on to metal the negative should be laterally reversed, i.e. prism-made, so that it is right reading on the negative.

OFFSET PRINTING

BY IMPLICATION, the impression is taken from the plate on to a rubber blanket and then 'offset' or transferred to the paper surface, so that the blanket is pressed against the plate and the paper, pressed in contact with the blanket, receives the image. It follows that on the plate the image must be right-reading and if the work is printed-down from a negative, the negative should be made without the use of a prism or reversing system. Contrariwise if printed-down from a positive for deep etch platemaking the original negative must be laterally reversed, i.e. right-reading or prism-made. The flexible rubber blanket – consisting of vulcanised rubber on a fabric base, treated to prevent stretch – gives a first-rate impression from the grained surface of the metal, with the minimum pressure. The rubber probes into the undulations of the grain and picks up the finest image detail, whilst the paper, pressed against the blanket, receives the impression which is forced into the grain of the paper by the flexible rubber. Thus a facsimile reproduction is obtained with minimum pressure and it is found that too much pressure spoils, rather than improves, the print quality. The use of the rubber blanket makes it possible to print on a wide range of surfaces – paper of varying textures, heavily grained cover boards, glass, etc. The use of highly concentrated, synthetic oils, varnishes and modern dye-stuffs enables impressions of density and brilliance to be obtained with minimum ink films and without squash. Set-off problems are minimised and the length of printing run is greatly increased. The normal zinc and aluminium plate will give 100,000–150,000 impressions and, compared with direct printing, because of the minimum pressure and the fact that the paper does not come into actual contact with the plate, there is less tendency to encounter distortion and paper stretch troubles.

Senefelder completed his book on the invention and art of lithography in 1817 and to him goes the credit for the introduction of the process. Carl Aller of Copenhagen in 1869 introduced photolithography. This did not develop to any appreciable extent until the 1920's, when it was combined with the offset process. Original and hand-transfer plates are seldom used today, having been almost entirely replaced by plates made photomechanically from negatives and positives. Earlier photolitho plates, prior to the last fifteen years, were unreliable, having little difference between the ink-and-water-receptivity of the image and non-image areas. Scum (sticking of ink to the non-image areas of the plate), tinting (the mixing of ink with the damping solution on the plate), blinding (non-acceptance of ink by the printing image), misregister, slow ink drying and short printing life were some of the difficulties encountered. Today, science has replaced a great deal of the old craft practice in platemaking and most troubles are due to carelessness and lack of systematic control and procedure.

Original and Hand-Transfer Plates

THESE PLATES are now confined to poster work and autolithography. The artist draws the image using a greasy crayon or tusche (a liquid greasy ink), also sometimes employing mechanical tints (Benday). The non-image areas are desensitised (made water-receptive and ink-rejecting) with a solution of gum, acid and salt (desensitising etch) to leave a non-visible film of gum on the non-image area which will attract water and repel ink. The same procedure is followed for hand-transfer plates in which, from the design, the required number of ink impressions are pulled on hand-transfer paper – one side of which is coated with a gelatin-like layer. The transfers are laid face down in position on a new plate and under heavy pressure the ink images are transferred to the plate. The paper is soaked with water, peeled off, leaving the images *in situ,* the non-image areas desensitised, and the plate is ready for proofing. Obviously the photolitho plate has superseded these methods because both quality of result and speed of operation are better.

PRINTING SURFACES

THE TYPE of printing surface has undergone a revolution during the century and a half of development since Senefelder. The original polished limestone of some 97% calcium carbonate and 3% magnesium carbonate, the best of which, formed in homogeneous slabs, was found at Solnhofen, Bavaria, has been replaced by thin metal plates solely on account of its weight, bulk and lack of flexibility. The smooth polished stone accepts fine line work without any tendency to broken edges that would be induced by a rougher surface. It absorbs moisture without flooding and does not oxidise, and whilst not requiring a grain to improve the water retention quality of the stone, it could be easily grained to obtain special effects and tone values for crayon and chalk work.

Plate Metals

ZINC AND aluminium in thin metal sheets, varying in thickness from 0·025 in. for 52 in. × 76 in. presses, 0·012 in. for 17 in. × 22 in. presses to 0·0045 in. for small offset machines, have superseded stone. In this country something over 75% of all photolithography is produced from aluminium plates and this state of affairs now appertains in the United States of America. Uniform thickness is very important and gauge tolerance for 0·025 in. plates should not exceed ±0·001 in. and for smaller plates ±0·0005 in. Of the two metals aluminium is capable of taking a finer grain than zinc and it also has the ability to protect itself against corrosion by the atmosphere. A thin layer of aluminium oxide quickly forms on the surface in air. This hard thin layer is 'keyed' on to the metal, protecting the reactive aluminium underneath from further attack.

The zinc and aluminium plates, which have replaced stone, do not have the water absorbing quality of the original stone surface. This requires the metal surface to be grained to induce the retention of moisture to dampen the non-printing areas and the grain, if not controlled, tends to reduce the straight clean edges of lines and dots into minute but ragged boundaries. The grain serves two purposes, it increases the surface area, thus presenting more surface to be moistened with the grain having a reservoir characteristic for the water on the plate surface, and the increased surface area provides better adhesion for the image, especially when the dichromated colloid type of image is being put down on to the surface. In recent years improved materials and a better understanding of the process of platemaking has much reduced the need for coarsely grained metal, indeed some plates now have no grain, their smooth surface being like the original litho printing stone. In addition to zinc and aluminium, stainless steel and chromium plated steel are used for long printing runs. For short-run work paper or plastic plates are made, being very suitable for the office type small offset machine. These small offset systems with their pre-packed chemical solutions and presensitised plates seem part of a different process from the original lithography, though the same basic water retention–grease rejection principle is still employed.

Zinc Plates

ALL METALS used in platemaking are produced by rolling either in strip or sheet rolling mills, but the metals themselves have very different characteristics. A zinc sheet is at least 99% pure, the remaining less than 1% of the metal producing an alloy with cadmium and nickel together with traces of iron and copper. Zinc is a reactive metal, the oxides formed do not usually adhere to the metal surface, thus the surface is left available for further reaction. Zinc stretches and creeps under printing pressure but it does not possess sufficient elasticity to recover completely from the stretched condition. It is somewhat more grease-receptive than aluminium which makes it easier to add work on a zinc plate with tusche (an emulsified ink that can be applied to the plate with a pen or brush). The stretchability of zinc plates makes it possible to correct misregister during printing by stretching the plate on the press cylinder. This stretch is permanent, and because all zinc plates are subject to some stretch round the cylinder when fitted on the press, if one plate of a colour set has to be re-made it is very difficult to register it with the older plates.

Aluminium Plates

ALUMINIUM IN an almost pure state is used for lithographic purposes, at a minimum 99·5% aluminium the remainder being silicon and iron with a trace of copper. Though aluminium is not as hard as zinc by the usual test methods, it does form a deeper and sharper grain than zinc. The natural oxide formation of aluminium produces a tough adherent non-reactive film over the metal surface. This layer is unusually difficult to remove compared with zinc, resulting in the two metals requiring somewhat different treatment in processing. Aluminium has sufficient elasticity to recover from a stretched condition which together with the anodising process makes the metal attractive to the lithographer. The anodising process improves the normal inert oxide layer by the fact that this layer is thickened and the surface made slightly porous, the surface being made more like that of the lithographic stone. Resistance to corrosion is improved by this process which is carried out by supply firms with the anodised plates being sold under various brand names. In some cases the plates have no mechanical grain, the chemical reaction only being relied on to have sufficient moisture retention.

Aluminium is ductile, malleable and one of the lightest of metals – about one-third the weight of a zinc plate of corresponding size and thickness. It has a brighter and whiter surface than zinc, which enables the image areas to be inspected more easily for flaws during processing. Aluminium, being more water-receptive than zinc (hydrophilic), is more easily and completely desensitised and is easier to keep running clean and sharp on the machine with less water and less tendency to scum. A characteristic feature, its resistance to stretching, is most important for colour register work. Because of its water-receptivity it is difficult to add work with tusche and, because of aluminium's sensitivity to chlorides, where the water supply is high in chloride content scumming trouble, due to oxidation, may result.

Stainless steel is an alloy of steel, chromium and nickel. It is a hard material which resists corrosion, the oxides which prevent corrosion giving it its good lithographic qualities. It is not an easily fabricated metal in that it bends at the cylinder gap and any subsequent flattening for re-use is a much more difficult operation than with either zinc or aluminium. The use of chromium-plated steel reduces the difficulty that is inherent in the mechanical properties of stainless steel. The idea of plating to produce multi-metal plates can be extended by lamination. In this the metal with suitable lithographic but poor mechanical qualities can be reinforced by lamination with a material such as one of the synthetic fabrics, which are particularly tear-resistant. This provides the necessary reinforcement at points where bending produces undue stress. A plate of this type is commercially available and though not of the lowest in first cost, it is economical when applied to web offset long-run work, where delays, owing to mechanical failure of the plate, would leave an expensive press idle for perhaps an hour whilst a new plate was being made.

CONTACT ANGLES AND PLATE WETTABILITY

THE EASE with which some metals accept ink and others more readily accept water is well known. This quality of the relative wettability of a metal by oil or by water has been evaluated by the study of the contact angle. This study and measurement has done much to enhance the performance of the lithographic plate. The usual methods of measurement consist of studying the angle produced when an oil drop comes in contact with a moistened metal plate, or the angle formed between water/metal boundary when a sample plate is placed in water.

The contact angle of the oil drop method is formed when a prepared

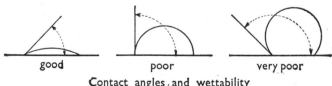

good   poor   very poor

Contact angles and wettability

Fig. 67

sample plate is placed face-down under water or fountain solution and a drop of oil is allowed to float up to and come in contact with the plate. Metal that is readily wetted by the oil will let it spread out on the surface. Metal surfaces or fountain solutions that inhibit oil wetting will cause the oil to assume a spherical form and make contact with the surface at only one point. Measurement of the angle between the oil drop and the metal surface gives the contact angle.

The G.A.T.F. evolved suitable apparatus for the measurement of the water/metal angle. In this method a small tank is filled with water with a supply arranged so that a constant flow keeps the surface free from dust, etc., which could influence the results. The sample plate is attached to an arm and lowered into the tank. A light reflected from a mirror shines across the water surface towards the user, the light being reflected off the water where plate and water make contact. The angle the plate makes with the water surface can be adjusted and the angle so made measured off on a built-in scale. The angle of the plate is altered so that the light beam meeting the water at the line of contact with the plate remains undistorted. Experience shows that results from this apparatus are in line with performance on the press.

GRAIN

THE GRAIN on the plate surface not only provides for improved adhesion of the image but in addition the depth of grain provides latitude in wear of the metal surface during printing. Deep coarse grain would provide maximum plate life but this would be at the expense of distortion of fine lines and halftone dots. A fine grain is necessary for minimum dot distortion, this resulting in improved image definition on the printed sheet. Coarse grain can be used for such work as crayon posters, large solid areas or any class of work where the image is not of fine detail. In these applications definition is not important but thick ink films may be required, and these need more moisture which is more easily arranged with a coarse-grained plate. For the majority of work a fine but deep grain is most suitable, the closeness of the grain giving good definition, whilst the deeply cut grain withstands wear. A fine but shallow grain can be used for proofing, the deep grain not being necessary for the few impressions required.

The recent trends and developments in lithography all lean to the use of less grain in the plates, improved techniques making this possible. Plates with minimum grain, or even no grain at all, require more critical adjustment of the ink/water balance. Commercial experience, over a wide range of conditions, favours some form of grain even if this is only a very slight grain effect. This is because practice has shown that this gives a more satisfactory control of damping; the slight roughness assists the retention of the residual desensitising layer. The grain can be produced by chemical or mechanical means.

CHEMICAL GRAINING AND ANODISING

CHEMICAL GRAINING is normally applied to aluminium and is usually associated with anodising, which consists of thickening-up to one-thousandth of an inch the film of aluminium oxide. The grain is produced by an alternate acidic and alkali treatment. The plate is cleaned with a nitric-sulphuric acid solution and suspended in hot sodium hydroxide, previously conditioned with aluminium scrap. Anodising consists of placing in an electrochemical circuit by suspending the metal in a 20% sulphuric (or chromic) acid solution and passing through it a low voltage current of some 12–14 volts as in electro-plating. This procedure can be used, if required, without any preliminary chemical graining, because the anodising itself produces a very fine electrochemical grain. The chemical graining of zinc can be done in 10–20 min. using an aqueous solution of hydrogen peroxide and sulphuric acid, providing the alloy composition of the zinc meets certain specifications (virtual absence of copper, etc.).

Apart from chemical graining, mechanical graining, sand blasting and brush-graining methods are used.

Mechanical Graining

THIS METHOD is the one most widely used. The procedure for zinc and aluminium, to provide a water-receptive surface, is similar with lighter marbles and finer abrasives used for aluminium. The graining machine works on the principle of an eccentric giving a circular rotating motion to the grain trough. Speed or 'throw' affects the grain as well as the grade of abrasive and the size of marble used. Most machines operate with a throw of $1\frac{1}{2}$ to 3 in. and at a speed between 150 and 250 revolutions per minute. The most important factor affecting the grain is the type and size of grain and the type and grade of abrasive used. Glass, porcelain and steel marbles are used. Glass marbles are cheapest, but are light and wear quickly – this is an advantage for thin plates. Porcelain marbles, widely used on the Continent, are heavier, more expensive and last longer. Chrome steel marbles are extensively used in the United States. They are hard, long-wearing and of much greater weight in proportion to their size. Thus smaller marbles can be used, giving a more closely-knit grain. A drawback is their tendency to oxidise; if left in the machine for a time without use they can deposit particles of oxide in the grain. Running the machine for a few minutes before use with a little abrasive and hosing the marbles before commencing graining should obviate oxidation. Wooden marbles, which are very light, produce a fine grain on thin aluminium plates. Unfortunately they develop flat spots, producing a flat uneven grain if not kept moving with the right amount of moisture.

Abrasives used are carborundum (silicon carbide) aluminium oxide and crushed flint (quartz) and pumice powder is also used for the production of a very fine grain. The former has great cutting power and extreme hardness. The cost is high and particles can become imbedded in the plate surface and cause trouble if they fall out on the press run. Aluminium oxide (or flint) is generally used. These must be correctly graded and free from iron particles. They are obtainable in a wide range of grades – between 40 and 220 or higher. The grade of abrasive has a

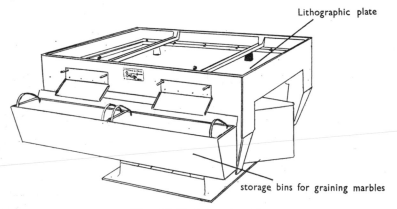

Lithographic plate

storage bins for graining marbles

Fig. 68 Graining machine

great effect on the final grain produced, but it must not be assumed that a no. 100 flint will necessarily produce a no. 100 grain. Other factors also play their part – speed and throw of the graining machine, size and weight of marble, grade of abrasive and the amount of water used. To produce a fine grain a small throw of about 2 in. maximum with a slow speed of 150–180 revolutions per minute, plus glass or porcelain marbles of $\frac{3}{4}$ in. diameter, or slightly under (steel $\frac{9}{16}$ in. or $\frac{5}{8}$ in.), and a good quality, evenly graded fine abrasive (120 or finer) is required. The minimum quantity of abrasive and water should be used during the graining time, which is about 55 min. The first application is made when the operation commences and repeated at 10-min. intervals, the final application being 5 min. before the plate is removed from the machine. If the machine is allowed to run with exhausted abrasive at this stage the sharpness of grain will be lost. The plate must be well washed with running water and wiped clean with a soft bristle brush or cloth. It is then either sensitised in the normal way or dried in a drying oven with good circulation or in a warm current of air, as quickly as possible to minimise oxidation.

Sand-blast Graining

CHEMICAL RESEARCH and the advent of the deep etch process have made it no longer essential to have a deep cut surface of myriads of water-retaining reservoirs. Chemical formulations, capable of imparting layers of insoluble hydrophilic (water-attracting) compounds to zinc and aluminium, have made it unnecessary in most instances for a deep cut grain. A surface microscopically distorted by slight abrasion, to give the greatest available surface with the object of holding these compounds by adsorption over a maximum area without disturbing the surface so as to affect the dot shape, is the requirement. Whilst grainless plates are now capable of giving first-class reproductions for normal printing the accurate machine setting required makes it an easier proposition to have some grain.

The combination of sand-blast graining and the electrolytic surfacing of aluminium are notable recent developments. Sand blasting uses a smooth abrasive with little cutting effect, the plate being grained by a sand-laden blast of dry, compressed air which eliminates any possibility of oxidation either during or immediately after graining. At no period is the plate wetted and there are no grain variations because there are no marbles to wear out or replace. As the abrasive is broken down below a certain weight it is automatically drawn off from the machine, graining being permanently carried out by a standard abrasive regardless of the number of plates grained. With the Howter graining machine the plate is fed into the machine through a narrow slot, picked up by the feed mechanism and automatically processed and delivered ready for use. With graining speeds in the region of four or five inches per minute a quad demy plate (35 in. × 45 in.) can be grained in about ten minutes with the machine ready for the next plate immediately.

Brush Graining

A VARIATION of sand blasting for mass production work is a wire brush scratch technique in which rotating wire brushes are used to produce a controlled scratching of the plate surface. The type of grain produced can be varied by the duration, speed, pressure and stiffness of the wire brush. A fine uniform grain can be obtained on aluminium plates using a nylon brush with an abrasive of either pumice or fine aluminium oxide (no. 500). The plate is wet with water containing a wetting agent, the abrasive is sprinkled over the plate and the motor-driven brush worked backward and forward over the surface.

EQUIPMENT

The Vacuum Printing Frame

THE MODERN printing unit, such as the H.P.L. Rotex, has been designed to provide semi-automatic high-speed metal printing, whilst conserving valuable floor-space. An open-type 75 or 110 amp. arc lamp with an electrical load of 22–30 amp. single phase with controlled carbon feed is

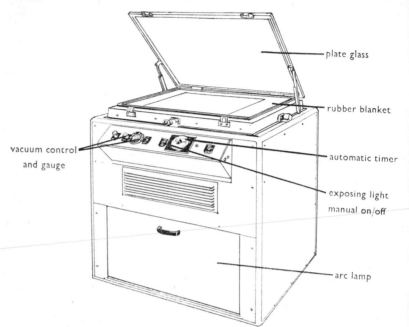

plate glass

rubber blanket

vacuum control
and gauge

automatic timer

exposing light
manual on/off

arc lamp

Fig. 69 H.P.L. Rotex vacuum printing frame

used. Plates are loaded with the frame in the horizontal position; once vacuum is obtained the frame is rotated through 180 degrees to face downwards. The required exposure is pre-set on a timer and after exposure the frame is rotated through 180 degrees for unloading. The cover glass of the vacuum frame is kept cool by a fan drawing cool air through the cabinet and variable vacuum pressure can be selected to facilitate the handling of film negatives. Maximum plate size is 43 in. × 33 in. (109 cm. × 84 cm.). The larger size units have motor-operated arc lamps, whilst the smaller units (24 in. × 20 in.) have solenoid-operated arcs. Dichromated colloid coatings are sensitive to ultra-violet and blue-violet light. Therefore mercury vapour lamps and open or enclosed arc lamps are suitable light sources. A single arc lamp is preferred for exposing. Multiple arc lamps or banks of fluorescent lights and mercury vapour bulbs or tubes tend to undercut, especially if there is tape or photopake on the negative or positive, thus the work is thickened. Motor-driven arcs overcome variations in light intensity, in that the gap between the carbons is kept uniform by the motor constantly feeding the carbons as they burn. With the older method of adjustment, by the use of a solenoid or electromagnet, the gap becomes longer as the carbons burn, until a point is reached when the solenoid

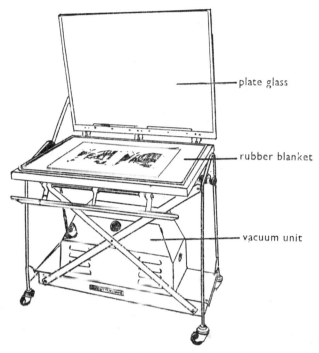

plate glass

rubber blanket

vacuum unit

Fig. 70A Vacuum printing unit

acts to shorten the gap. In this case the intermittent adjustment of the carbons would cause flicker and variation in the light intensity. The motor-driven arcs, because of their steadiness, minimise or eliminate the need for the use of a light integrating meter. These meters are needed with solenoid arcs. They measure the exposure in terms of light units reaching the plate irrespective of light intensity and can be compared to a water meter which measures water in cubic feet regardless of the rate of flow. Variation in light action, owing to fluctuation, can vary as much as 25% when clock timed, compared with a light integrating meter.

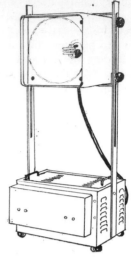

Fig. 70B Three-phase 3-carbon arc lamp with motorised feed to give the maximum evenness of illumination

Fig. 70C Ascorlux pulsed xenon lamp. Air-cooled with built-in timer, 2-phase 380–440 volts (H.P.L. Ltd)

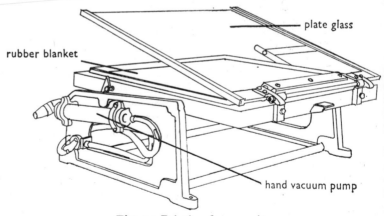

Fig. 71 Printing frame unit

The Whirler

THE USE of the whirler is to coat the plates which are mounted on the turntable. This is done by pouring the solution over the plate whilst it is turning. A coating arm, by which a coating funnel is centred on the turntable, is also provided. A positive variable speed drive fitted with a revolution counter for setting and measuring the whirler speeds is essential. The turntable consists of a non-corroding alloy and is fitted with a

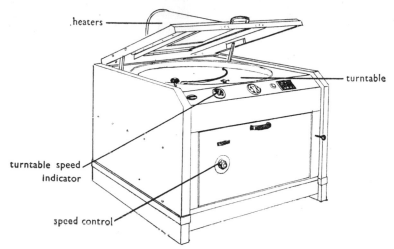

Fig. 72 Horizontal whirler

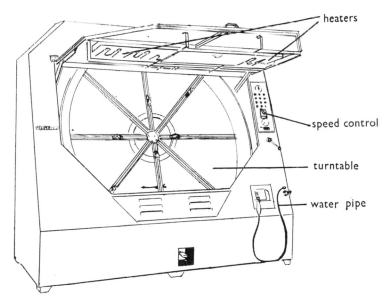

Fig. 73 Vertical whirler

water arm for flushing and cleaning purposes and a non-radiant heating and fan element positioned in the counterbalanced lid. Speed range should accommodate 20 to 150 revolutions per minute. Horizontal and vertical whirlers (space saving) are manufactured. The former distributes the coating solution by centrifugal force; the latter, which has the turntable at about 15 degrees from the vertical, relies on a combination of centrifugal force and gravity. Inside temperatures of the whirler should be controlled thermostatically and the water connected to the whirler should be temperature controlled.

XIII

The Chemistry of Platemaking

COATING SUBSTANCES

THE MAJORITY of plate coatings use *ammonium dichromate* as the sensitiser. It is formed by neutralising chromic acid with ammonia and is poisonous and can cause dermatitis. The oldest coating material employed is *albumen*, which is a protein derived from the white of eggs. A milk protein substitute for albumen is *casein*, which is insoluble in water and is dissolved in an ammonia solution. For printing-down use it must be free from fat otherwise scummy plates will result. A cheaper protein substitute than albumen or casein is *soyabean*, which is also dissolved in an ammonia solution.

Gum Arabic. This is a natural gum exuded from acacia trees in the Sudan. It is the main ingredient of deep-etch coatings and plate etches and should be clean with a high degree of solubility. The addition of a few drops of carbolic acid prevents sourness and it should be strained through muslin before use.

Glue. The general name for adhesives, especially those made by extracting hides, bones, cartilage, etc., of animals with water. Fish glue was the first material used for deep-etch plates, now replaced by the gum process. It was cheap, employing water development, but plates scummed quickly during printing.

Kodak Photo Resist (KPR). The image consists of an organic resin insolubilised by light. The light-sensitive resins are insoluble in water but soluble in organic solvents, such as trichlorethylene. On exposure the exposed parts are rendered insoluble in the organic solvents which dissolve away the unexposed areas. Like plates made by the electrostatic processes of Xerography and Electrofax, which consist of baked organic resins, KPR plates have good ink-receptivity and resistance to abrasion and blinding. Costs are high, but plates have a long shelf life, unaffected by temperature and relative humidity.

PRESENSITISED PLATES

DIAZO MATERIALS, polymerised by light action, form the basis of most presensitised plates. They have good ink receptivity and resistance to wetting by water and gum but poor resistance to abrasion, thus wearing rapidly.

Plate Performance

ZINC, ALUMINIUM, copper and chrome are the chief metals used for plate making. Zinc is quickly changed from a sensitised to a desensitised state, making it more suitable than aluminium for hand-transferring, whilst aluminium, in turn, is superior for receiving a tough anodic layer. The ductility or stretch of zinc helps to correct mis-register on the press, but in general the ratio of use in this country is 70% to 30% in favour of aluminium, with the merit of aluminium being the reliability of the image, its well-desensitised non-image area, longer printing run and a surface more water-receptive than zinc. The impact on the industry of the anodic aluminium plate has been marked. The oxide layer on the surface gives a tough water-receptive non-image area and, in addition, provides a porous honeycomb surface for the image. The plate stands up well to the abrasion to which it is subjected from the blanket, inking and dampening rollers. Copper is ink-receptive and chrome, being water-receptive, combines well with copper, so that in conjunction on a metal support they form a tri-metal plate to provide the ideal lithographic surface.

Excluding presensitised plates, which are discussed separately, the deep-etch gum process is most favoured in this country. Surface plates, mainly albumen, are still used. To be trouble-free edible flake is preferred, and once the ratio of dichromate to albumen has been decided, whirling speed should be standardised and excess water whirled off the plate before coating. If difficulty is experienced in removing the ink in the non-image areas, with the residual coating not being easily soluble in water and thus remaining in the grain, the cause may be too much dichromate, too thin a coating, or over-exposure. The opposite effect – easy development, resulting in lack of fine detail and short plate life – could be caused by low dichromate content, a thick coating, or under-exposure.

Deep-etched plates are considerably more robust, with the image, slightly in recess, consisting of a tough inert lacquer applied direct to the metal. For optimum results the coatings, chemicals, lacquers and inking solutions should be standardised and of proprietary brands. Relative humidity is more important in the plate-making department than temperature, and air conditioning is desirable. Humidity control is an important factor in obtaining a perfect gum stencil. Often relative humidity varies between 30% and 80%, or higher. For trouble-free working it should be not more than 65% for zinc and aluminium and 58% for tri-metal plates, otherwise weak images and surface scum on the machine can result. An atmosphere of higher relative humidity than that corresponding to the moisture content of the plate means that the plate after coating will accept moisture until a state of equilibrium is reached. This increases its sensitivity, makes development of the image more difficult and reduces the contrast of the result.

COATING SOLUTIONS

THE COMMON organic materials used in the making of light-sensitive coatings are of natural origin. These include for surface plates egg albumen, a modified casein, soyabean protein and horse blood plasma (Patracoat). For deep-etch plates gum arabic and polyvinyl alcohol (PVA) are used, the latter for Eggen plates. These materials are classified as colloids and when such coatings, in a thin film in combination with ammonium dichromate, are dried down on a plate they become light-sensitive and exhibit a tanning or hardening nature after exposure to ultra-violet light. Potassium dichromate can be used, but is less light-sensitive when mixed with the colloid than ammonium dichromate.

The chemical mechanism of the reaction is not well understood, but it is assumed that the dichromate, containing hexavalent chromium, is activated by light, oxidises the organic colloid and is reduced to tri-valent chromium. Most soluble trivalent chromium compounds have a tanning or hardening effect upon certain organic colloids and dichromates have no such effect. Thus it is assumed that the hardening of the dichromated film after exposure to actinic light is a result of the production of trivalent chromium compounds. The colloids are so complex, being mixtures not pure chemicals, that it is not possible to provide a chemical formula for them, and when a dichromate is added and the mixture exposed to light only a fraction of the dichromate (less than 10%) is changed. Some of this changed part loses its oxygen, which is assumed to be taken up by the colloid which is oxidised, and the reduction product of the dichromate attaches itself to the colloid. The new combination is much less soluble in water than the original mixture and it is this reaction to light, to render them partially insoluble in water, that makes them so valuable in printing.

STANDARDISATION AND CONTROL OF VARIABLES

IT HAS been assessed that there are at least forty-three different factors in platemaking which can vary and change the sensitivity of a dichromated coating between plate and plate. These factors include such general things as variations in the plate grain, whirler speed, amount of rinsing water on the plate, as well as specific factors such as dark reaction and continuing reaction, coating thickness, specific gravity and viscosity, pH of the coating solution, etc. Standardisation in essential factors is necessary.

(1) *Variation of Dichromate.* If the dichromate is increased without a corresponding increase in the colloid ratio the coating will be more light-sensitive. Conversely, a decrease in dichromate results in a decrease in sensitivity. The dichromate–colloid ratio should be 1:3 for surface plates and between 1:3 and 1:5 for deep-etch plates.

(2) *Coating Thickness, Specific Gravity and Viscosity.* Specific gravity is measured in degrees Baumé and is related to the amount of solid material in solution. Viscosity describes the solution's ability to flow. Both are influenced by changes in temperature – the higher the temperature, the thinner the solution, and vice versa. The thicker the coating, the more the exposure required, the light taking longer to penetrate the coating right down to the metal surface. A coating suitable for a fine-grained plate will be too thin for a coarse-grained plate, and the opposite also applies. The moisture content of the plate before coating affects the result. The plate must carry some moisture because a dry plate isn't instantly wettable by the coating solution, making coating difficult, but excess moisture dilutes the solution. Obviously the amount of coating solution affects the coating thickness, with excess solution giving a thicker coating – because it is diluted less by the moisture content on the plate. It follows that too little solution results in a thinner coating. The faster the whirler speed the thinner the dried coating will be, and vice versa. Also high relative humidity causes the coating to take longer to dry. Thus more solution will be whirled off the plate on humid days than on dry days, resulting in high humidity producing thin coatings and low humidity thick coatings. Plate coatings of uniform light-sensitivity demand an air-conditioned room, or at least an accurate hygrometer. The higher the relative humidity, the less the exposure required. If it goes down the exposure requires lengthening. A 20% change in relative humidity cannot be compensated for solely by change in exposure. This would require also a change in the coating thickness.

In general, relative humidity is the percentage of saturation in a unit of air. A relative humidity of 40% indicates that the air contains 40% as much moisture as it could carry if it were saturated (100% wet) at that temperature. Air carries more moisture at a high temperature than at a low one. The plate coating absorbs moisture from the air which varies directly with the room humidity. A plate could require double the exposure at a relative humidity of 40% as it requires when the relative humidity is 80%.

(3) *Alkalinity (pH) of the Coating.* The quantity of ammonia in the solution affects the light-sensitivity of the plate coating. In addition to ammonium dichromate, ammonium hydroxide is present because the dichromated colloid is acid and unstable, and would be useless after a

few hours if not made alkaline with ammonia which acts as a preservative. The majority of the ammonia evaporates a short time after the
coating has dried, the amount remaining depending on the initial pH
of the solution. Excess ammonia reduces the light-sensitivity of the
coating.

(4) *Age of Coating.* It is realised that the egg albumen or the gum
arabic and the ammonium dichromate are not by themselves light-
sensitive, but only the mixture of the two. When mixed, oxidation
occurs and the chromium of the ammonium dichromate is reduced to
chromic ion and may form chromic hydroxide. This reaction proceeds
slowly in solution, and if made alkaline with ammonia, the reaction is
slowed down even further. The reaction proceeds when the dried
coating on the plate is kept in the dark (*dark reaction*) but is speeded up
greatly when the dried coating is exposed to light. Light action changes
the solubility of the coating so that, in the case of albumen, casein and
soyabean, it is made insoluble in water. With gum arabic the exposed
parts become insoluble in a water solution containing salt, such as
calcium chloride (deep-etch developer). Dark reaction is a gradual
tanning or hardening of the coating, having the effect of an overall pre-
exposure which, if continued, will result in little difference in solubility
between the exposed and unexposed areas of the coating. Temperature
and relative humidity are the deciding factors in assessing how long the
coated plate can be kept before the entire coating becomes too insoluble
to be developed. The spontaneous hardening or dark reaction is faster
the higher the temperature and relative humidity. When the relative
humidity is below 50% and the temperature does not exceed 80° F
coated plates can be kept up to three or four days before developing.
If the relative humidity is about 70% development must take place
within 6 hours. High temperature produces an increase in dark reaction
as well as increased sensitivity. Low temperature or relative humidity
gives slow dark reaction so that a surface or deep-etch plate can be
stored for two months or longer in a refrigerator at about 10° F and still
be satisfactory, even though the relative humidity of the refrigerator is
high. It has been proved that a temperature of 40° F almost eliminates
dark reaction.

When the light-sensitive coating has been exposed to light the hardening of the coating continues after the arc lamp is switched off. This
phenomenon is known as *continuing reaction* and it means that the longer
the exposure plate is allowed to stand before development the larger the
halftone dots become in the case of surface plates. The occurrence is
only in areas exposed to light, whereas dark reaction takes place on all
areas of the plate. Furthermore, in the initial stages the action is as if
the plate were still being exposed, but it soon decreases and after about
an hour ceases altogether, whereas dark reaction continues, depending

mainly on the temperature and relative humidity. It is realised how
these two reactions can affect exposure in step-and-repeat platemaking.
Jorgensen and Bruno suggest that the plate is allowed to age for one
hour before the first exposure is made, and allowed to stand in the dark
for one hour after the final exposure, before developing the plate.

Acidity and Alkalinity (pH scale)

THIS IS a measure of the hydrogen-ion concentration. Density is expressed as degrees on the Baumé hydrometer scale and heat as degrees
on the thermometer scale. The pH scale records the intensity of acidity
and alkalinity. The scale is divided into tenths from 0–14. Midway between 0 and 14 is the neutral point, so that a solution having a pH of 7

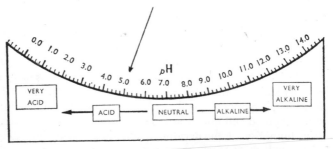

Fig. 74 pH scale of hydrogen-ion concentration

is neither acid nor alkaline. Below 7 signifies acidity, the intensity increasing with decreasing numbers. For example pH 6·5 is mildly acid,
pH 6 increasingly acid, pH 5 is ten times more acid than pH 6 and pH 4
is a hundred times more acid than pH 6. The numbers between 7 and
14 indicate alkalinity, the intensity of which increases proportionately
as the numbers increase toward 14. Colorimetric pH comparator control
sets for testing are available.

Sensitivity of Coating Solution

SURFACE AND deep-etch coatings are much more sensitive to blue light
(410–500 millimicrons) than to green light (500–560 millimicrons) with
very low sensitivity to yellow light (520–700 millimicrons) and completely insensitive to red light (600–700 millimicrons). The illumination
most effective for hardening the coating is one rich in ultra-violet; this
is in the region of the spectrum just below 400 millimicrons.

Safelights for Platemaking

DAYLIGHT, WHICH is rich in ultra-violet radiations, is unsuitable and if
used would result in inferior work. This applies for all light-sensitive
coatings, albumen, casein, gum arabic and diazo compounds. All of

them are more or less unaffected by light of wavelengths above 580 millimicrons, so that red, orange or yellow light could be employed. Safety, with maximum luminosity for ease of working, is the objective, so that yellow fluorescent lamps are most satisfactory. Sodium lamps are also used and windows should be glazed with pale amber glass.

Sensitivity Guide

THE USE of a numbered continuous-tone grey scale, such as the Kodak Step Tablet no. 2 or 3, enables the platemaker to assess how much the coating has been hardened under particular conditions of exposure time, coating thickness, temperature, relative humidity, etc. The wedge is printed-down alongside the work and the transmission of light is approximately halved each two steps upon the sensitivity guide. With a surface plate the first six steps should ink-up completely, followed by a dark grey and then a lighter grey until a step is reached (dense in the wedge) which will not hold ink. The step which still holds a solid film of ink is known as the 'critical step'. The number of steps visible conveys relevant information.

PREVENTION OF OXIDATION

THE CLEANING of the plate and the removal of metal oxide film, grease, graining sludge and the like are carried out by *counter-etching* the grained metal plate using weak hydrochloric or acetic acid or an alkaline solution such as tri-sodium phosphate. *Surface* treatment of the plate is carried out to stop unwanted oxidation or corrosion of the metal which prevents the gum arabic etch, used to assist the wettability of the plate with water, from adhering to the plate, so that the metal is not water-receptive or, in other words, is poorly desensitised. The *Cronak* process is designed for the surface treatment of zinc. It is realised that zinc would be unsuitable for platemaking without gum arabic. The adherence of the gum and its ability to wet with water (desensitise) are affected by the presence of other materials and by corrosion. If the metal is clean, the gum sticks making the zinc water receptive, i.e. well desensitised. Oxidised or corroded zinc plus foreign matter, such as residual albumen, prevent the gum adhering to the metal, hence poor desensitisation and water-receptivity, plus scumming on the press run.

Surface treatment uses chemicals which leave a tenacious coating on the metal, preventing corrosion and assisting the adhesion of the gum. The 'Cronak' method for the surface treatment of zinc uses a solution of sodium or ammonium dichromate, sulphuric acid and water. This converts the surface to an amorphous chromic oxide including chromium trioxide, which protects the zinc from oxidation during platemaking and press running. Because the dichromate could cause skin irritation (dermatitis) the *Nital* treatment has been evolved, which uses a solution consisting of ammonium alum (ammonium aluminium sulphate), concentrated nitric acid and water. This leaves on the surface of the zinc a very suitable base for the gum, consisting of colloidal or amorphous aluminium hydroxide. It is used mainly as a '*post treatment*' after developing and before etching. The word 'post' means 'after' and implies, in this instance, after development. Plates are also subjected to post-Cronak and post-Brunak treatment.

Aluminium plates are given surface treatment, not to prevent general oxidation – because it does not corrode like zinc – but to protect the normal oxide layer formed from the effects of damage. If the surface is damaged small holes or corrosion 'pits' form producing 'ink-dot scum' in these areas. The *Brunak* treatment was evolved by Bruno and Hartsuch, and full details of all the surface treatment methods for plates are published by the G.A.T.F. of America who developed the techniques in their research laboratories. The Brunak solution consists of ammonium dichromate, hydrofluoric acid and water and it removes residual solution, improving desensitisation. The hydrofluoric acid reacts with the aluminium oxide forming chromic oxide and chromium trioxide, releasing the residual coating of albumen or casein held in the aluminium oxide as well as checking the electrolytic corrosion of the metal when the aluminium oxide surface is damaged. The Patral treatment for aluminium, developed by P.A.T.R.A., is recommended. The film not only prevents corrosion, but completely desensitises lithographically, so that the metal surface is very ink-repellent when wet and the treatment also avoids skin irritation. The natural oxide film is replaced by one containing chromium and fluosilicic acid.

PLATE ETCHES

THESE AND fountain solutions are concerned with the surface character of the non-printing areas and they operate by depositing a film or coating on the metal surface. Unlike light-sensitive coatings they are extremely thin and invisible to the eyes (millionths of an inch thick). Whereas *counter-etching* is to clean the plate surface to hold the image, *pre-etching* follows counter-etching or surface treatment and is generally known as a *desensitising etch*. The function of this etch is to deposit a water-receptive film on the non-image areas which will last during the press run and wets with a minimum of water. The principal ingredient of the etch, which includes an acid and salt, is gum arabic, which contains free organic acid groups in the molecule (carboxyl) binding the gum to the metal and preventing it dissolving in the presence of water. A substitute is cellulose gum and the normal acid is phosphoric acid which converts most of the contents in the gum to carboxyl groups to give better adhesion. Salts like ammonium dichromate and nitrate salts and phosphates exercise a restraining effect, reducing the attack on the metal by the acid content of the etch and leaving some gum on the surface. Thus a good pre-etch solution for zinc consists of gum arabic acidified with phosphoric acid with some ammonium dichromate and for cellulose gum a cellulose gum–magnesium nitrate–phosphoric acid solution is preferred. P.A.T.R.A. introduced an etch based on Cellofas, which is similar to gum arabic but forming a thicker solution. This gives it very desirable properties for plate-etching but is not so acceptable for gumming up.

Thus the non-image areas which have been made water-receptive (hydrophilic) by 'plate-etching' are desensitised, which means that these areas will not accept ink as long as they have been previously wet with water. After 'plate-etching' the plate is 'gummed' and as the plate etch and the gum solution contain gum arabic, cellulose gum, etc., both operations assist in desensitisation of the plate. A plate given both treatments is better desensitised than a plate given one treatment only. The gum solution consists usually of gum arabic and water or acidified cellulose gum and water with a pH of about 4·0–4·5. The etch is much more acid (pH 2·0 to 3·0) and contains, as stated, inorganic salts such as bichromates, nitrates or phosphates, plus the gum arabic or cellulose gum. Gumming the plate gives an additional coating of gum to protect the non-image areas whilst it is being handled and also when it is washed out and treated with *asphaltum*.

This latter treatment replaces the ink on the image with a thin film of asphaltum if the plates are not to be immediately run on the press. Also after printing, before storage, replace the ink image with asphaltum. This is because the ink would become hard and glazed and difficult to wash out, whereas asphaltum remains ink-receptive and will dissolve without any trouble even after several years' storage. The ink image is washed out with turpentine and the asphaltum rubbed down in a thin, even layer.

FOUNTAIN ETCHES

PLATES CORRECTLY desensitised in platemaking can be run on the press with just plain water in the fountain. Ideally, when wet the surface film would provide permanent ink-repellency to the non-printing areas. Unfortunately, under practical conditions the film often breaks down and scumming occurs with ink adhering to non-printing areas. This is caused by abrasion on the machine and from paper fluff, plus chemical action such as a poor dampening solution or acid. Faulty machine setting, paper fluff, thin ink or ink containing excess of paste driers are probably the most common causes of scumming. Dichromates are included in fountain etches to reduce the continuous corrosion caused by acid solutions. G.A.T.F. suggest a fountain etch for zinc and aluminium plates consisting of zinc nitrate, phosphoric acid, cellulose gum and water at a pH between 5·0 and 5·5 with gum arabic or cellulose gum solutions added. This is for printing surface, deep-etch, or presensitised plates. A higher concentration of gum is used for bi-metal plates. P.A.T.R.A. recommend the use of gum solutions and similar non-corrosive dampening solutions right from the start of a printing run, with no salts such as ammonium phosphate or nitrate added, because they may prove harmful from a corrosion point of view. A fountain *solution* deposits a desensitising layer on the non-printing areas. It is non-corrosive and reduces the tendency of the dampeners to grease, which causes poor wetting and ink spread in non-image areas. A fountain *etch* is corrosive and relies on continuing corrosion, by acid, of the non-printing areas to keep scum under control. A recommended P.A.T.R.A. fountain solution consists of Cellofas (an organic colloidal desensitiser) combined with sodium hexametaphosphate, and does not need the addition of a dichromate, which is a health hazard. It is a fact that P.A.T.R.A. does not recommend the use of fountain etches except in real emergency because attack on the image is always liable. Dichromates in fountain etches minimise the danger of sharpening and a solution of nitric acid, ammonium dichromate and gum is, according to P.A.T.R.A., as effective as a phosphoric or phosphoric dichromate fountain etch and much less harmful towards ink drying.

SCUMMING

THIS CAN be defined as the adherence of ink to areas of the non-image portion of the plate, which include not only the large open areas but the minute spaces between dots which fill-in or scum. Non-image areas are desensitised so that they remain water-receptive. During printing, ink which includes certain pigments will tend to cause scumming, especially if the pigments are very greasy and contain, for instance, oleic acid, which will displace the gum arabic molecules and adhere to the metal making it ink-receptive at that point. Excess driers or ink driers containing lead, also an excess of alum in the printing paper, can cause scumming of the plate. A badly desensitised plate and the use of an incorrect fountain solution are also factors which can result in scumming.

BLINDING

POOR ADHESION between the metal and the image is a prime cause of plate blinding. Other factors are poor ink-receptivity of the image, partial desensitisation of the image, abrasion of the image areas and paper coating pick on the blanket which prevents the ink image transferring from blanket to paper. A weak or blind impression occurs when a deep-etch plate is over-etched or when thin developing ink allows the desensitising etch to penetrate part of the image. Non-blinding lacquers should be used which have an affinity for ink rather than gum and good quality developing ink must be used to ink-up the image areas of an albumen plate completely. With deep-etch plates it must be ascertained that the developer has removed all traces of the coating in the image areas before applying the lacquer, and no water or deep-etching salts must be left on the plate, which must be perfectly dry after treating with alcohol, before the lacquer is applied. If gum adheres to some of the image, water is accepted instead of ink. This partial desensitisation of the image causes the plate to blind in these areas and it may be caused by a too thin ink film, excess water in the ink, or excess gum or acid in the fountain solution. Too much pressure between the plate and the blanket causes an abrasion which leads to very serious plate blinding which cannot be rectified. This type of blinding can also be caused by hard pigment particles and fibres in the paper and, during a colour run, by minute particles present in the dry offset spray.

XIV

Platemaking Methods

SMALL OFFSET

Plate Classification

SEVERAL DIFFERENT methods are used to produce lithographic printing plates. *Direct Image.* This is for duplication needs, circulars, etc., requiring about 1500 copies, also for specialised large offset work such as posters. The printing areas are produced by drawing, transferring or typing on to the plate, which may be paper, plastic or metal. Typed plates require touch typing and the use of a good carbon ribbon impregnated with a special high grease content ink. The non-printing areas are made water-receptive from the damping rollers on the small offset machine. *Diffusion Transfer* (photo-chemical transfer plates). This small offset plate, maximum size $15\frac{1}{4}$ in. $\times$ $20\frac{1}{2}$ in., is produced in about three minutes with press runs up to 15,000 from paper plates and 30,000 from metal plates. Copycat, Agfa-Gevaert (Gevacopy), Kodak and others manufacture platemaking equipment. The original is exposed to an orthochromatic emulsion transfer paper, which is developed in conjunction with a sheet of offset foil by being fed into the processing unit. Initially (Kodak Ektalith) the two sheets are kept apart until the fully exposed silver salts of the negative are developed to metallic silver, leaving the residue undeveloped. They are then rolled together and the undeveloped salts dissolve and diffuse across to the coating on the foil and are developed to form a positive silver image on the foil. The processing is automatic, taking about one minute, and after stripping the transfer paper from the plate the positive image strongly adheres to the base (master). Fixative solutions are applied to produce the required ink-attractiveness of the silver halide and gelatin-based image areas, plus the water-receptiveness of the metal in the non-printing areas. *Direct Photographic Plate.* This photo-direct technique utilises silver halide as the actual plate substance and is a purely photographic procedure with the positive plate image processed automatically within one minute after exposure to the copy. Intermediate negatives or positives are obviated, with the plate materials consisting of plastic-coated paper bases coated with orthochromatic autopositive emulsion. Press runs approximate to 5000 copies and the method is suitable for the duplication of specifications, schedules, charts and screen work up to 100 screen ruling. The Kodak Verilith plate material requires an exposure of a few seconds. Maximum plate size is 10 in. × 15 in. and Addressograph-Multigraph (Multilith) and Kodak (Itek 10–15 Platemaster) market automatic equipment and the necessary plate processes for the purpose. For instance, Kodak now supply the autopositive silver halide emulsion in 250 ft. rolls and the new Platemaster camera Model 18/24 produces plates 18 in. × 24 in. The lighting consists of two sets of four 72 in. high output fluorescent lights. Maximum copy size is 36 in. × 48 in.; range of focusing scale 50% to 110%. The plates are prism-made, daylight spool loading, with two plates exposed and processed, in the activator-stop-bath, at the rate of two per minute and the plates ready for the press one minute after the completion of the exposure.

ELECTROPHOTOGRAPHIC PLATE

XEROGRAPHY WAS invented by Chester F. Carlson, an American physicist and lawyer, in 1937. The conception of utilising electrostatic charges as the basis for creating visible images was demonstrated by Selenyi as far back as 1928, but the first commercial application of photocopying founded on this principle was not introduced until 1950, based on Carlson's invention. The two most common photoconductors used are selenium and zinc oxide. In selenium systems the photoconductor is re-used many times, while zinc oxide in a binder generally has a paper substrate and is used only once. Selenium-based methods require six steps in processing, charging, exposing, developing, transferring, fixing and residual image cleaning.

Xerography depends upon the ability of selenium to hold an electrical charge until it is exposed to light. The plates are so made that they pick up a coating where light has *not* fallen – a coating that can then be transferred to paper or a printing medium. The thin metal sheet is coated with a layer of selenium about 0·001 in. thick and is 'sensitised' by passing it under fine wires connected to an electrical potential of about 7000 volts. When charged with electricity the plate is placed in a light-tight holder and exposed on the camera. The light sensitivity is primarily to blue light and the speed corresponds to that of fast bromide paper. The plate-holder is laid face down on the rotator, the slide removed, and a fine powder cascaded over the plate leaving a black deposit over the areas unacted upon by light – that is on those parts which hold the electrical charge. These correspond to the image areas which do not reflect or transmit light and thus do not destroy the charge. Developing (depositing) is then completed and the image can be exposed to light. A sheet of paper or the multilith mat is placed on the plate and the whole re-inserted in the charger, when the charge is taken up by the paper or plate, the particles which form the image being thus transferred. After removing excess deposit, the plate is placed face-up in the fuser – essentially an oven – and the copying resin fused on the medium as permanently as an ink impression from a printing press. The temperature varies from 225° to 375° F and the whole process takes 2–4 min. Thousands of such paper litho plates are now used, mostly on small duplicator type presses, and by using a modified process, good images can be transferred directly from the xerographic plate to a metal plate.

The selenium-coated plate is quickly cleaned and is then ready to take another charging and impression. Care must be taken not to expose it to light once charged and before the impression is developed on it. Overexposure in processing would reduce the electrical charge on those areas which should receive no light action, giving a lighter impression than is desirable. The exposure must be long enough for the light reflected from the white areas of the copy to eliminate the electrical charge from these parts so that no impression is recorded. Exposure is shorter under humid conditions and varies according to the amount of light reflected from the copy. A mixture of selenium with tellurium gives better photoconducting properties and higher red sensitivity. Vitreous selenium alone is sensitive to blue and green only. The powder consists of alcohol-insoluble base particles, having good dielectric properties (sulphur). A pigment is precipitated on the surface by mixing spirit-soluble nigrosine with an alcoholic solution of the organic base salt of either of two specified sulphonated diazo dyes. After ball-milling for the proper length of time the powder will adhere to a negative or neutral xerographic latent image on a positively charged background. The Haloid Company of America introduced improved plates using a carefully cleaned aluminium base plate, converting to aluminium oxide at 450° F in air and coating vitreous selenium on the oxide surface. One method of fixing or fusing the powder image is by cooling the paper by pressing it against a heat-conducting surface prior to its passage through a compartment containing trichlorofluoromethane vapour. Some of the vapour will condense on the cooled paper and dissolve or soften at least one of the constituents of the powder image to fix it to the paper or metal. Although charged, exposed and developed only once, the image can be transferred as many as six times from the one cycle of operations. In three minutes an offset master can be made and up to 7000 copies can be run-off from paper plates and 70,000–80,000 from metal plates on an office-type offset litho duplicator.

A number of xerographic continuous tone devices have been developed, the objective being to produce images of a quality comparable to conventional silver halide material, while providing rapid dry processing. The devices utilise aerosol development and selenium photo receptors. Continuous tone cameras and processors for high-speed reproduction have been made and used experimentally by the Haloid Company since 1950–1953. Many systems and techniques have been used to produce colour pictures, such as aerosol development using dry pigment toners with continuous tone or screen dot pattern exposures; also liquid spray aerosol development using colour solutions in suspensions. When used with screened electrostatic images, cascade development with the correct resinous toners produces colour prints.

In 1954 R.C.A. announced their version of an electrostatic copying process and called it 'Electrofax'. Though identical in principle to xerography, it differs from it in two fundamental respects. First it employs a different photo-conductor, zinc oxide in an insulating resin binder coated on paper, as opposed to á layer of selenium on a metal backing plate. Secondly it produced copies directly without the need of a transfer step. Thus because the image is fixed on the zinc oxide paper a system using ZnO does not require the transfer and cleaning steps, which gives certain operational advantages. Electrostatic photography or photo-electrostatics refers to the processes used to form images by means of light action and electrostatic charges. Methods based on selenium are known as 'transfer photo-electrostatic processes' and those based on zinc oxide 'direct photo-electrostatic processes'. There are three major applications – copying of drawings, documents, etc., preparation of offset masters, enlargement of microfilms. While direct-type equipment is simpler than transfer type (xerography) the latter has advantages in that it can be made selective. Also zinc oxide papers (Electrofax) require controlled conductivity in the paper and are humidity sensitive, while amorphous selenium on a metal substrate is quite insensitive to humidity. Zinc oxide papers can be rendered hydrophilic by chemical modification of the zinc oxide particles, so that copies produced in zinc oxide type machines can be used directly as offset masters. Xerographic images are easily transferred to most materials that are flexible and insulating and, not so easily, to anything that is rigid or conducting. The image is oleophilic (ink-accepting) and hydrophobic (water-rejecting), making an excellent imaging material for an offset lithographic plate.

The electrophotographic system (Electrofax) is described by M. L. Sugarman in an article in *The Penrose Annual*, vol. 50 (1956), page 128. Recently a number of companies have introduced office copies and microfilm enlarger printers using zinc oxide as a photo-conductor. The paper is charged negatively by corona charging (usually two-sided), the original is exposed and then developed by magnetic brush or liquid development, using a positively-charged powder. With magnetic brush development (iron particles) the image is fixed by heating, and resolution, obtained with a 200-mesh developing powder, approximates to 1000 lines per inch.

Ozalid Elfasol

THE ELFASOL aluminium plate has a surface layer of an organic photo-conductor and plate runs approximate to 100,000 copies. The material must be handled under red safelight conditions and the plates may be charged positively to give a positive image from a negative copy or more generally charged negatively to give a positive image from a positive copy. Special electro-photographic cameras, capable of size changes, are available and all colours, excepting yellow and predominantly yellow mixtures, can be reproduced. Exposure times are under one minute and the latent electrostatic image is developed using a developing powder. Unwanted areas can be removed easily at this stage using a fine dry brush or a moist swab of cotton wool, after which the image is oven-fused for some 30 seconds at about 180° C. A de-coating solution quickly removes the coating from non-printing areas and after washing under water the plate is gummed-up and is ready for the printing press.

LARGE OFFSET
PRESENSITISED PLATES

DICHROMATED COLLOID processes have, as previously discussed, a number of limitations to efficiency in working. These include dark and continuing reaction, which produces fogging, the influence of room tem-perature and humidity variations so that above 75% R.H. the procedure becomes unreliable, poor resistance of the image to acids and strong desensitiser in surface processes and involved processing in the positive process. Alternatives have been sought for both the dichromate and the colloid and plates which are available already coated with a light-sensitive material are termed presensitised plates. The use of these types of plates has increased tremendously during the past few years. A coating for a presensitised plate must be light-sensitive with minimum dark reaction so that it can be processed at least six months after coating with ease and simplicity. This requirement is met by certain diazo compounds.

The method consists of utilising the special properties of a large group of chemical substances known as diazonium salts (diazo from the German azote (nitrogen)), which are derivatives of coal tar, the 'diazo' referring to the two nitrogen atoms per molecule in a diazo compound. Most diazo compounds start from an aromatic amine such as aniline, and the method of converting amine to diazo compound is to react upon aniline in the presence of hydrochloric acid with nitrous acid, the chemical compound or product being benzene diazonium chloride (benzene (C_6H_6): aniline ($C_6H_5NH_2$): phenyldiazonium chloride ($C_6H_5N_2Cl$)). In photolithography naptha quinone diazides pre-dominate.

Many thousands of different diazo compounds have been synthesised and the subject is extremely complex. In general, for lithographic purposes there are two main classes of light-sensitised reactions. The first changes the chemical nature of the material in a fundamental way so that with a *positive system* the sensitiser molecule, which is initially oleophilic (ink accepting), is broken down and solubilised by exposure. In the second case light action causes an increase in the molecule without necessarily altering its chemical nature (polymerisation). With *negative working* systems the water soluble diazo material is polymerised on exposure to give an oleophilic resinous image.

Presensitised plates may thus be *negative* or *positive* working depending on the diazo used plus the type of developer. For *negative* working materials organic compounds are used such as 4-diazo 1, 1-diphenylamine treated with paraformaldehyde in the presence of zinc chloride and sulphuric acid to produce a light-sensitive diazo resin. Current diazo-sensitised negative working plates are on paper, cellulose, or aluminium, and are also available polymer-sensitised on aluminium. Aluminium plates are also diazo-sensitised for positive working. The aluminium plates are almost grainless thus giving first-rate image definition and using a minimum of water. Sizes 30 in. × 40 in. and 40 in. × 60 in. of 0·005 in. and 0·010 in. thickness are made. A disadvantage in that generally no image is visible after exposure, making difficulty in frame work.

Negative working plates are exposed to light through a negative. Light action causes the diazo nitrogen group to separate from the remainder of the molecule, escaping as a gas. Multiple reactions occur in the residue in that the light-changed diazo coating is insoluble in the developer and the unexposed coating is soluble in the developer with dark reaction negligible even after six months' storage before processing. The developer, which may be acidified gum arabic, removes the coating only from the unexposed areas. The image parts are made ink-receptive by using a reinforcing lacquer applied by rubbing, after which the plates are gummed-up and ready for printing. If aluminium is used in place of paper or plastic bases the diazo compound will slowly react with the aluminium surface (dark reaction). To avoid this the aluminium is lightly anodised or treated with a hot solution of 2–5% sodium or potassium silicate.

The polymer-sensitised aluminium plates for negative working are very successful, being coated with a light-sensitive material which has a resinous and grease-receptive nature, unaffected by water and aqueous solutions and only soluble in certain organic solvents. The resin polymerises on exposure to light, becoming completely insoluble yet retaining its greasy nature. Water splashes and finger marks do not affect the surface and grained surface can be used if required. Grainless plates on thin metal can be difficult to roll up and large plates are better with a slight but definite grain to provide both a water reservoir for damping and a key for the surface image. The plates are only soluble in organic solvents and the development and the desensitisation of the background are carried out by applying a single solution by hand. Polymer coatings are not quite as light-sensitive as diazo coatings but are much higher than dichromated albumen and their resistance to fountain etches and wear and tear on the machine is superior to diazo compounds. Potential press runs are in the region of 100,000 copies.

Positive working presensitised plates, such as the original Ozasol plate and the more recent 3M-SP plate, are used by firms whose reproduction departments are geared to the production of positives for platemaking. They are generally finely grained aluminium coated with a diazo-oxide type light-sensitive layer (ester of a diazo-oxide sulphonic acid). It is resinous, insoluble in water and fairly resistant to acids and alkalis. An alkaline developer is used to dissolve away the exposed areas, leaving the original resin as the image. The light action has formed phenolic groups which make the light-modified material soluble in dilute aqueous alkali. There are two kinds of positive working materials, of which one has been discussed, and from the foregoing, it is realised that with negative working presensitised plates, also normal surface and deep-etch plates, the developer removes the coating from unexposed areas, leaving the coating on the exposed areas. With the above-mentioned type of positive working presensitised plate the reverse applies, in which exposed areas are dissolved by the developer and unexposed parts are not affected by the developer and remain *in situ*. Thus a positive image results from exposing through a positive and vice versa. Diazo-naphthol is a diazo oxide compound which is soluble in organic solvents and insoluble in water. Exposed to light it loses nitrogen as nitrogen gas and changes to the carboxyl group making the exposed areas soluble in an alkaline-water solution to remove the coating in the light-exposed areas without affecting the unexposed portions.

WIPE-ON PLATES

THESE PLATES are similar to presensitised plates, with the light-sensitive diazo type coatings wiped on instead of being applied on a whirler. The coating dries almost at once and no special care is required in applying the coating which is negative working. The procedure is fast and easy and once coated the plates can be stored in the dark until ready for use. A zinc base (S.D. syndicate) can be used, or an aluminium base (Nicholson's Easicote). Both bases are surface treated with an anti-oxidant to prevent reaction with the diazo coating. If required the plate can be re-coated and new work printed in position. No dark reaction occurs, and good line and tone definition is obtained with printing runs in the region of 100,000.

K.P.R. PROCESS

THE KODAK Photo Resist light-sensitive coating was introduced in 1953 and is negative working from a negative printed-down usually on grained zinc. The coating is some three to four times faster than albumen and is a polymeric lacquer which is insoluble in water but soluble in trichlorethylene. The polymer cross-links on exposure to light and no ammonium dichromate is needed because K.P.R. is light-sensitive by itself. After counter-etching the zinc in weak hydrochloric acid, dry thoroughly and coat with the solution. When sensitised the plate is un-affected by moisture and keeps indefinitely stored in the dark. The tri-chlorethylene dissolves the unexposed areas and development is best carried out in a tank using the vapour degreaser principle. This is done by heating the trichlorethylene in the tank to its boiling point so that it vaporises and condenses on the plate to dissolve the unhardened K.P.R. Light rubbing of the image areas with cotton wool must be avoided, because this would weaken the image. The image is not affected by water or fountain etches and after development a desensitising etch should be used to avoid scumming on the press.

PVA PROCESS

POLYVINYL ALCOHOL can be substituted for gum arabic to pro-duce, in conjunction with a dichromate, a light-sensitive coating. The exposed areas become insoluble in water, the image being developed by washing away unexposed material. The polyvinyl alcohol chain has pre-dominantly a 1·3-glycol structure resulting from head-to-tail addition of vinyl acetate molecules. Insolubility is attributed to crosslinking of polymer chains by co-ordination of alcohol groups to 'nascent' chromic ions formed by reduction of the dichromate. PVA is used in the process-ing of Aller bi-metal plates (copper on stainless steel) and also for tri-metal plates (chromium on copper with an aluminium base). Water-spray development is used after exposure, a developing pad being avoided because of the softness of the image and the application of a dilute chromic acid solution is employed to strengthen the light-exposed areas. This treatment makes the exposed areas very hard and the etching solution can be applied in the usual manner with a pad. Dilute sul-phuric acid is used for Aller plates because warm water and scrubbing application is ineffectual and with tri-metal plates a hot lye solution is used. Because the chromic bath hardens so thoroughly, a PVA exposed coating is not often used in this country as a sensitiser for zinc and alu-minium deep-etch plates, owing to the difficulty of effecting its removal.

The coatings are positive working, and the method of water development is popular on the Continent with the touch dichromated PVA coating being suitable for bi-metallic plates in which the stencil has to withstand long etching in strong solutions. Less ammonium dichromate is used than applies for albumen or gum arabic processes, nevertheless the exposure, probably because of its transparent nature, is about one-half, and whirling speeds approximate to 80 r.p.m. for bi-metallic plates and 60 to 70 r.p.m. if used for zinc and aluminium. The coating is also less affected by high temperature and humidity and uses little or no expensive alcohol, which is quite an economy. When prepared, the solution has a shelf life of about five days. Drying time is fairly prolonged, the image is inclined to sharpen in development and development control is limited. Of the many non-ionic vinyl polymers tested by P.A.T.R.A. only one – the di-methyl-amine derivative of a polyvinyl ester salt – showed favourable platemaking and printing characteristics as a potential commercial negative working coating. Others were unsuitable because of extreme low sensitivity to light, or the inherent oleophobic (ink rejecting) character of the tanned coatings, or severe blinding at all stages of a plate run.

DRY OFFSET OR LETTERSET PLATES

THE TECHNIQUE of dry offset is not new and has been practised with varying degrees of success since its inception in 1915. It is known under various names: dry offset, relief offset, wrap-round letterpress, thin gauge relief printing, photoengraved offset, high etch and letterset. The leading exponents of the technique are packaging printers working from Dycril, Dow or Kodak plates with some security printing and magazine work also being executed. A better control of colour throughout a sheet of heavy solid packaging designs during a long run is possible. The result given is better than occurs with offset lithography and there is a big reduction in picking problems which limits the number of stoppages during a run and a much quicker return to production, after a stoppage, is possible. The use of odourless moisture setting inks with a reduction in ink requirement also applies. The Dycril Type 30 plate is most commonly used in preference to the thinner Type 25. This requires a machine with sufficient cylinder tolerance such as applies on Nebiolo offset machines. The dampening system is eliminated and blankets and inkers require a different shore hardness when running a dry press and accurate pressure setting is of vital importance. Litho and letterset can be combined, such as in producing from two plates a heavy solid from one plate and an accompanying fine vignette from the other plate.

Even before the introduction of the Dycril photopolymer plate by Du Pont in 1960 and the Kodak Relief Plate in 1965 the advent of the

Dow 'powderless' etching method brought about a revolution in the quality and output of shallow-etched plates on zinc and magnesium. Normal thickness is 0·025 in. and the plates are etched to 0·008–0·012 in. in the non-image areas. The ink rollers ink the relief image, which is offset to a rubber blanket and from the blanket to the paper. It is dry printing, no water being involved, with the printing areas in relief and the non-printing portions etched away. In fact it is not a lithographic but a letterpress process because no lithographic principle of grease affinity–water repellency is involved.

Printing runs of 4–5 million impressions and over are possible but the many advantages claimed for dry offset such as a wide selection of paper and ink, constant colour, less make-ready time, ability to use photo-composed line and halftone combination work efficiently, long plate life, etc., depend upon critical and extreme accuracy or 'near perfection' on the press run. Ink rollers must be accurate, the blanket uniform in thickness, very smooth and specially hard. The plates must be accurately curved and of uniform thickness and plate-to-blanket pressure is also an extremely critical factor. The shallow-etched plates have a tendency to fill-in under the best conditions and the dots squeeze-out on the blanket. To prevent this the printer is sometimes compelled to reduce the ink so that there is often a tendency for the result to print greyish and lack contrast and depth of tonal detail compared with orthodox letterpress or lithographic printing.

ALBUMEN PROCESS

OF THE surface platemaking methods for photolithography the albumen process is being superseded by presensitised and wipe-on plates. It is negative working, and is suitable for runs of 50,000 impressions on small and large offset machines. The process is cheap and rapid compared with deep-etch. With the deep-etch process the mechanism is such that faulty procedure results in an immediately detectable blind image or in scum which is obvious. The albumen image may appear firm when it is soft enough to be rubbed off very easily with a swab of cotton wool and it may look clear and free from ink when the grain is full of scum, which will readily ink-up on the press run with the soft machine ink. Lack of system and care cause these faults and, in the main, soft images result from too thick a coating and scum from a coating which is too thin and sensitive. The soft image may be 'held' by careful gentle development and scum removed with ammonia and the application of a felt pad. These expedients are to be deplored and consistency of method and technique should avoid their necessity.

Dirt and grease should be removed by counter-etching with a 5% acetic acid solution and after washing the metal is clamped to the turntable of the whirler, the motor switched on and regulated to spin the plate slowly. The dichromated albumen solution is poured slowly from a beaker on the centre of the plate and the centrifugal force of the spinning action causes the coating to be distributed uniformly and thinly over the surface of the metal. The whirling speed is increased to between 50–80 r.p.m. with the lid closed and the heater turned on to dry the coating. The size of plate and type of metal and grain determine the whirling speed, a coarse grain requiring a slower speed and always the peaks of the grain must be covered. A time of 10 minutes is average for coating and drying, with aluminium requiring less exposure and less whirling than zinc.

A standard solution is egg albumen flake (5 oz), ammonium dichromate ($1\frac{1}{4}$ oz), water (80 oz), 0·880 ammonia (2 oz). To prepare, suspend the albumen contained in a muslin bag in 60 oz of water and dissolve the dichromate in 20 oz of water. This prevents insoluble matter in the albumen fouling the coating. The density of the albumen solution will be in the region of 3·5° Bé, and the dichromate is added, followed by the ammonia. The density approximates to 4·5° Bé with a pH of about 9. The solution is best left overnight to stabilise. The coating is pale yellowish in colour and is now slightly alkaline. The sensitivity increases with increasing acidity, thus the ammonia, by reducing the acidity, functions both as a restrainer and a preservative. The most durable and hard image is produced by a thin coating which is hardened by an exposure of about 5 min. using a 50-amp. open arc at a distance of 3 ft. Relevant factors are coating thickness and acidity of coating, intensity of light and length of exposure, temperature, relative humidity, opacity of negative and the incidence of dark reaction (age and time factor).

When inked and placed under water, test before development outside the work area. If the ink, with moderate rubbing pressure, lifts cleanly after two or three minutes' soaking, this indicates correct coating thickness. A very thin coating will leave a stubborn scum and if the ink-covered albumen film disintegrates on being touched, the coating is too thick. Inking-in before development is best done using a stiff developing ink (3 parts re-transfer ink, 1 part press black) applied with a pliable nap roller. The ink should be as stiff as possible and well-knocked into the plate, rolling from all angles to give a good uniform film. Pure turpentine, never varnish, should be used if it is necessary to reduce the ink. Liquid ink, applied by rubbing using a soft rag to give an even thin film, is often used. Roller inking is preferred in that it produces a denser, firmer, cleaner and sharper image. The bulk of the surplus ink should be removed by gentle rubbing with a swab of cotton wool followed by gentle rubbing with soft, hairy wool felt which attracts ink and picks up all surplus ink without smearing or damaging the image.

After development dry immediately in the whirler or by fan heat, chalk the image, damp the plate and, to prevent scumming during printing, apply a desensitising etch of ammonium nitrate (2 oz), ammonium bi-phosphate (2 oz), water (80 oz). Sponge off with clean water and gum-up.

DEEP-ETCH PROCESS

THIS PROCESS is positive working and produces a recessed image on the metal, by a weak etching method, to a depth of 0·002 in. to 0·003 in. for normal aluminium and zinc plates and about half the depth of the anodic layer for anodised aluminium plates. The technique gives more control over the finished result, with sharper tonal definition and printing runs of 200,000. The plates print cleaner and carry a greater ink

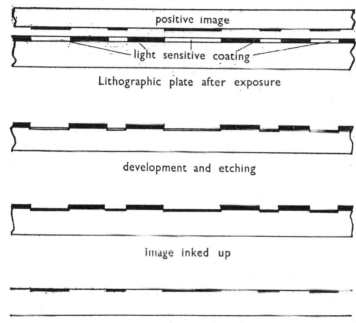

positive image

light sensitive coating

Lithographic plate after exposure

development and etching

image inked up

stencil removed

Fig. 75 Deep-etch plate

deposit with less wear on the image by friction from the rollers and dampers. Solutions were formerly mixed and prepared in the workshop but are now purchased from the suppliers ready for use. The solutions are thus formulated and controlled under strict laboratory conditions; this assists standardisation of procedure in platemaking. Prior to sensitising the metal is counter-etched with either dilute acetic acid or phosphoric acid (aluminium), or nitric acid and alum (zinc). Anodised aluminium may be prepared with weak hydrofluoric or sulphuric acid.

A deep-etched plate is similar to a gum reversal plate up to the development procedure. Before spiriting off after development the deep-etching solution is applied, followed by the application of the lacquer base after cleaning and drying. Inking and removal of the stencil are similar in both processes. Gum reversal is rarely used now solely because a deep-etch plate, which is far superior, is obtained by continuing the gum reversal process a stage or two further. Dr Julius Bekk (1930) first introduced deep-etch plates. The dichromated gum process has generally superseded the dichromated glue process in this country, probably because gum is a quicker and simpler process to work although, it is claimed, longer press runs appertain from glue reversals. PVA sensitised metal plates are increasing in popularity. In all instances the light-sensitive coating is hardened on to the metal to protect the parts which are *not* to carry the image and the image area is not exposed to light, but remains soft so that it may be removed from the metal. Thus the coating forms a stencil overlay, through the openings of which a caustic solution is applied to burn the image into the metal. When attached in this manner a lacquer followed by a dense ink is applied and the stencil, having performed its function of protecting the surface of the metal during the etching of the image, is removed.

The vinyl resin lacquer base held in the recessed areas during plate-making results in an appreciable increase in the quality and permanence of the image printing areas. The lacquer base is relatively less affected by acid and water than an albumen surface plate and the image being slightly recessed is not subjected in the same way to mechanical abrasion, and also carries more ink without thickening the print.

The coating solution protects the face of the metal during etching and must therefore be free from spots or holes. Bubbles and specks are avoided by carefully filtering the solution through cotton wool immediately before use. The solution is more viscous and dense than applies with albumen and average whirler speed is thus higher. On fine grain zinc or aluminium it is about 75 r.p.m. using plates smaller than double demy (double demy 60 r.p.m.; quad demy 50 r.p.m.). When using very smooth plates such as bi-metal and anodised aluminium the speed can be increased by about 50%. It is essential that the grain is properly covered; too thin a coating gives scummy plates, whilst too thick a coating can result in the background stencil breaking down through softness. This would cause at least a loss of definition, with probable large areas of scum, and the etching solution will undermine the coating causing the image to spread laterally. Exposure time approximates to 5 min. using a 50-amp. open arc at 3 ft. Over-exposure continues the hardening action so that incomplete development of the unhardened areas follows. This sharpens-up the image and loses the extreme highlights, and the shadows are grey and weak giving a pale, faded-looking print. Under-exposure produces a weak, soft stencil, so that the image thickens-up in development and results in stencil breakdown and a scummy plate.

After exposure areas of unexposed (unhardened) coating resulting from dirt or scratches on the positive or frame glass, or any unwanted parts of the image, are prevented from receiving the same processing as the image by painting them over (staging) with shellac or cellulose paint and thoroughly drying before development. Development removes the unhardened coating from the image so that it may be 'etched' to recess it slightly into the metal. This requires care and precision. No coating solution must remain on the image and the developer must be replenished several times. Note the time when effervescence appears on the zinc plate (lactic acid action) and double this time for complete development. Squeegee off surplus developing solution and when the image area is perfectly clean and light grey in colour the plate is ready for 'etching'. No frothing occurs on aluminium, development being judged by the whiteness of the metal. A standard sensitising solution consists of a stock solution (14° Bé) of (a) ammonium dichromate (18 oz), water (80 oz), and (b) a stock solution (12° Bé) of gum arabic (64 oz), water (160 oz), chlorocresol (5% sol. in spirit – 2½ oz). For use, take one part (a) and three parts (b), adding 2 oz of 0·880 ammonia to each 80 oz of solution. The chlorocresol, which preserves the gum, is mixed with the gum prior to adding the water.

The deep-etch solution is constantly brushed, or applied with a felt pad, over the image until etching is complete, when the etch is stopped immediately by using a neutralising agent of methylated spirit (industrial alcohol), isopropyl alcohol or cellosolve. This cleans the plate, dissolving the shellac stop-out without damaging the water-soluble stencil. Many changes of cellulose wadding are necessary, and the operation must be thorough, any traces of foreign material left on the image areas will result in image breakdown later; and the spirit must not be allowed to dry until the plate is clean, otherwise streaks will form which cannot be removed. Application of the alcohol is from the centre, rubbing towards the outer edges of the plate, so that no residue of the etch is left on the metal. A suitable deep-etch solution for zinc consists of calcium chloride (41° Bé) 35 oz (1000 c.c.), zinc chloride (dry) 9 oz (250 c.c.), hydrochloric acid ¾ oz (25 c.c.), ferric chloride (optional) 1 oz. Add the zinc chloride to the calcium chloride solution; when cool add the acid and ferric chloride. The density of the solution should be 47° Bé. For aluminium the density of the solution should be 50° Bé and consists of calcium chloride (41° Bé) 35 oz, zinc chloride (dry) 13½ oz, ferric chloride (50° Bé) 10 oz, hydrochloric acid (38%) 4 oz, cupric chloride 1 oz. Etching time for zinc plates is about 1½ min. and for aluminium plates 3 min.

After etching and cleaning or washing with alcohol (spiriting off) the printing image is formed. The plate must be perfectly dry and hard and the lacquer, based on vinyl resins, if correctly applied is virtually indestructible and forms a good grease-receptive image which is impervious to water, mild acids and normal solvents. The lacquer is poured as a pool in the centre of the plate and spread quickly and evenly with a lint-free pad over the image surface. The lacquer dries quickly and an even film must be obtained before it dries out. After finally fan drying with warm air, apply a heavy, black, greasy developing ink to protect the lacquer during stencil removal. Frenck chalk is then applied to prevent the ink spreading or smearing later. The gum stencil is now removed by soaking in warm water (90–100° F) and scrubbing with a stiff brush. If hard, a 10% solution of hydrogen peroxide or a 5% solution of citric acid may be applied as long as it is rinsed off the plate before scrubbing is commenced.

The plate is gummed up and dried in the normal way and desensitising will be required if acid has been used to remove the stencil, otherwise the residual gum film acts as a first-rate desensitiser. G.A.T.F. have published a copperising formula (isopropyl alcohol 99% – 1000 c.c.; cuprous chloride 31 gm.; hydrochloric acid 38% – 32 c.c.) for providing a stronger non-blinding image on aluminium. This is applied before lacquering takes place, after washing with alcohol and re-hardening the plate. The copper coating is applied over the image areas, the plate again treated with alcohol and normal processing continued. It cannot be applied on anodised aluminium and provides no advantage on zinc plates.

ANODISED PLATES

ANODISED ALUMINIUM plates, such as the Howter Duraplate, account for at least 75% of total plate sales to the larger offset printers in this country. First introduced about 1950, they are used mostly in conjunction with the deep-etch process and, having a fine grain, are coated at about 90 r.p.m. Deletions can be made on the plates using equal parts of amyl acetate and hydrochloric acid, and abrasives, which would destroy the anodic deposit, must not be used. The plate has superior printing quality to zinc or ordinary aluminium deep-etch plates. The grain (mechanically or chemically produced) being extremely fine, allows the finest tones to be printed, and the tough inert surface withstands friction, weak acids, alkalis and gum. Less water is required during the press run and a well-desensitised, non-image area is maintained throughout. Anodising increases the surface hardness, resistance to corrosion (does not easily oxidise) and gives increased wettability on account of the capillary cell-like structure of the anodic layer. This ensures that water is more easily adsorbed on the plate, minimising the

need for damping during the printing run. Consequently emulsification
of the ink, paper stretch and pick, are all minimised, plus the use of a
finer surface grain on account of the ready wettability of the metal. Press
runs of 400,000–500,000 are possible. The aluminium is anodised in a
bath of sulphuric acid, the plate being the anode with lead plates the
cathode. The plate is electrically oxidised with the anodic coating produced being substantially aluminium oxide; the electric charge liberates
oxygen ions at the cathode which travel through the sulphuric acid
electrolyte to the aluminium plate (the anode). When the plate has a
suitable thickness of aluminium oxide (approximately 1/1000 in.) it is
taken out of the electrolyte and sealed in hot water or in a special solution
which also functions as a desensitiser.

BI-METALLIC PLATES

THE MAINTENANCE of a grease–water balance on the plate during
printing is an essential requirement in lithography and in the past the
ink-receptive (oleophilic) printing image and the water-receptive (hydrophilic) non-printing background have been sited on the same plane
using either zinc or aluminium. Faults in printing are usually traced to
defects in image ink-receptivity or non-image water-attractiveness. The
causes are legion – both physical and chemical – and are often unpredict-
able. Hence the need for a more positive separation between printing
and non-printing areas led to the development of the bi-metallic or
multi-metal plate. The applied principle in bi-metallic platemaking
involves the use of two different metals at the printing surface, one to
receive the image, the other for the non-image areas. Use is made of
the natural affinities of metals, thus copper which is oleophilic (grease-
attracting) is generally used for the image areas, with chromium or
stainless steel, both hydrophilic or water-attracting metals, used for the
non-image areas. The lithographic behaviour of a metal is its degree of
preference for grease or water in the presence of both, plus a desensitising
agent such as gum arabic. Tests indicate that a metal with a strong preference for grease in plain water may be much less receptive when the
water contains a desensitiser, producing a poor image easily blinded. It
has been proved by the measurement of contact angles that copper at
one end of the scale and chromium and stainless steel at the other end
combine the maximum opposition of grease–water affinities with hardness and resistance to corrosion.

Basically there are three different methods available for multi-metal
plate production; the first being by selective etching through an electro-
deposited surface metal, the second by chemical deposition of a thin
metallic film usually in the image areas and thirdly selective electroplating of metals in the image or non-image areas during plate processing

after exposure. The first method is the one most used. Negative and positive working plates are made with press runs of 1,000,000 copies possible and the plates can be stored and re-used indefinitely. Bi-metallic, tri-metallic or poly-metallic plates are all two metal (bi-metallic) in their lithographic principle – the printing surface always consisting of two different metals, one ink-attractive and the other water-attractive. Tri-metal indicates that the two operational metals are plated on a third supporting metal. This is done for cheapness, nevertheless the third supporting base must have strength and durability to match the other two. Poly-metallic is a misleading term and usually means a tri-metallic plate with a special protective copper plating between the supporting metal and the image copper. The most widely used plate consists of a chromium surface with a recessed copper image and print-ing-down is normal deep-etch with special etching solution for removing the chromium from the image areas. The ultra-hard chromium takes the wear and tear of printing, and whereas a copper image in relief soon loses fine lines and dots, consistency is maintained throughout the run because of the protection of the image by the chromium. A matt chro-mium surface obviates the need for graining and provides very suitable traction for the inking rollers with the added advantage that because of the smoothness of the surface (absence of grain) the most faithful repro-duction is possible.

Exposure to light action hardens the deep-etch light-sensitive coating, producing a hard, acid-resistant stencil which allows the unexposed areas to be dissolved from the plate. After development an acid solution is applied to attach and remove the electroplated surface metal to bare the image metal beneath. The Aller plate (negative or positive) is a stainless steel base plate electroplated with a thin coating of copper. The BIO-M (Eidesco) positive working plate has a brass base electro-plated with a diamond hard chromium surface and the Lithengrave (PDI) negative working plate consists of an aluminium base coated with an electroplating of copper. A Mylar plastic backing lamination is bonded to the back of the aluminium so that if the aluminium should crack along the gripper edge, the plate would still be held in register. This also applies with PDI Lithure plates.

In tri-metallic plates Algraphy (Chromoffset), Coates Bros. (Nu-chrome) and PDI (Lithure) supply positive working plates in which the base metal is electroplated with copper on which a second and surface electroplating of chromium is made. Different base metals are used which take no part in printing and are solely supports for the ink-attractive copper and the water-attractive chromium platings. In all instances the image areas are recessed.

With the Aller *negative* process the copper surface is prepared with a 2% solution of sulphuric acid and Tripoli powder, baring the plate for coating. After washing the deep etch coating is applied. The plate, being grainless, requires a thin coating which is whirled at about 110 r.p.m. After exposure develop and spirit off to leave a hardened dichromated gum image with bare copper in the non-image areas. Re-harden for several minutes by arc lamp, and etch to remove all traces of copper from the non-image areas to bare the stainless steel. Remove the coating resist and make the copper image grease receptive by rubbing with a greasy ink cloth and dilute sulphuric acid (2%) followed by rolling-up

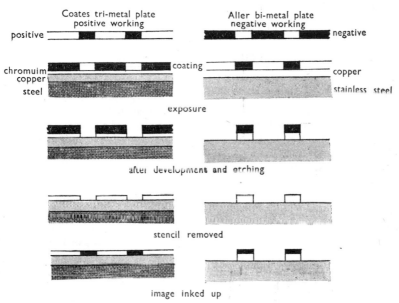

Fig. 76 Bi-metal and tri-metal processes

and gumming. In the *positive* process, after developing apply a special silvafix solution, treat with alcohol and lacquer and dry as with normal deep-etch. Roll-up thinly, french chalk and treat with nitric acid (10% sol.) to dissolve the background stencil and excess ink, taking care to remove all the unwanted resist. Complete the process by inking and rolling-up in a similar manner to the negative process. If necessary deletions can be affected with strong nitric acid.

The Nuchrome (Coates) *positive* process is tri-metallic, having a mild steel or aluminium base which is plated with copper and then with matt chromium. The plate is cleaned with a dilute solution of hydrochloric acid (1½%) which slightly etches the surface and requires careful controlling. The technique of sensitising, exposing, developing and spiriting off follows the Aller procedure, resulting in a hardened background stencil with the image portions exposed to show the chromium surface. Re-harden the stencil as previously and etch with calcium chloride–hydrochloric acid solution for a period averaging ten minutes until the image areas are clear, showing bright copper. Effervescence ceases when all the chromium is dissolved – which signifies etch completion. Remove the stencil using warm water or a citric acid solution (5%). Finally treat with a phosphoric acid solution before inking. This assists copper–ink receptivity and chrome–water affinity. The electroplated chromium deposit is about 1/20,000 in. in thickness (0·00005 in.) and the electroplated copper approximates to 1/2000 in. (0·0005 in.).

KODAK RELIEF PLATE

FOUR TYPES of 'wash-out' plastic plates are available – Colliplate, Dycril, Horner-Nylon and Kodak. Each differs from the other, but all have certain characteristics in common. The molecules of a plastic material are sensitised; the plastic surface exposed through a negative to a high-intensity light; exposed areas are hardened and made insoluble; unexposed areas are removed by washing-out and developing procedures. These are discussed in *Camera and Process Work*, Chapter IX.

The Kodak Relief Plate is a recent addition in this field of development. The plate has a thickness of 0·025 in. giving a depth of 0·010 in. to 0·012 in. Other plate thicknesses include an 0·030 in. plate to provide an etch depth of about 0·016 in., also a thinner plate (0·017 in.). The plate construction consists of an integral sandwich of an enamelled steel base, on top of which is a modified acetate butyrate layer, with a top layer of high-contrast silver-halide photo-sensitive emulsion.

Exposure for 30 seconds through a Kodalith negative produces the desired visible image on the plate. This is then activated for about 90 seconds in a special activator solution and sprayed with warm water (120° F) to wash away the unexposed emulsion. The exposed and thus hardened parts of the emulsion remain behind to act as a resist to the solvents used in the Kodak Relief Plate Processor. The dried plate is fed on to the drum of the Processor and held by magnetic hold, maximum plate size 60 in. × 40 in. Solvents and physical action remove the modified acetate unprotected by the exposed and hardened emulsion. The processing is completed in 15 to 20 minutes. Each revolution of the drum takes two minutes, giving a depth of 0·0015 in. (8 revs. = 0·012 in. depth). Negatives should be photolitho type negatives with 5–10% highlight dots and 95–100% shadows. Printed results are first-class with full gradation including fine highlight and dense shadow tones.

XV

Machine and Press Work

PREPARATION FOR PRINTING

THE PERFORMANCE of a litho plate on the proof or printing press depends to a considerable extent on the non-image areas being made completely ink rejecting, that is insensitive or desensitised to ink reception. The litho stone or the paper plate have non-image areas which are easily and naturally desensitised with moisture, but metal plates require that this characteristic is imparted to them.

The solutions used in desensitisation contain water-soluble gums, acid or acid salts, various other salts and water. Each of these constituents has a definite purpose and in combination they provide the water wettable surfaces. The number of formulae is legion with many of doubtful value. The best solutions are generally of few components with simple methods of making and application.

The best known desensitising material is gum arabic, this being strongly adsorbed on to metal surfaces, but only under certain conditions. Arabic gums do not absorb unless they are in an acidic condition, it is the released acid grouping of the gums which has an affinity to the metal surface. The acid usually used is phosphoric acid; this also forms an insoluble phosphate film on the metal surface. This film is ink-repellent when wet, but if dry and without gum being on the surface, this quality is much reduced. The zinc phosphates become insoluble when the desensitising etch rises above $3 \cdot 5$. The pH must be below $3 \cdot 5$, therefore when the solution is first put on the plate, the liquid must remain in contact with the metal sufficiently long for the reaction between metal and acid to take place. The concentration of free phosphoric acid becomes reduced and the pH rises, allowing the zinc phosphates to become insoluble.

The addition of salts such as nitrate, phosphate and bichromates of ammonia, calcium, magnesium and zinc is to reduce the solubility of the zinc phosphates. By doing this they ensure the metal surface is covered very quickly by the phosphate film thus inhibiting excessive attack on the metal itself. This in turn means that the rise in pH is not too rapid, enabling the solution to continue effective action until all the metal surface is phosphated. The different metals used in lithographic plates mean that slight changes are sometimes required in the desensitising solutions, for example a good aluminium desensitiser is effective on zinc, though not usually vice versa.

Dichromate salts in desensitising solutions are a hazard in that there is the danger of painful dermatitis which, once contracted, requires the person to be permanently removed from all contact with processes using these compounds. Dichromates should not be allowed to dry on the skin, gloves being worn to ensure freedom from the hazards of their use. In addition, the dichromate salts prevent the desensitising solution from being rubbed down as a plain gum solution; the presence of dichromate would cause gum to become ink-receptive due to light or age hardening.

The gums used are either gum arabic or a cellulose gum, the latter being a manufactured product with the advantage of greater uniformity over the naturally occurring gum arabic, which varies in solubility, viscosity, and has insolubles such as sand or other contaminating foreign matter. The cellulose gum is sodium carboxymethyl cellulose, being developed over the last twenty years for lithographic purposes. It is claimed that cellulose gums give a better bond to the metal surface and though many formulae are available for both zinc and aluminium, it is considered to be more satisfactory on zinc. In use the lower concentration of cellulose gums means that it is much easier to obtain streaks when rubbing down. To avoid this a more liberal amount of gum must be put on the plate and lighter rubbing out to obtain as thick a layer as possible. Thick layers may have to be built up by two applications of the solution.

Phosphoric acid is generally used; it releases the arabic acid in gum arabic and the carboxymethyl cellulose from its sodium salt. When the acid attacks aluminium an orthophosphate of aluminium is formed and on zinc, zinc phosphate. If an acid like hydrochloric is used the reaction forms zinc chloride which is water-soluble. This is removed into the dilute hydrochloric acid solution, leaving the surface free for further attack until all the acid is exhausted. The phosphate formed combines with the metal to produce an inert layer on the metal surface.

Sometimes etch solutions are used which are called non-corrosive, often referred to as salt etch, a typical one for zinc or aluminium being: ammonium dihydrogen phosphate ($2\frac{1}{2}$ oz), ammonium nitrate ($2\frac{1}{2}$ oz), water to 100 oz. A more corrosive etch solution consists of: water (7 oz), phosphoric acid 85% (1 oz), ammonium dihydrogen phosphate (1 oz), ammonium nitrate ($1\frac{1}{2}$ oz), gum arabic (14 Bé) to make 80 oz. A suitable cellulose gum etch contains: phosphoric acid 85% ($\frac{3}{4}$ oz), magnesium nitrate (1 oz), cellulose gum (4 oz), water to 80 oz. For aluminium a simple phosphoric acid-gum etch is satisfactory, such as the G.A.T.F. formula of gum arabic 14 Bé solution (80 oz), phosphoric acid 85%

(2½ oz). For gumming any of the above can be used, the gum arabic–phosphoric acid being satisfactory for both zinc and aluminium, or a plain gum arabic solution can be used, about 12° Bé being satisfactory. The final gum layer should be thin, otherwise there is the danger that a thick gum arabic layer may crack when dry.

When the plate is on the press and for any reason the printing must be stopped for a considerable period such as a meal break, it is usual to put the plate under gum. Before stopping the press allow the plate two or three revolutions without paper then a further two or three with the dampeners off. Powder the image with equal parts rosin and french chalk, then apply a plate gumming solution rubbing out to produce a thin gum layer, a suitable solution being: gum arabic 12° Bé (80 oz), phosphoric acid 85% (⅔ oz), phenol (¼ oz). The phenol (carbolic acid) is used as a preservative.

At the end of a run when the plate is to be removed from the machine the same technique is followed except that when the gum has dried down the ink is removed with turpentine or a wash-out solution, such as Lithotine. Asphaltum is applied, rubbed out smooth and dried. The asphaltum is usually bought from a supply house but can be made from: asphaltum powder (2 oz), beeswax (½ oz), tallow (½ oz), benzine (2 oz), turpentine (10 oz) and oil of lavender (1 oz).

THE OFFSET BLANKET AND ROLLERS

THE PURPOSE of the blanket is to transfer the ink from the printing plate to the paper. This has to be carried out without any noticeable distortion of the image, either in size or quality. The blanket has to continue to do this over a large number of impressions without damage to the plate and with no change to itself owing to the ink, water, or paper. Development work to the fabric backing, the bonding agents, and the rubber surface has enabled the manufacturers to make offset blankets that are tailored to the requirements of all branches of lithography.

The fabric backing is built up from three, four or five layers of material. This is to enable the backing to be sufficiently strong and stretch resistant without the use of one layer of a coarse fabric. The fine cotton fabric is pre-stretched to remove some of the stresses in it from the spinning and weaving, when the required number of layers of fabric can be bonded together to produce the flexible backing which will fit well on the cylinder. The adhesives have to be such that there is no chance of the bonding parting however arduous the service conditions. At this stage the backing has to be even thickness so that the accuracy of gauge can be achieved which is required of a good blanket.

The surface coating is applied in numerous thin layers by means of an accurately set steel blade. The roll of material is then hung to allow the solvents to evaporate before vulcanising, a process which, by control of temperature and duration, influences the final type of product. The surface coating is made up from a mixture of natural and synthetic rubbers, with the inclusion of the synthetic rubbers greatly improving the surface coatings. Butane, of the acrylo-nitrile type for example, has low oil absorbency, as has Neoprene; this reduces the chances of the blanket swelling. Butane has less resilience than natural rubber but by judicious selection of natural and synthetic elastomers the 'rubber' can be tailored to almost all requirements. Plasticisers and stabilising materials are incorporated in the mix as well as pigment. Pigments can also

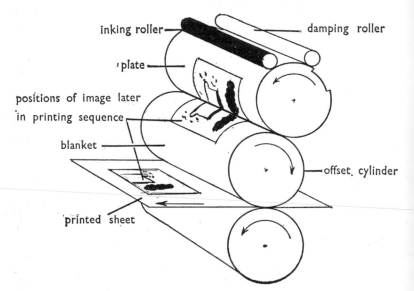

inking roller
damping roller
plate
positions of image later in printing sequence
blanket
offset cylinder
printed sheet

Fig. 77 Offset printing principle

act as a filling and toughening agent in addition to the function of identification by colour. Colour can vary from black to light cream. Carbon black, a common black pigment, gives toughness to rubber but black is not a popular colour owing to the difficulty of seeing the impression during the printing of dark colours. Manufacturers use the colour to identify their range of blankets or even grade within a range. Red, grey, green or brown have no particular significance except that a certain red, for example, is an identification for a particular type and make of blanket. The grades of blanket within a range include such things as hardness. Hard blankets are changed for tin and carton printing to soft ones for a quick start to printing. This is due to the soft resilient surface having a greater affinity for ink than a harder one. The degree of affinity to ink is a function of the blanket hardness and surface. The fine matt surface of a blanket can be damaged by careless handling in use, the surface becoming glazed and of low ink affinity and at the other extreme being softened and made tacky. These conditions are brought about by the use of the wrong solvents, driers, ink vehicle or improper cleaning. Solvents that cause trouble include turpentine, benzol, toluene, and carbon tetrachloride. Cobalt driers are harmful, paste driers on the other hand are comparatively harmless.

The thickness of the blanket has to be suitable for the machine. Some machines are designed for use with one blanket and some have sufficient cut-out for two. Originally one blanket was used, but later the use of two became a more or less standard practice, the under blanket being a semi-permanent one, though replaceable paper or manila packing can be used instead. A single blanket of considerable thickness has to be under greater tension than a thin one, for in order to tension the back correctly, the front has to be stretched even further so that it is under a much greater tension.

The effective thickness of a blanket on the press is very important. Off the press difficulty arises in measuring the effective thickness owing to the fact that the thickness of a blanket will vary according to the amount of tension it is under, plus the natural resilience of the material which makes the simple micrometer unreliable. Instruments have been designed to measure the thickness, though to measure a blanket under tension presents practical difficulties. The method is to use a compressive load to simulate the effect of tension on the blanket. As applies with printing pressure the thickness of the blanket under printing conditions is then known, so that packing can be arranged to give the correct blanket height on the cylinder of the printing machine. The improvements in manufacturing techniques have lessened the frequency of low spots in the blanket but when these are encountered the low areas have to be eliminated by thin tissue applied locally on the underside of the blanket.

The normal type of 'rubber' used in blankets, whilst waterproof in itself, is still 'wettable' by water. This means that water is also transferred to the paper from the plate and this loss has then to be replaced by the damping system. The addition of silicons to the rubber reduces the amount of water transfer, the water shedding property varying between different types of blanket. The transfer of much water to the paper can cause difficulty in the drying of the ink, this being particularly noticeable when the fountain acidity is high or when certain salts have been added to the solution.

The damping rollers are part of the system whereby the correct amount of water is applied to the plate. The maintenance of the system in a clean and good condition is an essential if printing is to be carried out in an economic manner. The usual damping system consists of two cloth-covered plate dampers that contact the surface lightly and so feed the moisture to the plate. These rollers receive their moisture from a power-driven metal roller which in turn obtains its moisture from a cloth-covered oscillating roller. This last roller is intermittently in contact with a metal roller that revolves in the fountain solution. The amount of dwell between these two rollers is adjustable, controlling the quantity of water transmitted down the train of rollers to the plate. A variation to this arrangement is for the speed of rotation of the fountain roller to be altered for water adjustment.

The plate or form rollers are covered with material which can act as a moisture retainer or reservoir and to feed this moisture to the plate surface. The more usual material is a cotton cloth supplied in various textures and either used in the form of a tubular knitted fabric or in the flat. The tubular material has to be worked on to the roller stock, but material in the flat has to be cut to size and sewn on to the roller so as to leave no raised seam. Rubber-covered roller stock requires only the cotton outer cover but because this does not always give sufficiently even damping, particularly on stop and start conditions, an undercover material of flannel is applied. On steel stock two flannel undercovers are sewn on, particular care being taken to measure the circumference at each layer so that the covers will fit snugly when sewn.

Paper-covered dampers can be used on a soft rubber-covered stock, the relative cheapness of paper being attractive. This type of cover is wound round the roller in a spiral manner and, in the same direction as the roller normally rotates. The thin paper cover lacks the water reservoir quality of the more conventional roller covering and therefore requires more care when the press is stopped and started, and the roller dries out rapidly when the press is stationary. A minor advantage is that the plate responds more quickly to changes in the adjustment of the fountain feed. The Shore hardness of the rubber stock should be between 8 to 16.

The damping rollers, being in contact with the litho printing plate just before the image is re-inked, sometimes become contaminated with traces of the residual ink that is still on the plate from the previous inking. This ink film on the damping system needs to be removed from time to time if the rollers are to maintain their efficiency. There are two methods of doing this, washing the ink off when the rollers have been removed from the machine, or removing the ink whilst the rollers are on the press by an ink attractive scavenger roller. The latter method is to have a brass roller in the damping train, which unfortunately conflicts with the desired quality of the roller's water affinity. To avoid the necessity of using additional rollers above and outside the moisture transfer chain to the damping rollers, a spiralled chromium-brass roller has been suggested. This is the Coates Spiralchrome damping and scavenging roller, three-quarters of a brass roller being covered with chromium plate, the plating being spiralled like a barber's pole.

Small offset machines of the so-called office type dispense with the damping system as such and use the inking rollers to carry out both functions. Though this results in a lowering of the efficiency of the inking system, for the type of work usually carried out on the machines the system is perfectly adequate. This method is known as the fount system and consists of a reservoir containing an aqueous solution which is fed through the nip of a rubber-covered roller and the ink-carrying

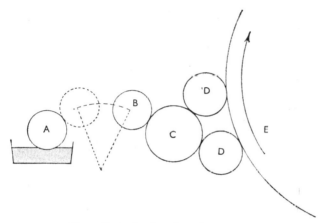

Fig. 78 Orthodox damping system

A, fountain roller; B, feed roller; C, distributing roller; D, plate dampers; E, plate cylinder.

roller. The latter makes contact with the inking train of rollers, the dwell between the two rollers and the inking rollers controlling the quantity of water travelling forward.

The inking rollers carry out the distribution of the ink from the ink duct to the printing surface. The ink reaches the plate surface from two or more forme rollers, which are steel shafted metal cores covered with a resilient rubbery material. The ink travels to the forme rollers through a series of rollers whose function is to distribute the ink evenly, which is done by sideway oscillation. The rollers are made of steel, copper or a suitable plastic, and in addition to providing a rapid replacement of ink to the forme rollers, the ink is broken down by its passage over the numerous rollers. The supply of ink is controlled from the ink duct by means of an alteration to the gap between the steel roller and a thin steel blade, which makes near contact with it. The ink supply can be changed

locally by adjustment to the gap between blade and roller. This adjustment is made by means of thumb screws which make the blade bear
more or less heavily on the roller. Overall control over the ink supply is
achieved by changing the dwell between the vibrator roller and the ink
duct. The design of the inking system varies between presses of dif-

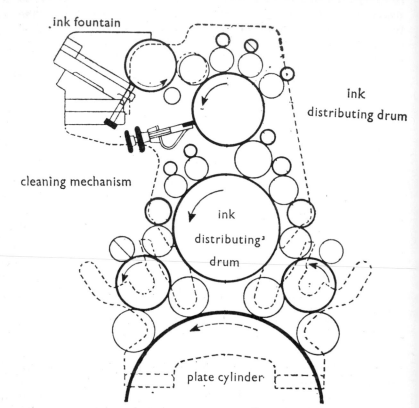

Fig. 79 Inking system on an offset press

ferent manufacture, the aim being to give good rolling power so that,
for example, large solid areas can be printed without loss of weight of
ink on subsequent sheets or between gripper and back edges of the same
sheet. In addition the ink should be broken down so as to feed quickly
and evenly to the forme rollers, without the need for more than a small
quantity of thinners being added to the ink.

The rollers which contact the plate are of rubber, vulcanised oil or
plastic. These materials are chosen because of their resistance to ink

and solvents. In addition these materials possess the qualities of the optimum resilience and ink affinity whilst still being relatively easy to clean. Steel rollers have two faults in litho printing, corrosion and failure to take ink, which is known as stripping. The moisture from the fountain solution causes the corrosion, whilst an excess acid solution or one containing too much gum desensitises the steel, resulting in its failure to accept ink. The lack of ink then allows further desensitisation, so the fault can be self-generating. Whilst control over the fountain solution can overcome both these problems, replacement of steel by another material can also be carried out. One alternative is the use of ebonite-covered steel rollers, another the employment of copper-plated steel. Both these materials have a greater ink affinity than steel.

Rubber rollers are built up on steel stocks, using thin sheets of oil-resistant synthetic rubber wrapped around the roller stock. Finally when the roller is a larger diameter than the required finished roller, the whole is bonded together by vulcanising. Afterwards the roller is ground true to size on a lathe, the final finish producing the required fine nap to the surface. Vulcanised oil rollers can be made so that a hard outer skin is formed over a softer body, the latter being nearer to the roller stock. The method of casting varies, one method being to use a cardboard liner in a steel tube. The assembly is spun on a lathe whilst a suitable polymerised dry oil is poured in. After this the steel stock is centred in the tube and further vulcanised oil is fed in to form the core. The finishing follows similar lines to that of rubber rollers, the cardboard outer casing being first stripped off.

Roller cleaning can be easily neglected, so that minute traces of ink that are not removed at wash-up gradually produce a glaze on the rubber or oil rollers. The press wash-up system is designed to clean the rollers and is satisfactory for colour changes. However, at fairly frequent intervals, a more thorough hand wash-up can be used to prevent the build-up of ink glaze which reduces ink affinity and lowers printing quality. During this hand wash attention must be given to the ends of the rollers where dried ink very quickly builds up. The automatic wash-up usually consists of a steel blade which is designed to remove from one of the steel rollers ink that has been diluted by solvent. Ink particles, by their very nature, are difficult to remove so that over the years the problem has received the attention of research institutes. One method of washing-up developed by research is the use of three solutions. The first solution floats the pigment particles from the rollers, leaving them suspended in the solution. The second solution removes the first solvent without destroying the suspension of the ink particles, and the third solution (isopropyl alcohol) is used for the final cleaning operation. This technique requires supplementation by hand cleaning to keep the rollers in really first rate condition.

OFFSET PRESS OPERATION

THE FINAL stage in the production of printed matter is the printing process itself. All the previous operations are processes preparatory to printing and constitute a means to that end. Although the plate itself is now ready for printing, the machine has to be prepared to perform its essential function of ensuring that the printed sheet exactly corresponds to the image on the plate. The methods of preparation for printing and the printing procedure differ in detail according to the make or age of the press and the ideas and experience of the operator. The essential requirement of the press operator is that he should be methodical in order that he will perform the various operations in a logical sequence. In addition, a good colour sense and a keen critical faculty are necessary so that he can examine the printed sheet and assess it for print quality, colour, register image fit, drying, etc.

The preparation for printing can include those items of preventive maintenance which bear more directly on printing, such as cleaning, lubrication and routine adjustment. It is important that the manufacturers' handbook should be consulted for information concerning lubrication. Modern machinery has many components – gears for example – which require special lubricants, such as extreme pressure oils which are designed to withstand the high pressures generated between the gear teeth. In the matter of lubrication it should be remembered that to ensure long, trouble-free running of modern high-performance machinery the correct oils and greases are of primary importance. The choice of lubricant based only on price is a short-lived economy because, with many other faults, cheap oil may have low film strength. The lubrication of the press can be divided into daily, weekly or monthly periods, or upon a system based on the number of sheets printed. Whichever method is followed, old oil or grease should be removed together with any excess from the present lubrication cycle, as dirt together with paper lint and coatings form abrasives which induce serious wear on moving parts. This lubrication should not be carried out when a press is running because not only is this dangerous but many lubrication points are in positions where it is not possible to reach when the press is in operation.

Dirt in any form is inadmissible on a printing machine. The ink fountain must be kept free of dirty ink because rollers can be damaged by dried ink particles and these may also cause faulty fountain blade adjustment. To prevent this happening it is necessary to dismantle and clean all the ink mechanism from time to time. This cleaning should also include inspection of the inking rollers, hand cleaning of the ends, and a close check of the surface for any traces of glazing. The water fountain must be checked and also the rollers for loose, worn or uneven covering and the whole for accumulation of dirt and ink. When this occurs the rollers and fountain need cleaning and the frequency with which this is necessary depends on the type of ink and work involved.

The cylinders of the press have to be inspected and cleaned from time to time. Slight amounts of corrosion or dirt can seriously affect printing quality, owing to dirt or moisture being allowed to accumulate under the blanket covering. If the press has bearers these too will require to be kept clean. In addition, the feeding and registering mechanism will require some attention, for here dirt soon builds up to cause faulty functioning of this important part of the press. The dirt comes from such sources as paper fluff and can soon make difficulties in register. The air lines for the vacuum system of lifting the sheets also accumulate dirt which, if not eradicated, will result in inefficient working of this portion of the press.

With the dampening and inking systems cleaned and ready for another job the blanket system of the press must be inspected. The pressure imposed upon the paper being printed is very important as, amongst other things, it can cause the paper to lengthen under printing and partial contraction of the paper afterwards causes the image to shorten. Changes in print length may be required to make an impression fit other printing, or for the impression to match exactly the original image. The usual method of making these changes is in the packing of the plate and blanket cylinders.

Printing press design is such that the machine may or may not employ bearers, depending on the ideas of the manufacturer. The plate cylinder and the offset blanket cylinder have a space machined out of each cylinder which is designed to accommodate the plate and, in the case of the offset cylinder, the space may be greater in order to receive the offset blanket. In a simple example the plate cylinder may be designed to take a plate of 22 g. or 0·028 in. whilst the blanket cylinder may take one or two offset blankets to a total thickness of 0·070 in. From this it is presumed that as the two cylinders are driven together the ink would transfer from plate image to blanket, but without some pressure being available the ink will not be transferred. The pressure can be increased to any desired amount if packing is inserted under either the plate or the offset blanket. The pressure could be so great that the cylinders themselves would be forced apart and to avoid this some datum position has to be taken. When the press is first erected, and afterwards at suitable intervals, the pressure with which the bearers are pressed together is set. The lock nuts and adjusting screws are released in order that, for example, a 0·006 in. feeler can just be inserted between the bearers on both sides of the cylinders. The 0·006-in. feelers are now replaced with 0·003-in. feelers, after which the adjusting screws are tightened to give the same light pull on the feelers as before. The number of turns the adjustment screws are moved to accomplish this are noted and it is a simple matter to rotate the adjusting screws the same number of turns again to bring the bearers into perfect contact. The accuracy of the setting can be checked by putting spots of ink on to the clean bearers so that a few rotations of the press will show if the setting is even by means of the ink transfer between the metal surfaces. The press is then set to ride on the bearers by means of a slight further increase in the adjusting screw pressure so that the ink dabs transfer well from bearer to bearer. Alternatively, if the adjusting screws are moved to give an additional

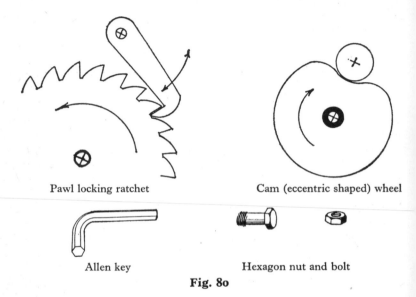

Pawl locking ratchet   Cam (eccentric shaped) wheel

Allen key   Hexagon nut and bolt

Fig. 80

0·003 in. with the bearers just in contact, this would assure that they would be under 0·003 in. pressure.

The plate can, if required, be packed to bring the surface level with the bearers. This packing is arranged by the insertion of relatively incompressible material under the plate, which can be hard manila or super-calendered paper. The amount of packing can be calculated if the cylinder cut-out is known and an ordinary hand micrometer used to measure the plate thickness. The packing of the offset blanket cylinder is not as simple as for the plate cylinder. The main difference is that the blanket is, to a certain degree, compressible. Measurement of the blanket thickness has to be made by an instrument which subjects the blanket to a certain or fixed amount of compression. If this is not possible, then any packing material put under the blanket to produce a good impression will have to be found by trial – which wastes valuable time.

For printing purposes the offset blanket is arranged to give between 0·002 in. to 0·004 in. pressure, which means that the offset blanket should be packed to bring it 0·002 in. to 0·004 in. above the bearers. This amount of over-packing varies according to the blanket, soft blankets requiring less over-packing than hard blankets. Another factor is that smooth (grainless) plates require less pressure than grained plates. The design of the press also influences the packing required and a lack of rigidity shows itself in the need to set more pressure when the machine is static, to allow for the elasticity under impression.

The actual fitting of plates, and when necessary new offset blankets, is a matter of care. Machines vary in the method of fitting a plate or blanket in that the plate or blanket can fit directly or some form of clamp is first used. In whatever detail the design of press varies, the main point is that both plate and blanket have to be under even tension. Excessive force must be avoided if the plates are not to be stretched or cracked, or the blankets strained.

The impression cylinder does not ride on bearers. This is to allow variation between impression and blanket cylinders in order to accommodate stocks of different thickness. The same rule applies to impression cylinder pressure as applies to all other pressure in printing, that is, as little as possible consistent with obtaining a good impression. Excessive pressure will always cause above-average wear. The pressure at the impression cylinder will need to be varied according to the paper surface and the hardness of the offset blanket. Any excessive pressure is likely to show in such faults as stretched paper and, on smooth paper, by slurred impression, which will also be evident on the offset blanket. This is a condition which can eventually reach the plate and will sensitise the plate causing scummed areas on the plate itself. Pressure adjustment of impression is by some form of screw mechanism because the majority of presses do not use any covering in the form of a blanket on the impression cylinder. Machines that use a blanket-covered impression cylinder require a hard blanket which is very much harder than the offset blanket.

FLAT-BED PRESSES

THE MAKES and types of press now used for offset lithography are legion and it is beyond the scope of this book to go into the details of them. The proof press is the most simple type of offset machine, though even here one line of thought is to have a press which is as automatic as possible. The essentials of a proof press are two flat tables, one to hold the plate, the other to hold the paper and also form an impression slab. An offset cylinder rotates across the dampened and inked plate, taking up the image and, as the cylinder rotates, further transferring the ink to the paper. In this type of press both the dampening and inking is by hand – which can result in many variations in, for instance, colour proofing. To avoid this, as mentioned later, the modern proof press has automatic dampening by rollers, as applies with a production press, and an inking system which allows a consistent ink film thickness to be maintained.

The three essentials in a good proof are exact reproduction of the dot size (sharpness), correct overall values of individual colours, and a perfectly flat pull obtained naturally. Incorrect dot reproduction can usually be traced to bad settings of the press. A reduced dot (oversharp) must not be confused with sharpness, which infers the correct transposition of dot size. A squashed dot can be caused by over-inking, over-pressure

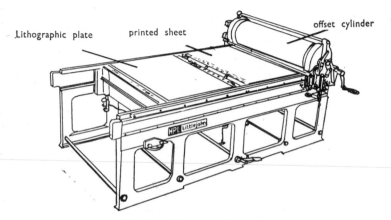

Lithographic plate   printed sheet   offset cylinder

Fig. 81 Offset proofing press

between plate and blanket, or a slack blanket. A weak dot is the result of lack of inking or pressure which simulates a flat effect. In general flat-bed proofs have a tendency to appear flat.

Over fifty litho proof press models and sizes are available in Britain at the present time. The carriage motion is the heart of the machine, controlling the precise relationship between the cylinder and the beds, and it must move smoothly and easily. Bearers should be wide, gear tracks ground and polished. The press is actually a simple transfer press, one bed for the plate, one for paper on which the image is to be transferred. The beds must be level to the cylinder to a very fine degree of pressure, adjustable to allow for different plate and paper thickness without any trouble. The control for register is located on the second bed and the lays should be simple and exact, with micrometer setting and quick locking.

The majority of flat-bed offset presses ink on both the up and down

stroke and the use of two plate rollers is considered to give an approximation in result matching the offset printing machines' four-roller inking
from one stroke. Some proof presses are equipped with three plate
rollers inking normally on one pass only, with the advantages claimed
that one rolling with three rollers is a far closer match with the production machine operation and reduces the likelihood of repeats.

The traditional method of damping with a sponge is being superseded.
The older method of a damping pad acting as a small reservoir to keep
the rollers reasonably damp, plus a water feed from a trough, has been
replaced. The pad is now used to receive excess moisture and the water
trough has a constant rotating roller, with a nipping roller to control the
supply, and from this the dampers pick up water. Mechanical damping
does away with the human element, and apart from saving time, ensures
controlled damping as applies with offset litho production machines.
Some litho proof presses are now fitted with automatic sheet delivery.

SINGLE-COLOUR MACHINES

ALTHOUGH A number of manufacturers no longer make single-
colour offset machines, there are still many in use in the industry. Most
machines are similar in design, the plate cylinder, in general, being
mounted above the blanket cylinder with the impression cylinder behind
and slightly below the blanket cylinder. The illustration shows an alternative arrangement. Perfecting machines, used a great deal for book production from film settings, operate on the blanket-to-blanket principle.

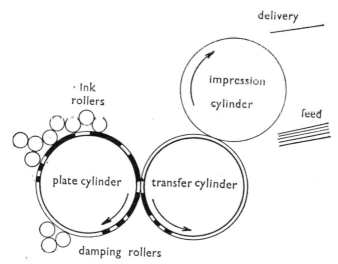

Fig. 82 Principle of single-colour offset machine

The sheet to be printed is conveyed between the two blanket cylinders, the upper cylinder having grippers to hold the sheet, so that each blanket cylinder operates as an impression cylinder to the other.

Small Offset Machines

ONE AREA where single-colour machines still retain all their appeal is in the so-called small offset field. These machines, generally of smaller sheet size, were at first treated as a form of office duplicator. Now that the limitation and potential of the machines are understood many large printers use the machines for black-and-white line work and type reproduction, especially where repeat orders are likely and runs are not large. Speed of printing can be up to 5000 sheets per hour and sizes include 11 in. $\times$ 14 in., 15 in. $\times$ 20 in. up to a plate size of $18\frac{3}{4}$ in. $\times$ 24 in. In order to increase the range of work that can be undertaken by these presses some manufacturers have made available additional roller attachments to increase the rolling power of the equipment. This improves the ink coverage over the whole of the printed image. Plates are usually thin gauge aluminium with holes or loops on the clamping edge, which means that they can be fitted to the cylinder in a few seconds.

TWO-COLOUR MACHINES

THE WIDE use of lithography for colour work has resulted in the development of two-colour machines, which usually follow the lines of the manufacturers' single-colour presses. Some machine makers simply couple two single-colour presses together in tandem, whilst others arrange the colour units vertically above each other, or even invert the top unit in an endeavour to improve ease of operation. Two-colour machines go up to paper sizes of 43 in. $\times$ 63 in. with running speeds of up to 5000 sheets per hour. With smaller sheet sizes, for instance double demy $25\frac{1}{2}$ in. $\times$ $37\frac{1}{2}$ in., the running speed may reach 10,000 sheets per hour.

The demand for colour, especially four-colour halftone work, either for catalogue or carton use, has brought about the development of four- and six-colour machines. These machines are generally four single colour units coupled together, or two or three two-colour presses in tandem. The technical difficulties of designing these presses seem to have been overcome, for instance, one detail which requires both skill in design and manufacture is the sheet grip mechanism. This can be appreciated when it is realised that on a multi-colour press, built on the unit principle, the sheet may have to be transferred between as many as eight different gripper mechanisms between the feed pile and delivery.

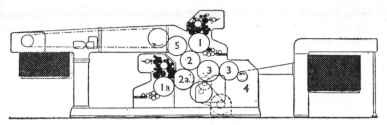

Fig. 83A Crabtree Ambassador offset perfector press

1 Plate cylinders; 2 blanket cylinder; 3 transfer cylinders; 4 feed gripper; 5 chain delivery grippers.

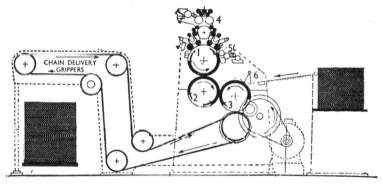

Fig. 83B Mann Fast Three rotary offset machine

1 Plate cylinder; 2 blanket cylinder; 3 impression cylinder; 4 inking system; 5 damping system; 6 swing grippers.

WEB OFFSET

THE SEARCH for higher output at lower cost and the need to meet the requirement of newspaper production have seen the development of the web offset press. Here the paper, in a continuous roll, is fed into the machine. At the delivery end the paper can be either cut into sheets or re-reeled for finishing elsewhere. The web offset press can be a single-colour machine printing on both sides of the paper at once for newspaper production. To this another web offset press may be coupled, which is a four-colour machine to supply colour covers and inside centre pages. The design of the colour press may be of the unit type or it may have the four colour units arranged round a common impression cylinder. When web offset is used on newspaper work ink drying is not a serious problem, the stock being sufficiently absorbent to allow the ink to be handled immediately after printing. When glazed or coated stock is used, however, the press has to have a drying unit coupled to it. This is generally gas-heated, the interior temperature automatically rising as the speed of printing increases. Rapid cut-off of the heat has to be arranged, because a sudden loss of running speed would result in the paper bursting into flames in the dryer. One limitation of the web offset press is that the cut-off or circumference of the printing surface cannot be changed so that if a press has a $22\frac{3}{4}$-in. cylinder circumference then work must be arranged to suit this, or a suitable sub-division. For example, the page size could be $22\frac{3}{4}$ in., $11\frac{3}{8}$ in., or $5\frac{11}{16}$ in. but not 21 in., 10 in. or 4 in. It is realised that the latter could only be done if the paper was trimmed to waste off the printed pages.

Web offset can be defined as a method of lithographic printing in which the machine is able to print one or more colours on one or both sides of a web of paper in a single operation, converting the product, at least in part, to its finished state. It has been estimated that there are about a thousand web-fed offset machines, engaged in newspaper, magazine and book work, in use throughout the world. The principle of web printing is not new, the firm of Vomag in Plauen, East Germany, having marketed web offset machinery in the early 1920's and Fritz Wolff is recognised as the initiator of this method of printing. There are two basic types of web offset machinery, blanket-to-steel and blanket-to-blanket, which can be defined as the three- and four-cylinder systems respectively. The three-cylinder blanket-to-steel is the traditional offset system where the web passes between the blanket and impression cylinders to receive a print on one side of the paper only. For multi-colour work a succession of three such cylinder units (open units) are used, or alternatively a large common impression cylinder around which several colours are grouped. Then several colours are printed on one side of the web, the web moving round the large central cylinder taking its colour successively from the smaller blanket cylinders ranged round it. Maintenance of register is good, and if both sides of the web are to be printed, the paper is taken round another impression cylinder with the blanket cylinders similarly ranged round it. The main disadvantage is a lack of accessibility.

Perfecting

THE FOUR-CYLINDER blanket-to-blanket system of unit constructed press is in demand because it is a much more compact and versatile method. It operates by 'perfecting' which means printing on either side simultaneously with the blanket cylinders running together with the web in between and each one provides the impression cylinder for the other. Thus two plate cylinders transfer their images to two blanket cylinders with the paper passing between these two cylinders so that each blanket cylinder, as stated, acts as an impression cylinder to the other. Second and further colours are added at the next unit, and since the printing is on a web and not a sheet of paper, there is no need for transfer grippers, etc., with the web passing from the first couple to the next and on to the third, if required.

The advantages of web offset over sheet-fed litho are that output is three to four times faster, plates are cheaper, and a wider range of papers – from imitation Bible papers to coated and uncoated stock – can be printed. In newspaper printing the latitude of the offset blanket gives greater freedom from speckle than does rotary letterpress and a more even print is obtained. This improved coverage with better-class inks gives denser blacks. For news work, often the use of 100–110 screens is preferred to 120–133 screens to avoid the possibility of the filling-in of halftone detail. Folding, punching or perforating can be combined in one machine and completed in one movement through the machine. Roll paper is cheaper than sheet paper and reel-fed machines use less ink and less water so that cheaper paper can be used. Also smaller floor space and less power are required for printing and, it is claimed, make-ready time is reduced.

SHEET-FED AND REEL-FED MACHINES

IF THE principles of the sheet-fed offset machine are understood, there is no difficulty in following the principles of the reel-fed press. The web of paper replaces the sheet and in place of the sheet feeder the web is drawn into the machine by measuring rollers which guarantee the correct food of paper into the machine at each succeeding revolution of the cylinders. Various tensioning devices are incorporated so that the web stays taut and with uniform tightness whilst running through the machine. Register rollers, to lengthen or shorten the paper between units, are incorporated, so that without moving the plate the paper can be retarded or advanced to bring colours into register.

There is a high wastage factor which can outweigh the advantage of speed on short-run work so that less than 50,000 copies is uneconomical. Unlike sheet-fed work the product cannot be re-run through the machine to add further work and, as previously stated, the printed length is restricted to the circumference of the cylinders whereas the sheet-fed machine will accommodate any odd size of working.

XVI

Ink and Paper

PRINTING INKS

PRINTING INK, the medium by which the results of mental processes and effort can be duplicated visibly, was first used by the Chinese, who discovered paper between A.D. 100–200. The basic ingredients were essentially soot in natural gums and oils, applied with a bamboo tube and later a brush. The inks of Gutenberg (A.D. 1450) differed very little in essential constituents, consisting of bodied linseed oils (70%), carbon from oil, bones and vegetable matter (30%). Modern ink formulations contain all or some of the following components – pigment (to give colour); vehicle (to ensure transfer of ink to paper); thinner (to assist working on the machine); drier (to enable drying of the print); anti-drier (to control drying rate on the machine); modifier (to give properties in the print other than colour properties).

The pigments are usually finely divided solids, also dyes and their inclusion in the ink affects the colour, opacity, gloss, working properties, consistency, penetration and light resistance. The vehicle carries the pigment on the ink-transferring areas of the machine and affects the consistency, transfer, penetration, colour, hardness, gloss, resistance, setting, drying, life and working on the machine of the ink. The thinners, usually separated from the vehicle, influence consistency, working, penetration, gloss, drying and setting. The driers quicken hardening in oxidative inks and are the solvents to control the rate of drying in gravure inks. Anti-driers retard drying on the machine and modifiers such as waxes and oils control setting, flow, consistency, gloss and rub-resistance.

The basic ingredients are pigments and vehicles and once the mixture, in the form of a viscous liquid, has been transferred to the printing stock, the image must be made permanent by drying the ink. Thus driers are added to speed up solidification of the ink film, plus other additives to meet special requirements.

Pigment

PIGMENT IS the solid matter in ink visibly recognisable as colour, black, white or grey. The pigment is discernible on the printed sheet but the

vehicle is near transparent and not visible. Pigments are mainly inorganic and organic. Inorganic pigments are the naturally occurring
pigments or earth colours which together with manufactured pigments,
achieved by the chemical reaction between two or more water-soluble
substances, form a coloured precipitate that is insoluble in water. Because
they are abrasive and difficult to work very few naturally occurring pigments are used today. Pigments produced by precipitation (chrome
yellow, cadmium red, bronze and prussian blues and whites) are in
limited use – such organic pigments being used more in paint making
than in printing. They are low in cost but tend to be coarse. William
Perkin (1856), a chemistry student, discovered the first synthetic dye-
stuff, thus introducing organic pigments which are now widely used in
printing ink manufacture. They are mostly derived from chemicals extracted from coal tar and most hues of the visible spectrum can be
matched by these dye-stuff pigments.

Vehicle

THE CHOICE of vehicle or carrier for pigment depends on several factors,
including the speed at which the ink film is required to dry. The
methods by which the liquid ink solidifies or dries are as follows:
(a) *Oxidation:* in which the vehicle absorbs moisture from the air,
changing from liquid to solid. This is speeded-up by the addition of
driers. (b) *Absorption:* which refers to the penetration of a thin fluid
vehicle into soft absorbent paper, with the thin film of pigment left on the
surface of the paper. (c) *Evaporation:* which means that the vehicle or
solvent evaporates quickly into a gas, owing to using substances which
have a very low boiling point, or by applying mild heat to the ink film
after printing. (d) *Precipitation:* which is the method used in moisture-
setting and wax-setting pigments where glycol type solvents and suitable resins in the ink react with any moisture causing the resins binding
the colouring matter to be separated on to the paper so that the moisture
and solvent are absorbed by the stock.

The vehicle carrying the pigment and binding it to the printing stock
is generally responsible for controlling the feeding, distribution, transfer and coverage of ink, also the method by which it dries. These
vehicles consist mainly of drying oils, such as linseed, heated for different periods and varying temperatures to give different varnish con-
sistencies, which are given number oo–10 to indicate viscosity. Petro-
leum, resin and castor oil are the absorption oils used in the ink vehicle
for printing on soft absorbent papers. Oils such as china wood oil, fish
oil and cotton seed are used for special purposes.

Synthetic resins have, in recent years, replaced the drying oils, or are
combined with them to give a more uniform product which acts and

dries faster. Another vehicle consists of a resin-solvent combination which causes the ink to dry, partly by penetration and partly by evaporation, without the use of driers. This type of vehicle or solvent is used mostly for photogravure and flexographic printing and employs either hydrocarbons (benzene and toluene), alcohol (methyl alcohol), acetone or amyl acetate. They possess a low boiling point and thus speedily evaporate, but their flash point is low and they constitute a health danger and a fire hazard and the vaporised solvents should be drawn off by extraction ducts.

Driers

THESE ARE added to printing inks to assist oxidation drying. The small amount of drier within the ink acts as a catalyst, assisting chemical change without altering itself. In the initial stages of drying the drier acts as a carrier of oxygen to the vehicle. In the latter stages of drying, the drier or catalyst helps in the polymerisation of the ink film, in that it assists the molecules to join up with each other, resulting in solidification of the printing ink. Most driers are compounds of cobalt, manganese and lead and are known as 'soaps' which are soluble in the various vehicles with resinates, linoleates and naphthenates. Cobalt is the strongest drier, drying the ink film rapidly from the surface down. In some instances, however, it gives the dried ink film a hard unresilient surface (termed crystallised), causing difficulty when overprinting succeeding colours. Manganese has a much slower drying action but the surface of the ink film is left more open, which enables better superimposition of succeeding colours. Lead is efficient but dries slowly and is seldom used, chiefly because of its harmful effect in the form of lead poisoning.

Drier action is increased with increasing temperature, thus inks dry faster in hot weather than in cold weather. Relative humidity affects the drying time of printing pigments, too high a R.H. value will increase drying troubles. Speed of drying is also affected by the pH of the paper coating; as the pH decreases and acidity increases drying time is lengthened.

Lithographic and letterpress printing pigments have much in common, with the exception that letterpress inks can be of a much thinner nature and moisture set inks are limited to the letterpress process. Gravure inks are different in make-up, being very fluid, finely ground, non-greasy and drying mainly by evaporation. The majority of letterpress and litho inks dry by oxidation and polymerisation and absorption.

The film of ink printed lithographically is normally only one-third the thickness of ink deposited by letterpress printing. Thus it is essential that litho pigments have first-rate colour strength. They must also be of a more greasy nature to carry out satisfactorily the lithographic principle. It follows that resistance to water, to prevent the ink 'bleeding' into the fountain solution (causing emulsification), must be strong. Inks for offset printing must have considerable 'tack' or stickiness in order to give clean, sharp impressions without filling-in on the press run. The requirements of modern lithography require the production of inks which are probably more exacting than many other printing processes. They must be highly pigmented, hydrophobic and capable of a rate of drying to suit the type of machine and paper.

Inorganic pigments formed by precipitation include white pigments to form extenders to control the saturation of a hue, and they vary between being fully transparent to being completely opaque. Alumina hydrate is a transparent and good working extender, whilst titanium dioxide, a very popular pigment, is opaque. Barium sulphate by itself has poor working qualities, but co-precipitated with alumina hydrate it forms a first-rate gloss white. Black pigments are derived from carbon black, which is a product of the burning of crude mineral oil or the gas from the same under restricted amounts of air. The soot formed is collected and the slightly brown colour modified by the addition of pigments such as Prussian blue.

The ink has to accommodate many different operating conditions, both in type of press, paper surface and running speed. To accomplish this compounds of metallic soaps, greases or waxes are added. By shortening the ink, that is reducing the distance the ink can be pulled without breaking, they reduce its tack. Ink of low tack fills in shadow areas more readily, whilst high tack may pull the surface of a coated paper, if the separation is quick as applies on a fast-running machine. Ink colour for multi-colour halftone work now follows the British Standards Institute recommendation, and inks made to these standards represent the best compromise of fade resistance, cost, ease of working, etc. For certain classes of work, such as showcard printing, flat tints are usually obtained by special ink mixing to produce the desired effect.

A vast amount of research has been, and is being, carried out on the effects of ink on paper and in the way it dries and behaves afterwards. For industrial purposes it has been found that an actual printing test is the solution for unusual ink–paper combinations. The P.A.T.R.A. test bench has been designed to enable these and other tests to be carried out in conjunction with general printing operations. Where practical experience is limited or a test bench not available, the ink manufacturer should be consulted on the choice of an ink to give the optimum ink–paper relationship.

TRANSFER OF INK TO PAPER

THE PRINCIPAL factor affecting the transfer of ink to paper is concerned with the smoothness of the paper surface under the conditions of printing. A smooth paper transfers more ink than a rougher surfaced paper. Increasing pressure aids the transfer of ink to paper, increasing speed of printing decreases the transfer and decreasing the viscosity of the ink medium also increases the transfer.

The distribution of ink over the roller resulting in the partition of the ink between plate and paper involves a series of splitting operations, the forces of which can be measured by an Inkometer. The main force in ink splitting is not ink viscosity but tack, subsidiary factors being speed, temperature and film thickness. Where ink tack is greater than the forces holding the paper together, picking will result. This is best defined for a given paper and ink by the speed at which it occurs.

The thickness of the ink film transferred to paper is about 0·0001 in. to 0·0002 in., with only the liquid ink vehicle absorbed into the pores of the paper. The penetration possibly equals the ink-film thickness which averages about one twenty-fifth of the paper thickness. Excess moisture, insufficient driers in the ink, excess acid in the paper and fountain solution and resistance of the paper are factors which interfere with satisfactory ink drying qualities on paper.

In general, papers with pH values between 4·5 and 5·5, which are slightly acid, do not cause scumming owing to counter-etching trouble. This acidity in uncoated paper can be traced to aluminium sulphate, which is added in the beater or hydrapulper during paper manufacture to precipitate the rosin size.

PAPER FOR PRINTING

THE BEST ink and machines are of no avail without good paper, which affects the result with regard to its colour, smoothness and absorbency. Basic requirements are that the paper should have a smooth surface, softness, pick-resistance and freedom from fluff. It must absorb uniformly and quickly the setting part of the vehicle, retaining the gloss vehicle on the surface, and it should not interfere with the drying properties of the ink nor have too high a moisture content. The paper should also possess maximum whiteness and high reflectance properties. In general cast-coated papers show most of these properties although the filtration through the coating may seem very fierce compared with some of the cheaper grades of coated paper, and can result in chalking and a loss of gloss. This is because a more complete penetration by the vehicle leaves the pigment on the surface of the coating. The stock is made smooth by calendering and brush-coated paper is smoother than machine-coated (M.F.) paper.

The first paper mill in England is reputed to have been built at Stevenage in the middle of the fifteenth century. Several mills existed by the seventeenth century. Rags provided the fibrous raw material, the only machinery used being the water-mill which worked heavy hammers to pound the fibre, the rest of the operations being carried out by hand. In 1799 a Frenchman, Louis Robert, had an idea for a machine which would produce a continuous sheet of paper. It was not a commercial success, but a partnership of John Gamble (Robert's brother-in-law), Henry and Sealy Fourdrinier and the engineer Bryan Donkin resulted, in London in the year 1803, in Robert's idea becoming a practical proposition. Instead of single sheets of paper being made one by one in a hand mould, a continuous sheet of paper was formed on an endless wire cloth, after which it was pressed between rollers and reeled up in the wet state, to be subsequently unreeled, cut into sheets and dried in a loft, as was the custom. This basic design, known as the Fourdrinier type (although their main contribution to the machine was probably financial), has remained unchanged and continues today. In 1821

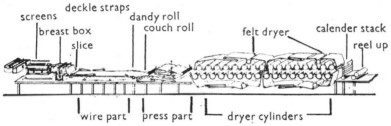

Fig. 84 Paper-making machine

Crompton took out a patent for a machine which would enable the sheet to be continuously dried by being passed over steam-heated cylinders. This technique again has remained unchanged.

Thus the basic paper machine, in which a very dilute suspension of fibres and water (known as slurry) is poured on to one end of a rapidly moving endless wire to be reeled up a few seconds later at the 'dry end' of the machine, after passing firstly through a simple press to remove the bulk of the water, and then over steam-heated drying cylinders which rotate at the same speed as the paper comes out of the press. On modern machines 250 tons a day at speeds of up to 2000 ft. per min. are produced. As soon as the sheet of water and fibres (slurry or stock) ($99\frac{1}{2}\%$ of water to $\frac{1}{2}\%$ of fibres) lands on the wire, the water starts to drain away, leaving a weak fibrous mat. To enable the very wet sheet of newly formed paper to be strong enough to support its own weight without tearing by the time it is pulled off the wire in a few seconds' time, suction is applied to the underside of the wire to assist drainage, bringing the moisture content down to about 80%. The sheet is then fed into the press section where giant presses with top rollers usually made of granite and the bottom ones of a rubber-covered steel shell, incorporating suction boxes, extract further moisture, so that the paper passes to the drying section with a moisture content of about 60%. Here up to 40 cast iron (hollow and polished) steam-heated drying cylinders, against which the paper is held by endless felts, reduce the moisture content to 6–10% and the paper is wound into reels which may be 10 ft. across and 3–4 ft. in diameter, before being slit into smaller reels.

CELLULOSE FIBRES

SCANDINAVIA AND Canada are the principal suppliers of paper pulp made from wood. All woods and grasses are largely composed of cellulose fibres, and provide the largest and cheapest source of organic polymer raw material, already in fibre form. These fibres are mostly between 1–4 mm. long and are separated by chemical or mechanical treatment. The fibres of straws, bamboos, sugar cane waste (bagasse) and palms can be used for paper-making, but about 90% of the fibrous raw material used is from wood, about three-quarters of it being new wood pulp and one-quarter waste paper. Of the remaining 10% about 1–2% is rags, and the rest is composed of pulps from straw, sugar cane waste, esparto grass and bamboo. Some high-strength, good quality paper is made from cotton and linen. Nearly 90% of the wood used is 70-year-old coniferous – spruces, firs and pines. Conifer fibres are relatively long, 2–4 mm., and have fairly thin walls arising from their low density. For many papers these characteristics are excellent, but for printing papers the shorter fibres of the broad-leaved woods (hardwoods) – poplar, sycamore, birch – plus straw and esparto grass, often with thicker walls, are also required. The resinous southern pines and the north-eastern hardwoods of the United States are now used for newsprint, previously the preserve of spruce and fir, and Australia has founded a paper industry based on the short-fibred eucalyptus tree. India and Pakistan have similar records of technological achievement with their indigenous bamboos, grasses and broad-leaved woods. Broad-leaf fibres average 1·2 mm.; coniferous 3·5 mm.; flax fibres 9 mm.

PAPER PULP PRODUCTION

IN TREES or in the stalks and leaves of straw and esparto grass the millions of fibres of which they are composed are rigidly held in place – pointing up and down the stem similar to matches packed in a box. The fibres themselves and the substance (lignin) which binds them contribute to the strength of the wood or straw stalks. The fibres must be loosened from one another before being reformed into paper. This is done either by pulping by mechanical means, whereby the fibrous material is ground or rubbed to pull the fibres apart, or 'cooked' by chemical methods using chemicals to dissolve the incrusting lignin to allow the fibres to fall apart. Individual fibres are composed of smaller units called fibrils which are similarly arranged and made from cellulose (carbon, hydrogen and oxygen). The exact arrangement of the cellulose molecule in the fibril characterises the plant and influences the paper quality.

About one-third is prepared mechanically by pressing bolts of barked wood against a revolving grindstone in the presence of water. Only wood is suitable for grinding, and the stone is a blend of an abrasive 'carborundum', grit and cement, about 5 ft. in diameter with a 4 ft. face. Two stones driven at approximately 300 r.p.m. by a 5000 h.p. motor can produce 70 tons of mechanical wood pulp (ground wood) per day. This can be drained off and pressed into wet pads (laps) and baled for transport to a paper mill. Woods, straw, bamboos and grasses can be prepared chemically. The wood must be first barked and then chipped into $\frac{1}{2}$–1 in. pieces, and straws are chopped and dusted before being 'cooked' for periods varying from $\frac{1}{2}$ to 16 hours at high temperatures under pressure with certain chemicals. Different processes use different chemicals caustic soda, sodium sulphide, sulphur dioxide, calcium bisulphite, sodium sulphite – to dissolve the incrusting lignin and disperse the fibres easily during washing operations. The pulp may be bleached with chlorine compounds, especially if required for printing.

Ground-wood (pulp) manufacture requires expensive and elaborate grinders, screens and refiners; chemical pulp manufacture needs powerful chippers for the logs, steel pressure vessels up to 15,000 cu. ft. in size, boilers, blow tanks, screens, and rotary filters, plus extensive storage and barking facilities. Paper pulp means the dry fibres themselves before they are further treated for paper-making and in Britain paper mills import most of the pulp used. A few mills in this country make pulp from waste paper by 'reslushing' and some make chemical pulp from esparto grass imported from North Africa, and also from a number of other materials – straw, rags, sisal (old ropes) – by pulping with caustic soda.

The advantage of chemical pulping over the grinding process is that individual fibres are undamaged and it is their length and strength which make them suitable for tougher paper. Often the two kinds of pulp are carefully mixed to produce particular papers. If the paper and pulp mills are close together, the liquid pulp is pumped direct to the paper mill. Otherwise, the pulp is partly dried, pressed into sheets for dispatch and when received at the paper mill reconverted into fluid form in hydrapulpers and subjected to 'beating'. The machine used for this purpose breaks up the fibres to the required length, fibrillates the individual fibres and frays them out where necessary. The character and strength of the paper are determined at this stage by the type and length of beating given ('free beating' – short cut lengths; 'wet beating' – bruised long lengths). Exact judgement is required; the difference, for instance, between blotting paper (soft and porous) and greaseproof (dense and impenetrable) is mainly the result of different beating.

The actual paper-making machine on to which the slurry of fibres in water (after being treated to remove lumps of fibre, dirt, etc.) is filtered, through a moving wire mesh, consists of a wet end, press section and drying section. The machine may be over 400 ft. long and can cost well over a million pounds.

Apart from fibres, water and fuel are the most important paper-making raw materials used. Most of the water is discharged as effluent and from 30 to 300 tons of water (often chemically treated and filtered first) are required to produce every ton of paper. For power and steam generation coal or oil is required – according to the quality one half to three tons of coal are needed to make a ton of paper. Thirty to one hundred tons of air (often filtered) pass through a ton of paper during processing. It is taken in cold and discharged warm and moist and modern drying systems are designed to use as little air as possible, as this heat is all wasted.

Materials other than fibres are added to printing papers to give them the required properties, because fibres and water alone produce absorbent papers. The first method, surface sizing, is done by dipping the paper in a bath of gelatin or starch to block up the pores, and the second method uses internal or 'beater' sizes, which are added after beating in the hydrapulper. These alter the way water spreads on paper by increasing the 'contact angle' and rosin treated with alkalis is added to the paper stock with aluminium sulphate. China clay is added as a 'filler' or 'loader' to increase the opacity and with expensive lightweight paper titanium dioxide is used. This pigment, having a high refractive index, is very white and opaque. Precipitated chalk is used in some instances and synthetic sizes, which are inclined to be expensive. Dyes and pigments are added to introduce colour, also fluorescent chemicals and plastics of various kinds. Melamine and urea formaldehyde resins can be incorporated to provide 'wet strength'. Paper readily disintegrates under water treatment but it is found that a wet strength paper remains strong and serviceable.

SURFACE CHARACTERISTICS

COATED PAPERS are papers to which an additional surface has been applied using dispersions of inorganic pigments in water, gums or resins in water or solvents, or melted solids. These include clays, natural or synthetic resins and cellulose derivatives, and asphalt or polythene waxes. A typical pigment coating is a combination of an inorganic pigment, an adhesive and various additives in small amounts, dispersed in water, with the solid components varying from 40 to 70% of the entire coating weight. Kaolin clays are the most widely used pigments, followed by calcium carbonate, then titanium dioxide and barium sulphate in lesser amounts. Adhesives are starch or casein, plus some of the synthetic resins. The adhesive holds the aggregates of pigment together, binds them to the paper surface and adjusts the flow properties of the coating to give a uniform and level surface. Dispersing agents used sparingly transform the coating from a thick, almost solid mass, to a flowing dispersion, whilst the use of plasticisers reduces the inherent brittleness of the adhesive.

Either one side or both sides of the paper may be coated in a single operation using (a) an excess of coating and then removing the excess by a scraping device; or (b) applying the exact amount by means of a series of metering rollers. Using the first method a metal blade, a jet of air, or a pair of squeeze rollers remove the excess coating which has been applied by puddling the coating on the sheet, or by dipping the sheet into a bath of coating. With the second method the coating is applied in the end of a train of rollers; as the rollers revolve the coating film continually splits until the correct amount of coating reaches the applicator roller. Oscillating brushes operating perpendicular to the paper travel, or a roller rotating in the opposite direction to the paper travel, can also be used to level the coating, remove any 'patterning' and produce a special high gloss finish. After drying the paper using hot air or steam filled drier rollers the final surface can be developed by polishing or super-calendering, using a vertical stack of alternating steel and softer composition rollers which are pressurised so that the softer rollers squash. When in motion the slippage of the hard and soft rollers produces a polishing action on the paper surface. Cast-coated paper, on the other hand, obtains its surface by having the wet coated sheet pressed to a highly polished hot metal cylinder and dried in contact to give a high-gloss coated paper.

During paper-making free fibres can tend to protrude through the wire mesh, giving rise to fluffing trouble subsequently on litho machines. To overcome this, and to give the paper similar characteristics on either side of the sheet for litho work, a machine with two wire meshes is used. The two webs are joined back to back in the rear end of the machine so that identical paper surfaces are obtained.

The choice of fibres, differences in beating, loading, pressing and finishing, alter the characteristics of the paper as required for different processes. For lithographic printing the coating has to be water resistant and repellent without having any detrimental effect on the ink-receptivity of the paper. To achieve this the adhesives are made insoluble in water by the addition of materials such as latex, and chemical treatment can convert a water-soluble cellulose coating to an insoluble salt. Litho paper should be fairly soft, receptive to colours, have minimum expansion and lie flat. The paper maker uses esparto and wood pulp to give this required softness combined with strength; the addition of straw would give a rather harder sheet, and rag would produce added strength. The paper should be fully matured by humidifying to release the various strains and stresses which may have been set up on the paper-making machine, and litho papers are usually humidified to 6–7% moisture content, which is the average content of the air in Great Britain. If the paper is stored at any time under unnatural conditions, the flatness and stability of the paper will be affected. Paper dried from a high to a low moisture content has less tendency to pick up moisture and is thus more dimensionally stable. The quality of fibre used also affects dimensional stability; rag and esparto have good stability, alkaline and sulphate pulps are only fair, and sulphite pulps provide poor dimensional stability in the paper.

The paper surface may be completed whilst on the paper-making machine by pressure from polished steel rollers (calendering) which flatten any fibres on the paper surface to provide a machine-finished (M.F.) paper. Imitation art papers employ suitable loadings in the paper introduced by water spraying during the machine finishing of the paper. Other finishes, such as super-calendering, are carried out as a separate operation after the paper has been made on the paper-making machine.

As previously stated, uncoated offset paper is surfaced-sized during manufacture to eliminate the lint or loose fibres on the surface. Coated offset paper is non-pick and 'waterproofed' by special treatment of the adhesive during coating to prevent the white coating pigment sticking to the blanket during printing. Because the grain is long it is important that, whenever possible, the grain direction of the stock size for printing should be in the direction of the cylinder axis. The paper should be pre-conditioned, that is, the moisture content must be controlled during manufacture to avoid press troubles. This is because the sheet passes between two cylinders under pressure and also some moisture is added to the sheet from the damp plate, through the intermediate blanket cylinder. To avoid register trouble a paper hygroscope is essential to determine the moisture content of a pile of paper before printing.

Super-calendered (S.C.) paper is made by running M.F. paper through the super-calender. Surfaced-sized or tub-sized paper is made by passing the moist paper (15–18% moisture) through a trough containing starch solution. This is located in the drier section of the machine. A layer of mineral pigment (china clay, calcium carbonate, titanium dioxide) bonded with an adhesive (casein, vegetable protein and latex) is used for coated papers and the machine-finished paper is super-calendered. High quality enamel papers are often double-coated, first on the paper machine and then in a separate coating operation.

Colour, brightness, opacity, smoothness and gloss are qualities in paper affecting the sharpness, clarity and contrast of the printed result. Yule, Nielson and Clapper of Kodak Limited have shown that light reflected from paper is the sum of both surface and internal reflections. Some light falling on the paper penetrates the paper and is scattered, part is trapped behind the dots and fails to emerge. Thus the white areas between the dots lose brightness; the deeper the light penetration, the greater the scattering with lower contrast, particularly in the shadows. Mineral filler and coating pigment (such as titanium dioxide) are more refractive than cellulose fibre and thus give maximum contrast of result.

XVII

Appendix

CHROMOLITHOGRAPHY

THE EXPRESSION obviously means lithography in colour as distinct from monochrome. Present-day usage infers that it applies to anything lithographed, whether colour or black and white, where the image is produced by handwork and not by the application of photography. Chromolithography was originally a manual operation, involving numerous stones printed in different hues and tints. Senefelder laid the foundation of this art in 1800, producing chromolithographs in eight and nine colours. Later experiments used twenty or more colours, creating a technique and skill which was unchallenged until the advent of the three-colour halftone process.

Until 1900 most litho work was produced by drawing with grease, crayon and ink on limestone. When completed, the stone was desensitised by sponging with acidified gum arabic and dried. This prevented the ink attaching itself to the non-printing areas on rolling-up the image. The impression was transferred to paper by pressure using a press like a mangle or wringer. The stone was re-damped and re-inked for each impression.

Metal plates were first used for 'hand transfer' purposes. An impression was pulled from the stone on to a specially coated paper, which was re-impressed on to clear grained metal to give a printing surface. An image drawn on stone could be pulled on numerous sheets of 'transfer' paper to give duplicate images, which in turn could be assembled on a template, face-up and positioned to a pre-determined sheet layout. A clean grain metal plate (zinc or aluminium) laid face-down on the template would yield, when passed through the press under pressure, a transfer from the paper to the plate. The next stage would be for the plate to be laid face-up and damped to remove the paper, leaving the ink image on the metal. After desensitising the non-image areas with a mixture of water, gum arabic, an acid and a bichromate of phosphate salt, the plate would be damped, inked up and, after touching-up and correcting, made ready for printing. The 'hand transferred' ink image in contact with the grained zinc or aluminium proved a satisfactory printing medium.

Keys and Set-offs

CHROMOLITHOGRAHY IS still used, mainly in the poster trade, and also in certain classes of label work and in autolithography. Accurate fit and registration of colours are most essential. The practice is to make a detailed outline copy of the original – termed a 'key' – using a first-rate transparent French transfer paper over the copy and fixed in position. The tracing is done using, either separately or in conjunction, fine pen, brush and litho drawing ink. The artist assesses the number of colours required to reproduce the copy, and the required number of plates are prepared on which to transfer an impression of the key or outline in a non-greasy dye or powder. All the subtle changes of tone and colour present in the original must be indicated on the key by the use of thick and thin, broken and dotted lines, etc. Register marks and corner ticks are added before transferring the key image to the respective number of plates.

The tracing or key is sometimes executed on sheet gelatin, the image being traced with a fine needle point, which scratches an impression in the surface of the gelatin. The lines are finally filled in with ink and the surface cleaned and polished before transferring.

Some understanding of the complexity and skill entailed will be realised when it is appreciated that, generally, yellow will be required in the greens, browns, oranges, greys and flesh colours; light blue in the greens, greys, browns and blacks; flesh in the greys, browns and blacks; pink in the reds, oranges and flesh colours, some greys and also in browns and purples.

The colour printing sequence in chromolithography generally follows the pattern to print opaque colours first, followed by tints, body colours and shading colours. Thus an average sequence for ten-colour printing would be, in order of printing, yellow, flesh and black (opaque colours); light blue, pink and green (tints); red, blue and brown (body colours); grey (shading colour).

For same-size reproduction impressions are taken from the key plate on special paper. These are powder sprinkled and run through the press on to damp plates, to give dye images for each colour. The dye has no chemical effect and will not print.

The finished result may also be required either enlarged or reduced in size, in relation to the original design. A poster, for example, would be generally enlarged. In this instance only one first-class impression would be required from the key image, or, alternatively, the key drawing could be used as copy for the making of a line negative.

For large poster work a reduced negative would be made, small enough to be accommodated for projection in an enlarger. The image, enlarged to size section by section for the number of sheets required, is observed in a suitably darkened room, and is projected on to the requisite sheet of white paper, the image being traced in a litho crayon on the paper. When completed it is placed face-down on the plate and rubbed down by local pressure. The image is then re-drawn over this impression using litho ink and, from this, impressions are pulled to give the required number of set-offs.

Litho drawing inks, or tusche, are usually obtained in small slabs, the best being Lemercier and Charbonell. Mixing with distilled water or turpentine will make the ink liquid. Distilled water is preferable to tap water, especially if the tap water is hard, as it flows more freely and dries evenly. Turpentine is mixed with ink for use over a gum resist, as gum is not soluble in turpentine. Water-based ink used over gum results in the water in the ink dissolving the gum so that the ink goes through it.

Various techniques are used for producing drawn plates, including crayon, hand and mechanical stipple, airbrush, mapping and ruling pens, as well as the artist's brush. This latter is probably the most controllable – sable, hog bristle oil painter's brushes and a wide variety of brushes for various effects being used.

CHALK DRAWINGS

LITHO CHALKS are made in a number of hardnesses, ranging from very soft, no. 0, to very hard, no. 5 or copal. The chalks made by William Korn Inc. are in general use. They should be smooth and homogeneous with a rich grease content, so that for delicate and fine work the smallest deposit will print. Chalks are usually made in small, square-sectioned sticks and should be placed, for use, in a crayon holder. Sharpen by cutting back from the tip and not towards it – this causes it to break. Soft chalks give a coarse, open texture, hard chalks a close-grained texture – depending upon the grain of the plate. Dark even tones are produced by building them up slowly, using a fairly hard chalk, working lightly in one direction and then at an angle. Thus, by working in a series of different directions, the grain is filled in evenly, giving a rich deep tone. Chalks are capable of producing a wide range of effects and the tonal range is completely controllable, which does not apply with ink. Goya, Daumier, Rodin, Picasso were, amongst others, wonderful exponents of this medium.

Gum-resist

STAGING OUT with gum is a well-known method for producing intricate, detailed, light areas inside dark areas, without hand painting. This entails drawing the required shape with a gum-etch solution, working over with litho chalk, proving ink, wash-out solution, or turpentine-based ink and when the plate is processed the gum will lift away from it with the coating of ink or chalk, thus giving a clear, white area surrounded by tone. Water mixed ink is no use over a gum-resist, the gum is soluble in water and it is actually unable to resist it. On metal plates gumming-out is a very suitable method to produce light, complicated shapes or white areas on a dark background. The margins of all plates should be gummed-out to keep them clean, after putting in the register marks.

For stonework, high-lights are best scraped into the solid or toned areas using an engraving tool or etching needle. Areas can be made lighter by scraping with the flat of a razor blade, or the use of a friction rub with pumice powder or snakestone. This can be done, because the grain has depth, whereas on plates the grain is shallow and scraping or rubbing, in particular, would remove it, making the plate too smooth to hold gum and water, so that it would fill-in.

When making the key plate, the surface of the metal must be prepared or sensitised with a counter-etch to ensure cleanliness and adequate ink-receptivity. The metal should have a fine grain and zinc is prepared by flooding for one minute with a solution of nitric acid, ammonium alum and water. For aluminium – a 5% to 10% sulphuric acid solution is recommended for this purpose.

Same-size Working

To OBTAIN the outlines of the key plate, for the separate colours from the original sketch, a transparent transfer paper, either French or Vegetal paper, can be used for tracing the outlines in litho drawing ink. This is an alternative to scratching or cutting the lines with a fine point on gelatin before inking-in with a mixture of transfer ink and thin varnish. The plate is damped and the image transferred to it, by means of a transfer press. When dry, the artist adds corner marks and register marks and squares-up the work. It is then 'rolled-up' – gummed, dried, washed-out with wash-out solution, inked-up, chalked and etched ready for pulling set-offs. This treatment replaces the water-soluble drawing ink with a greasy printing ink and also desensitises and makes the non-printing areas water-receptive.

Using the transfer press, the key plate is used to obtain the impressions for making the set-offs. The paper used for the impressions has a hard smooth surface, such as manila or white enamel paper, and is dimensionally stable. The plate is rolled-up with a minimum amount of slow-drying, black ink; the paper is laid on the plate and pulled through the press. The impression is immediately dusted with a set-off powder, such as Red Addle powder, jeweller's rouge, or blue aniline powder. This adheres to the ink and loose powder and is removed from the un-inked paper by dusting. The required number of set-offs are pulled from the plate and each in turn pulled through the press on to a metal plate. To fix the set-off permanently when using aniline powder, the plate should be just damped using a small quantity of methylated spirit. The preparation of the individual colour plates then follows using litho ink, crayon, etc., and shading mediums, such as Ben-Day, may also be used.

BEN-DAY MEDIUMS

THESE CONSIST of a wooden frame over which is stretched the medium consisting of a transparent gelatin sheet with a raised pattern of dots or lines on one side. The equipment used has micrometric adjusters, so that when the shading medium has been inked it can be laid face-down in accurate register with the plate constantly in view through the transparent medium whilst the work is being carried out. The medium is placed on a flat surface, lightly rolled with black litho transfer ink thinned with lavender or linseed oil, using a composition roller, placed in the hinged frame and suspended face-down above the

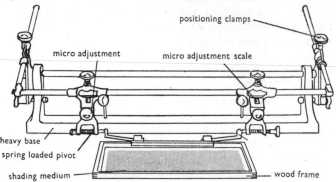

Fig. 85 Shading medium and holder

plate. The plate is carefully gummed out before inking with a thin gum arabic solution over areas where no tint is required. The medium is located over the ungummed areas and pressed into contact by burnishing with a leather or rubber stump, or a small roller. If the back is french chalked, the burnisher will move smoothly and easily. The result is a smooth, even ink image of lines or dots on selected areas of clear plate.

The white or non-printing areas are desensitised with a gum arabic solution, which in turn removes the impression of the shading medium where it has fallen on the locally gummed areas. The plate requires the normal treatment of being rolled-up and completely desensitised before printing.

TRANSFERRING

THERE ARE at least two dozen types of transfer paper, used for many different purposes. Charles Harrop, in his fully documented treatise on Transferring, first written in 1912, has listed the objects of the use of transfers.

1. To draw the work in its normal position. This was the origin of transfer paper. It has been most useful to artists for pen and ink sketches and for crayon drawings on grained paper.

2. For manuscript, whether for the fine copperplate writing, as used on visiting cards, etc., agreements, contracts and so forth, autograph letters and similar personal matter.

3. For tracings. The application of this method covers a wide range. Commencing with the facsimile copying of any manuscript or drawing, preparation of key plates for chromolithographs either by pen and ink work upon a coated tracing paper or by engraving in gelatin, up to the elaborate work in grain or stipple on films.

4. For obtaining portions of a design from various sources and mounting them as one complete transfer. This can be seen in the preparation of plans with line work, to which is added type and copperplate engraving transfers. This has been still further developed by offset printing, in bringing together transfers of the finest copperplate engravings, type, lithographic work, and transfers from intaglio plates or halftone blocks. The scope is practically unlimited.

5. For building up patterns. Most elaborate and intricate work is produced by copper and steel-plate engraving, stone engraving, drawing and photolithography, which can be patched up accurately to form corners, borders, backgrounds, tile and carpet patterns, and similar designs, without having to complete the whole of the original work.

6. For repeating the original work, any number of times, by patching up a large number of transfers upon one key sheet and transferring them on one plate or stone. It is a means of economic label production.

7. For repeating all the original drawings or engravings of the colours of a chromolithograph to print a number of the same subjects at one time, which is a variation of the above.

8. For placing prints upon china and other earthenware, on tin, iron plates and fabrics, etc. These methods come under the general heading of decalcomania.

9. For obtaining photolitho transfers. In this manner documents may be accurately reproduced, same-size, larger or smaller. Continuous tone subjects and photographs may be reproduced on grained surfaces and chromolithographs reproduced in varying sizes. Patterns may be reduced to working drawings.

10. For lateral reversal – from right to left.

11. For obtaining backgrounds. This is useful when a large surface or a series of small surfaces require tinting with dot, line, or grain patterns. It may be attained by transferring from ruled or other copper plates, or by rubbing down from films.

12. For cheapening the production and reducing the task and labour of stippling, by rubbing down grained (metzograph) tints where required. Especially useful for chromolithography.

13. For enlarging or reducing a subject. In a mechanical way, transfers may be made upon a rubber sheet, enlarged or reduced, then re-transferred to plate or stone.

14. For easy portability and for preserving work.

Transfer paper, which consists of a dimensionally stable base paper with one side having a water-soluble coating, is manufactured for various uses. Berlin paper, French paper, varnish paper, yellow Everdamp and transparent Everdamp are well-known types, the first two being transferred on to a damp plate, the remainder being dry transferred. Chalk or grained transfer paper has a thick coating with a rough texture, formed by brush marks or patterned from an embossed steel plate. It can be worked on with either litho chalk or ink. There is a tendency for the grain of the paper to clash with the grain of the plate, flattening the result. Translucent type papers are useful in patching up, to register with key images, and transparent or opaque yellow Everdamp paper and Scotch paper are quite heavily coated and much used.

Yellow everdamp can be purchased either smooth or slightly rough surfaced and embodies a thin non-dry coating, which obviates the need to damp. It is a versatile medium and easy to handle. Mainly intended for ink work, the rough surfaced kind is suitable for drawing on with litho chalks. The transparent everdamp is very suitable for key drawings. It also consists of a non-drying coating. The transfer paper is placed face-up on the subject and traced with a pen or fine brush using litho writing ink. On completion, place face-down on the plate and transfer the image.

A sheet of damped paper is placed over the transfer which, as stated, is face-down on the plate. The combination is passed through the press two or three times, increasing the pressure each time. The transfer adheres to the plate, the backing paper is removed, the transfer sponged and taken through the press several times under pressure. The coating dissolves and the paper is peeled off. Any coating sticking to the plate must be washed off with clean water. It is usual for a good conditioned everdamp paper to require no damping. If it has been kept too long, or dried out owing to high temperature conditions, it needs damping. Lukewarm water, or alternatively warming the plate, can help with difficult transfers. It is recommended that counter-etching of the plate is carried out before putting the transfer down. Also damping the plate with acidified water sharpens the transfer, because the acid sets the ink preventing it spreading. In general the procedure followed in processing a transferred image is similar to that appertaining for a direct one, with the exception that the first etch requires a weak gum-etch and the plate requires a thorough washing out with asphaltum, or a mixture of chalk, black ink and wash-out solution.

A heavy mangle-like press is used for copper-plate transfers. The copper-plate engraving is heated to soften the hard copper-plate transfer ink, which is then 'worked into' the recesses of the engraving using an ink pad. A clean pad is used to remove excess ink from the surface. After finally polishing the surface of the metal, the transfer is made on well-moistened Scotch transfer paper, using heavy pressure. The transfer paper is positioned face-down on the plate and covered with blotting paper and very thick layers of printer's woollen blanket. Gentle warming is applied so that when separated from the plate, the image is in very slight relief.

Before retransferring from litho plates or stones, a thin layer of retransfer ink should be applied with a nap roller to the image, the non-printing areas being first moistened with water. The transfer is pulled using a transfer press with the pressure usually applied with the aid of a steel scraper bar. Ability and skill are required in pulling a series of identical transfers for 'patching-up' to form a large sheet. The soft, tacky gelatinous Everdamp paper makes for easier working, being semi-moist and ready for use.

Final retransferring consists of laying the transfer sheet face-down on the prepared surface and passing through the transfer press, using soft packing combined with heavy pressure. The transfer should adhere with intimate contact to the plate. This requires the operation of passing through the press under pressure several times. Everdamp transfers are pulled on to a dry plate, whilst other types of transfer paper require re-damping to make limp and tacky for adhesion, or the plate itself is slightly moistened before placing the transfer sheet, or sheets, in position. The next operation is to remove the packing carefully and damp the back of the transfer using a sponge. Again pass through the press several times, re-damp and repeat the procedure until the transfers can safely be removed by water soaking. The plate is then dried by heat to prevent oxidation. Retouching and corrections are carried out, using a sable brush and litho writing ink, after which the non-printing areas are desensitised with a thin gum solution.

Preparing the Plate for Machine Printing

THE TRANSFERRED image requires strengthening before printing and the non-printing areas require fully desensitising to guarantee clean printing in the white areas. This operation in plate preparation is termed 'rolling up'.

Various methods can be used, depending upon the type of work and also upon workshop practice. In some instances the job can be rolled up right away, subject to there being no delicate halftones and dependent upon the transferer being confident regarding the state of his transfers and plate. One method entails washing the gummed plate over with a wash-out solution or asphaltum, until the ink of the design has been dissolved. After drying, the plate is washed with clean water, which will leave nothing but a deposit of bitumen on the work itself. The plate is then rolled up so that the image is fully charged with a layer of ink. The ink film may be reinforced by dusting with a finely powdered oil-soluble resin, for example colophony, or alternatively bitumen may be used.

A further method varies the procedure. Instead of washing off the asphaltum or 'wash-out' solution, this is allowed to dry and then the plate is rolled solid with ink. A piece of thick felt, charged with weak gum arabic solution, is applied all over the plate. This removes the film of ink and wash-out or asphaltum from the blank parts of the design. The plate is then washed over with clean water, rolled up briskly with a sparsely charged ink roller and strengthened as previously mentioned.

DESENSITISING (ETCHING AND GUMMING)

THE IMAGE is dusted with talc or french chalk to reduce the possibility of accidentally smearing the ink. This also allows desensitisation to react fully in close proximity with the edges of the work. The action of etching differs for stones and plates. With the former nitric acid applied to stone gives a rougher and more porous surface. With metal plates the grain has been applied and a corrosive etch, such as chromic acid, could be harmful. A non-corrosive etch for aluminium consists of phosphoric acid and gum arabic, and for zinc ammonium biphosphate, ammonium nitrate and gum arabic. The etching solution can be applied with a soft sponge for one to two minutes. It is then washed off, the plate gummed up and the image rolled up, cleaned up, or washed out once again before rolling and cleaning up. The acid etching solution cleans the metal, removing ink spots and unwanted residual layers to ensure full desensitisation. Complex phosphate and chromate films, formed during the chemical reactions, are removed by washing and desensitised by the final gumming process. On drying, a glue-like water-swellable layer, relatively insoluble, is produced.

During cleaning up, care must be taken to preserve the grain. Pumice powder moistened with a caustic solution is preferred for zinc to the use of snakestone or any hard abrasive material. Sometimes a steel needle or scraper is necessary. This should be followed immediately by a local application of the nitric acid and alum sensitising bath to prevent the parts removed filling in again during printing. The plate should be again thoroughly etched after correcting, to give a protective grease-resisting surface to the clear parts of the plate. It is then gummed up and dried, to provide the maximum chemical and mechanical protection of the non-printing areas.

Alterations are more difficult to carry out on metals than upon stones because the plate grain must be preserved, whilst at the same time removing the unwanted area. On aluminium erasing is done with sulphuric acid, care being taken not to rub the grain more than is strictly unavoidable. After washing and drying, the area is resensitised with a strong sensitising solution of hydrochloric acid, alum and water. After washing and quick drying, the alteration is made or the new transfer run down in position. Gumming, rolling up and etching follow.

On zinc plates the work is removed with caustic potash, using a resensitising bath of either nitric acid and alum or, for preference, phosphoric acid and alum. Additions in lithographic writing ink require a weak etch after transferring.

TRANSPOSITION, FROM BLACK TO WHITE

THERE ARE several ways of producing a negative image from a positive one which are fairly involved and complicated. The following is a fairly simple procedure.

1. A good impression is pulled on the press from the original that requires transposing. The print must not be too heavy. A hard-surfaced paper, such as manila or art paper, is preferred and a non-greasy black ink is used.

2. The impression is dusted with finely powdered gum arabic or, better still, dextrin, which is prepared from starch. Flick the back of the sheet to dislodge any particles of powder covering the blank parts of the sheet and dust carefully with a soft brush.

3. Damp the plate slightly and place the dry print face-down on it. Pass through the press to transfer the image to the plate in the form of a gum or dextrin-resist positive stencil.

4. Gum off the edges of the plate and all areas to be left white when dry. Roll the plate up in developing ink, or chalk black thinned with asphaltum or, alternatively, wash-out solution.

5. Treat with wash-out solution and process in the normal way. The ink or solution is washed off with water and the plate rolled up with ink. Where the impression was in gum the ink will be repelled. The image is strengthened before etching, with rosin and french chalk.

VANDYKE PROCESS

THIS REVERSING process from black to white is based on the sub-stitution of a resinous and greasy ink resist for a dichromated gelatin resist and was originated by Vandyke at the India Survey Office. The metal is grained, cleaned (nitric acid alum bath for zinc, alum bath or fluosilicic acid bath for aluminium), water washed and coated with di-chromated glue solution. After whirling and drying it is exposed under the image, developed in the normal way and stained with aniline violet dye, making sure that no scum is left where the metal should be bare. The clearing solution, or a weak ferric chloride solution, may be used to ensure a perfectly clean and satisfactory surface. After washing, dry and ink-up the plate thinly using a firm composition roller charged with stone-to-stone retransfer ink. The ink must strongly cover the surface of the bare metal and after inking the plate is warmed to about 100° F and allowed to cool. The plate is then immersed in a 3% hydrochloric acid bath and gentle rubbing with cotton wool removes the semi-soluble coating of glue, washing away at the same time its over-covering of ink, leaving the metal bare in these areas and thus bringing about a transposition of tone. The bare metal is then etched, gummed and dried in the usual manner.

POSTER WORK

THE SIZE of a poster is determined by the number of sheets involved. The individual sheet size is double crown (20 in. × 30 in.), quad crown 30 in. × 40 in. (2-sheet) and eight crown 40 in. × 60 in. (4-sheet). The latter size involves the use of the largest printing machine in normal use, which is for poster work. Most large hoarding posters are 40 in. × 60 in. sheets, so that a display using four 40 in. × 60 in. sheets is termed a 16-sheet poster (eight = 32-sheet; twelve = 48-sheet). The sheets normally overlap from right to left and the top row overlaps the bottom row. When printed the sheets are folded in the correct order for assembly on the hoardings.

Posters are produced from a single colour working to ten or twelve printings and include photolithography in four colours for cinema ad-vertising, also silk screen techniques using up to six or more colours. Hand-drawn methods are still widely employed, often printed direct, although offset printing is superseding it on account of the latter's ability to print finer detail and simulate a better photographic effect. Quarter-tone 'dot for dot' methods are also used, in which the work is reproduced to a smaller size using a finer screen ruling; the negatives are then 'blown-up' on the enlarger camera, giving coarser screen dot positives which are dot etched and corrected and final negatives made for printing down to metal, either by contact or by transmission if further enlargement is required. Alternatively the dot positives may be printed-down by the deep-etch method after stripping-up and joining or assembling the positives on the light table (shiner).

Chromolithography methods are employed in poster reproduction, the only difference being that intricate fine detail work is replaced by

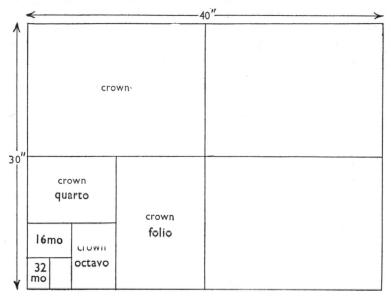

Fig. 86 Quad crown sheet

broader treatment. Chalk and crayon techniques and the use of a coarse spray air-brush are part of the poster workers' applied skill, which is used in producing the required result. Set-offs and key outlines are obtained in the usual way and many posters are a combination of photolithography in four colours and chalk drawn work including solid and tint colours.

SCRIBING METHODS AND AUTOLITHOGRAPHY

BEFORE THE advent of the photographic processes maps were produced from copper-plate engravings. This was a tedious, highly skilled process and map and security printing, with the introduction of photolithography, is today a combination of both methods. Many of the advantages of old-style engravings have been recaptured by using the Astrascribe technique which is a scribing process using a vertical stylus and special coated sheets of Astrafoil. Stylus points are obtainable in various thicknesses corresponding to the line thickness required, including twin points for roads. The sheet is dimensionally stable, transparent and impervious to extremes of temperature and humidity. The work is scribed through the non-actinic coating exposing the transparent Astrafoil beneath. Straight lines can be ruled at very close intervals and thicknesses varied by selecting the appropriate stylus point. Curves and irregular shapes can be executed using the swivel action incorporated in the stylus holder. The stylus point is held in a perfectly vertical position and line thicknesses are completely uniform. When completed the image is automatically a negative and can be used for printing-down direct to metal. Alternatively, by applying dye to the exposed scribed surface and removing the resist, a positive is produced to which town names and other details can be added to provide an image for printing-down direct to metal for deep offset platemaking.

Any image which is produced directly on to a stone, metal or plastic surface and uses lithographic principles to provide the printing medium, comes within the general classification of *autolithography*. It is a creative method of employing manipulative and artistic skills in which the artist has complete freedom of expression and application to produce an image from which impressions can be obtained lithographically. Sometimes, for commercial work, the artist provides the basic key plate or plates and other colours are introduced, under his supervision, by photographic methods, so that the final result is a combination of hand-drawn and photolithographic work. Transfer paper, as well as litho stone, was used initially and, more recently, the artist now produces images on transparent or translucent media such as plastic materials suitably grained on one side to provide a drawing surface. These include Astrafoil, Ethulon, Kodatrace and ground glass surfaces, and the drawing medium can be lithographic chalk or crayon, paint, ink or liquid opaque. The drawn plates may be printed-down direct to metal and by using one colour as the key and overlaying other sheets of plastic film and registering to tick marks, numerous colours can be drawn to fit, producing a multi-colour job.

THE VARIO-KLISCHOGRAPH K181

THERE ARE a great number of these electronic machines in use in photolitho establishments where they carry out the work hitherto performed by the camera operator and the negative-positive retoucher, producing tone-corrected and colour-corrected and balanced negatives and positives suitable for printing-down to metal in the usual manner.

The Vario-Klischograph was first exhibited at Graphic 57 in Lausanne. It operates on the same basic principle as the other models in the Klischograph range of electronic engravers, but was the first to provide variation in size from the original copy, enlarging up to four diameters and reducing to one-third size with a maximum plate size of 12 in. × 16½ in. One of six screen rulings may be used (60 to 137 lines per inch) and by the addition of various appropriate accessories it can be employed for reproducing from colour reflection copy or transparencies, or used for line and monochrome work.

The copy is illuminated by a fixed discreet light source, past which it travels at a constant speed and at a constant distance. Light reflected from the copy is scanned by a photocell, the output voltage of the cell being proportional to the brightness of the area scanned, thus controlling the action of the engraving stylus. When one line has been scanned, the optical head containing the light source and photocell moves by the

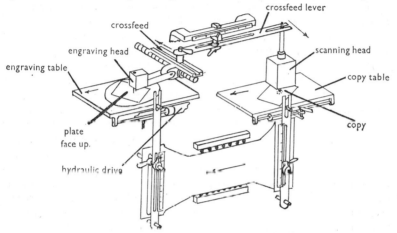

Fig. 87 Vario-Klischograph – schematic diagram

required amount, which is determined by the screen size and scale desired. The stylus is a sharply ground, three-sided point, which moves rapidly up and down and, in combination with the horizontal movement of the plate table, produces a succession of indentations in a straight line.

A coated scribing medium such as Astrafoil or Astrascribe is employed. This medium, with its waxlike coloured deposit on the scribing surface, can be 'screened' electronically to produce negative images, although positive images suitable for printing-down may be produced direct from the copy. From the dot negatives, made by the stylus cutting through the coloured 'wax' coating suspended on the clear Astrafoil, normal photographic positives are made by contact or transmission (for enlargement or reduction). These positives can, if necessary, be further dot corrected by the retoucher using orthodox chemical reduction techniques to sharpen the dot structure or effect tonal or colour correction.

The foil thickness is ten, twenty or thirty thousandths of an inch, coated with various colours – orange, blue-violet, mauve and brownish-black – which can be assessed for dot size similar to photographic negatives and positives.

The normal practice, based on experience, is to scan, for instance from a colour transparency, to produce a direct dot positive image. This is contacted back by normal photographic procedure to a screen negative, which is retouched and corrected where necessary. It is then contacted back to a positive image before printing-down to metal. This method allows much more latitude in retouching and dot correction.

In operation the copy to be scanned and the medium on which to record the impulses set-up are laid on two flat tables which move backwards and forwards during this scanning process. The tables are mechanically linked, but so arranged that the copy table can move below the foil table which is moved by a hydraulic drive at a speed that remains the same, independent of picture dimensions. This moves the copy table by a stable linkage system consisting of two vertically arranged levers and a horizontal drive. The pivots of these two levers, which are fixed at their upper ends to the copy and plate table respectively, are attached to the front lower edge of the chassis of the machine. Reduction or enlargement is achieved by adjustment of slides situated between the levers and the main horizontal guides, as shown in the diagram. The scanning and engraving heads are connected by a further horizontal lever, the pivot of which can be adjusted according to picture dimensions, thus causing the scanning head to move faster or slower than the cutting head at each line feed. The copy table and the engraving head can be released from their operating levers and set to any desired position, making it possible to enlarge or reduce separate parts of the original if required.

The medium to receive the scanned image is held by vacuum on the engraving table. A pair of feeler contacts, adjacent to the engraving head, measures the size of the plate and ensures that the direction of the table is reversed at the moment when the stylus is approaching the edge of the plate. When scanning and cutting are completed the machine stops automatically. The copy is held by vacuum face upwards against a glass plate by means of a rubber blanket. Scanning is from above. By the use of controls, tonal corrections and sharper definition can be obtained, moiré effects can be minimised by adjusting the scanning light spot. Under colour removal, colour correction by electronic masking computation and adjustment for screen angles, are embodied in this exceptionally versatile instrument.

Bibliography

General

Graphic Arts Technicians Handbook (Hunter-Penrose-Littlejohn Ltd).
'Handbooks to Printing' series (Ernest Benn Ltd).
Ilford Graphic Arts Manual, vol. I, by H. M. Cartwright (Ilford Ltd).
Modern Illustration Processes, by C. W. Gamble (Pitman & Sons Ltd).
Penrose Annual (Lund Humphries & Co. Ltd).
Photomechanics and Printing, by J. S. Mertle and G. L. Monsen (Mertle
　　Publishing Co. Ltd, U.S.A.).
Practical Printing and Binding, 1965 (Odhams Books Ltd).
Printing Science, by F. Pateman and L. C. Young (Pitman & Sons Ltd).
'Printing Theory and Practice' series (Pitman & Sons Ltd).
Reproduction of Colour, by R. W. G. Hunt (Fountain Press).
Science of Photography, by H. Baines (Fountain Press).
Structure of the Printing Industry, by A. Delafons (Macdonald & Co.
　　Ltd).

Photolithography and Lithographic Printing

Graphic Arts Technical Foundation Publications (U.S.A.).
Lithographers Manual (Waltwin Publishing Co.).
Offset Lithography, by L. E. Lawson (Studio Vista Books).
Offset Lithography, by B. E. Tory (Pitman & Sons Ltd).
Photolithography, by B. E. Tory (Pitman & Sons Ltd).
Proceedings of the P.A.T.R.A. Offset-Litho Conference, 1960
　　(P.A.T.R.A.).

Periodicals

British Printer.
Graphic Technology.
Journal of Photographic Science (Royal Photographic Society).
Litho-Printer.
P.A.T.R.A. Journal.
The Photographic Journal (Royal Photographic Society).
Print in Britain.
Printing Trades Journal.

Glossary of Terms

Abberation   Fault inherent in the lens construction in which a point is reproduced as a patch and straight lines appear curved. Principal axial aberrations are chromatic and spherical. With the former blue light comes to a focus nearer the lens than red light. All lenses have some form of residual aberration.

Absorbency   Ability of paper to absorb or receive liquids.

Achromatic   Refers to a lens partially corrected for chromatic aberration, bringing two spectrum colours to the same focus.

Acid   Substance which contains hydrogen which may be replaced by a metal to form a compound known as a salt. A solution with a pH value below 7 is acidic.

Actinic   The property of some light radiations to change the nature of materials exposed to them. In photography the rays at the blue-violet end of the spectrum are most highly actinic.

Acutance   Physical measure of image sharpness intended to correlate with the visual assessment of sharpness.

Adsorption   Concentration of a substance on a surface such as dissolved or suspended particles on the surface of a solid, e.g. gum arabic on the surface of zinc or aluminium.

Airbrush   A type of paint spray used by artists when retouching photographs, etc. Produces smooth tones by blowing a liquid pigment in a spray using compressed air.

Alkali   Soluble metallic hydroxides with certain characteristics in that they feel soapy, neutralise acids and react with them to form salts. Potassium or sodium hydroxide should be handled with care, due to their ability to destroy skin tissue when in high concentration.

Alloy   A composition of two or more metals.

Anastigmat   A lens corrected for astigmatism, which is a defect in which light rays in one plane may be in focus while those in the other are out of focus, giving distortion.

Anhydrous   Without water; usually salts without water of crystallisation.

Apochromat   A lens corrected for the three primary spectral colours, red, green and blue, as opposed to an achromatic lens which is corrected for two colours only.

Art-paper   Smooth-surfaced paper, produced by coating with a china-clay-based material. Used for fine screen work.

Asphaltum   A bituminous mixture used to make printing images on press plates permanently ink-receptive.

Astrafoil   A registered trade name for a dimensionally stable base film used for 'patching-up' work where accurate size holding is necessary. An image may be printed-down on it.

A.T.S.   Animal tub-sized, applies to good quality paper sized by passing the sheet through liquid gelatin.

Back pressure   The squeeze pressure between the blanket cylinder and the impression cylinder. Also called 'impression pressure'.

Baumé   A scale of specific gravity of liquids.

$$\text{Degrees Baumé} = \frac{144\cdot3\ (\text{S.G.} - 1)}{\text{S.G.}}$$

Benday or *Ben Day*   A method of tint laying on negative, positive or print on metal. Benjamin Day was the name of the inventor of the process.

Bi-metal plates   Lithographic plates in which the printing image base is formed of one metal and the non-printing area of a second metal. Usually the printing area is formed of copper and the non-printing areas of nickel, chromium or stainless steel.

Blanket   A sheet of vulcanised rubber on a fabric base, specially treated to prevent stretch when wrapped around the press cylinder. Receives the inked image from the plate and transfers it to paper.

Bleed   Term used to describe printing surfaces which extend beyond the edge of the trimmed printed page.

Bleach-out-process   An under-developed bromide print used as a basis for a line drawing in waterproof or fixed Indian ink.

Blind   A plate condition in which the image ceases to be ink-receptive.

Bloomed lens   Lens which has the outer air to glass surfaces coated with a thin film of metallic fluoride. This eliminates stray reflected light, increasing the light transmission by reducing the light lost by internal reflections which lower contrast. Average loss of light for glass of refractive index $1\cdot5$ and air, refractive index $1\cdot0$, is 4%.

Blue-key   A blueprint on glass or vinyl acetate used as a guide for stripping colours to register.

Bristol board   First-quality cardboard consisting of thin boards pasted together with smooth high finish, suitable to take pen or brush work with sharp clean lines.

Broadside   Any sheet of a standard size which is not cut or folded.

Cam   The projecting part of a disc or wheel adapted by means of grooves or teeth to convey eccentric or alternating motion.

Catalysis   A substance which can accelerate or retard a chemical reaction without itself suffering any chemical change is called a catalyst, and the process is called catalysis.

Catching-up The non-image areas begin to take ink due to insufficient water film.

Chalking Powdering or rubbing off of the ink as a result of improper drying. The pigment crystallises due to lack of binding vehicle caused by too rapid absorption into the paper. Too little vehicle is left on the paper surface to bind the pigment together.

Chiaroscuro The distribution or the blending of the lights, middle tones and shadows in an original or reproduction.

Chromolithography A nineteenth-century term for multi-coloured printing using as many as 20 colours. A reproductive process as opposed to a creative one, the term was coined by Engelmann in 1817 and the method patented by him in France in 1837.

Colloid A substance such as albumen, starch or gelatin which seems soluble in liquid, but is actually in a state of fine dispersion.

Collotype A surface printing process from a continuous-tone negative using dichromated gelatin, the reticulated gelatin forming the printing image.

Composition roller An inking roller of gelatin and glue; very susceptible to moisture. Now being superseded by rubber or plastic.

Candela Unit of luminous intensity replacing the international candle.

Candlepower The luminous intensity of a light source in a given direction expressed in terms of the candela.

Copy The original drawing, painting or photograph for reproduction. Also a term used in printing for the manuscript which is to be set in type.

Counter-etch The chemical treatment of a lithographic surface with diluted acids to remove oxides and dirt to make it sensitive to grease prior to producing an image on it.

Cross-hatching A method of shading, in drawing and engraving, by a series of crossed parallel or near parallel lines crossed with others at varying angles.

Cross-line screen Half-tone screen of parallel equidistant lines engraved at an angle of 45 degrees on two pieces of plate glass; cemented together so that the lines cross at right angles, forming transparent and opaque squares.

Dampeners Cloth-covered rollers that distribute the dampening solution received from the ductor roller of the dampening unit to the lithographic press plate.

Deep-etch Lithographic platemaking process in which the work areas are slightly etched (about 0·003 in.) into the surface of the plate. Positives are used for printing to metal using special solutions, with the etches supplying space for the lacquer base of the ink-receptive printing image.

Density The quantitative measure of the blackening of a photographic emulsion.

Desensitise The chemical treatment of the plate that makes the background or non-image areas insensitive to grease, oleophobic and also hydrophilic.

Developer Converts the latent image formed during exposure into a visible image by changing into black metallic silver the silver salt compounds affected by light action.

Diaphragm A variable opening in a lens system related to the focal length of the lens.

Dot etching The process in photolithography corresponding to fine etching in photo-engraving. The dots are not etched but chemically reduced, usually in the positive stage.

Double printing Two exposures on one piece of metal or film to register ticks. With metal the exposures can be on one coating, or the first print developed and the metal recoated for the second print.

Douthitt A diaphragm control system in which the lens aperture is accurately set in co-ordination with the camera extension.

Drop-out A technique in exposure in which the dot formation is eliminated in the high-lights of the negative to produce clean whites.

Duotone Two half-tone plates printed at 45 degrees and 75 degrees made from a monochrome copy to produce two-tone effect. Key plate printed in dark colour, second plate printed in light tint.

Dummy A sample of a proposed job made up in the correct material, cut and made up to size for approval by the customer.

Electronics The applied physical science dealing with the electron. Concerned with electrical circuits using thermionic valves and transistors dealing with the movement and control of electrons.

Emulsion Finely divided particles in a uniformly and stable dispersion: in a liquid. Photographic emulsion is a suspension of finely divided grains of silver bromide in gelatin.

Emulsification The dispersion into each other of two mutually insoluble liquids, for example, greasy ink in damping water.

Em The widest character width in a fount of type – usually 12 point (0·168 in.).

En Half the width of an em.

Etch or *Gum-etch* The chemical treatment of a plate to make the background or non-image areas grease-resistant, that is, desensitising.

Exposure The product of the intensity of light and the time during which light reaches the photographic emulsion.

Ferrotype sheets Iron sheets coated with black glossy enamel to produce a glaze on bromide prints. Polished stainless steel or chromed steel sheets now preferred.

Film   The flexible base of celluloid or plastic upon which the silver bromide emulsion is coated.

Flare   That portion of light which having passed through the lens is no longer part of the image formation, but is scattered over the whole area of the image.

Flash exposure   The short introductory exposure necessary to overcome the inertia of high-contrast material used in half-tone negative making.

Flat   A number of negatives stripped-up or assembled in position for printing-down on to a single sheet of metal.

Flat-bed press   A printing machine in which the printing surface is flat.

Flexographic   Pertaining to letterpress printing from rubber plates.

Fixing   The dissolving of the unexposed and unreduced silver halide to make the image stable, after washing, in white light.

Forme   Blocks and type matter made up and locked in position in a metal chase preparatory to printing.

Frisket   A thin paper covered with a rubber cement which adheres to artwork and is used as a stencil by cutting away wetted areas so that the areas underneath can be airbrushed. After retouching the frisket is removed, leaving the unexposed areas as they were originally.

Gallery camera   The older type of process camera sited in the studio, the photographic material being loaded into the darkslide in the darkroom away from the camera.

Galley   Three-sided steel trays used for the assembly and storage of type before page make-up. Hence galley proofs – long proofs without any separation for pages.

Gamma   A sensitometric quantity obtained from the characteristic curve of an emulsion. It is the ratio of negative contrast to subject contrast and is used as a measure of the development of a developer – emulsion combination.

Glue enamel   A dichromated fish-glue resist.

Graining   The process of roughening the surface of the plate by grinding with marbles or sand blasting with an abrasive to increase the capacity for holding moisture.

Gripper margin   The front margin of a sheet of paper fed into the machine gripper. Approximately $\frac{3}{8}$ to $\frac{1}{2}$ in. on the front edge of the sheet. This cannot be included in the printing area available on the sheet.

Gumming-up   Protecting non-printing areas with a solution of gum arabic to prevent oxidation and damage during wash-out and subsequent operations.

Halation   The reflection of scattered light back through the emulsion from the support so that bright areas have a halo consisting of a circle with a diffused outer edge.

Halftone The process whereby the illusion of continuous-tone gradation is conveyed by means of dots of varying sizes effected by the medium of a screen. The name is attributed to F. E. Ives.

Halftone dot and line tints A positive tint is a tint laid on the non-image areas of a plate. A negative tint is a tint laid on the transparent parts of a negative which correspond to the solid black areas of the copy.

Halfsheet work Both sides of the sheet printed from the same plate. After cutting two complete copies are produced.

Hickeys Faults in the printed result which show as irregular spots with white surrounding haloes, caused by dirt or hardened specks of ink.

H. & D. curve The characteristic curve of a photographic material. Hurter and Driffield carried out the first reliable method of accurate sensitometry, measuring the sensitivity of photographic emulsions, involving the measurement of light intensities and the resultant densities.

High-light negative A screen negative in which the dot formation is a true negative of the required print on paper. The size of dots on the positive will not accommodate any side etching or reduction.

Hue Colour or tint. The quality of colour which differentiates it from grey of equal brilliance.

Hydrometer Instrument for measuring the density or specific gravity of liquids.

Hygroscopic Attracts and absorbs water, a feature of gum arabic.

Hygrometer Instrument for measuring the relative humidity of the atmosphere or of other gases.

Imposition The term used for the positioning of the pages in correct position for printing.

Inertia Lack of sensitivity. All photographic emulsions require a certain exposure before a developable image can be obtained.

Ink print The method of printing on metal to give an ink image – overlaying the albumen image obtained by exposure and development.

Intaglio The printing area, as in photogravure, incised or cut into the metal with the non-printing part above. The opposite from relievo or relief plate, in which the non-printing area is below the surface.

Justification The arrangement and spacing of type so that the lines are of the same width.

Key drawing A line drawing in outline, usually for colour work, the colours being produced from set-offs, or blue-keys which are filled in as required on a positive or print on metal.

Latent image The invisible image present before development, after exposure to light of a silver halide emulsion.

Lateral reversal The reversal of the final printed result left to right relative to the original.

Layout The plan or sketch showing the position of the component parts of a printing forme.

Lens An assembly for forming an image of an object – usually glass or plastic bounded by a plane and a curved surface, or two curved surfaces.

Letterpress The printing process which has the non-image areas below the printing surface. Prints direct from movable type.

Levy Bros The makers of the first commercially ruled and etched glass halftone screen. Also of etching, blooding and burning-in machines.

Lithography or *Planographic printing* The method of printing from plane surfaces, as distinguished from raised or relief plates, or intaglio or sunken surfaces.

Litho varnish Linseed oil treated to form a varnish.

Lumen The amount of light falling per second on a unit area placed at unit distance from a uniform point source of one candela.

Luminous flux A measure of the intensity of a light source in lumens.

Lux The illumination per square metre of a surface. One metre from a point source of 1 candela is 1 lumen.

Machine finished (*M.F.*) Paper finished on the paper-making machine without any subsequent surface finishing such as supercalendering.

Make-ready The preparation of a printing machine to give the optimum impression from a printing surface.

Moiré The formation of undesirable symmetrical patterns produced by conflict between the screens and the lines or dots of the copy.

Monochrome Single colour.

Newton's rings The interference colours which occur when the separation between two surfaces in close proximity is of the same order as the wavelength of light.

Offset printing The printing surface first prints on to a rubber blanket and is then transferred to the paper, resulting in the ink covering the fibres of the paper more efficiently.

Opacity The reciprocal of transparency. If $\frac{1}{10}$ of the incident light is transmitted through a medium the transparency is $\frac{1}{10}$ and the opacity, being the reciprocal of the same, is 10.

Opaque A water-soluble paint used to block out areas on negatives to make them non-transparent.

Original The term applied to the copy-photograph or drawing – which is to be reproduced.

Pawl A sliding pin which drops into the notches of a ratchet wheel so as to allow movement in only one direction.

Perfecting Backing-up or printing on the second side of a sheet. A perfected sheet is one printed on both sides and a perfector press performs this operation.

pH value The degree of acidity or alkalinity measured on a scale from 0 to 14, with 7 as the neutral point.

Pica Unit of measurement of the British-American point system, 0·166 in. – $\frac{1}{6}$ in. or 12 points.

Point The smallest unit of measurement in the British-American point system, 0·014 in. – approximately $\frac{1}{72}$ in.

Prism Transparent medium bounded by polished plane surfaces inclined one to another. A right-angle prism has two faces at right angles, and the silvered third side at 45 degrees acts like a plane mirror, losing very little light.

Process engraving A general term used to describe an engraving made by photographic, chemical or mechanical methods, such as the halftone or line (zinco) block.

Polymerisation The combination of two or more molecules of the same kind to form a larger molecule which has different physical properties.

Quill brush A brush containing no metal, suitable for local application of etching solutions.

Quoin A wedge or other mechanical device used to secure type in a chase by exerting side pressure.

Rapid fixing bath The replacement of sodium thiosulphate with the more expensive ammonium thiosulphate speeds up fixing by a factor of between 5 and 10.

Ream In stationary 480 sheets, normally regarded in printing as 500 sheets. A quire is one-twentieth of a ream.

Reciprocity law failure Maximum blackening is produced on development by exposure of moderate time to a moderate intensity of light. Very low intensities of light with correspondingly long times, or very high intensities of light with very short times, do not produce similar blackening of the photographic emulsion.

Relative humidity The hygrometric state of the atmosphere. A measure of the moisture in the air as a percentage of the moisture the air would contain, at the same temperature, if saturated.

Refractive index The ratio of the velocity of light in air to that in the medium.

Register The correct relative position of two or more colours when printed.

Resist The sensitised coating which becomes acid-resistant after exposure to light in the printing frame.

Resolving power The ability of a lens to reproduce fine detail. A process lens of high efficiency will resolve about 200 lines per millimetre, with average 110 lines per mm. at $f/16$ (wavelength 550 mμ).

R.O.P. An American term (run of paper) applying when colour half-tones are printed at the same time as the type matter.

Safe light The illumination in a darkroom by which a particular photographic material can be safely handled without fogging.

Salt The chemical compound formed when the hydrogen of an acid has been replaced by a metal. A salt is named according to the acid and metal from which it is obtained, e.g. copper sulphate, derived from copper and sulphuric acid.

Screen The term used to denote the particular screen ruling to be used for reproduction. Screens are ruled. for practical purposes from 50 to 200 lines per inch, the character of the paper and printing process determining the selection of a suitable screen ruling.

Scum Unwanted traces of the colloid on the non-image areas of a print on metal or a layer of grease forming on the non-image area.

Sensitometry The study measurement and testing of photographic materials to determine the relationship between exposure and density.

Sheetwise Printing two sides of the same sheet with a different plate for each side.

Silk screen A method of printing in which a stencil adheres to a tightly stretched piece of bolting silk.

Size Substance added to paper to affect its ink or water absorbency. Starch, alginates and glue used in surface sizing.

Slurry A water suspension of fibres and the suspension of pigment and adhesive used to coat papers.

Spectrum colours The colours visible in the continuous spectrum of white light: red, orange, yellow, green, blue, indigo, violet.

Staging Applying a protective coating to plate areas not to be disturbed by the etch (gumming-out).

Stop The diaphragm setting of the lens associated with a corresponding f/number. Originally perforated metal plates, now usually a variable iris diaphragm.

Stripping The removal of the photographic emulsion from its support to assemble with others on to another base to form an etching flat.

Supercalendered (S.C.) Refers to the smooth finish obtained by passing a web of paper through calender rollers.

Tack Stickiness, the resistance of an ink film to being split between two surfaces, such as rollers, plate and blanket and blanket and paper.

Three-point lay The arrangement used in reproduction to ensure that the surface receiving the image or impression always falls in the same position relative to the original.

Tint A solid area of printing plate or a flat tone produced by a regular dot formation.

Tone-line A photographic process by Kodak to convert a continuous tone photograph into a line original.

Trapping The adhesion of printing inks one over the other in wet printing.

Tri-metal plates Plates with three layers of metal. The top layer is etched away in the image areas during processing to expose the middle layer which is grease-sensitive. The lower layer is merely a support.

Tusche A greasy lithographic writing ink used to draw on plates or stones.

Ultra-violet The invisible radiation of shorter wavelength than violet which has a marked effect on photographic material.

Vacuum back A perforated metal plate used to hold film flat during exposure in the camera employing suction induced by a suitable motor-driven unit.

Vignette A gradual shaded-off edge from dark to light. The screen dots blend into an invisible finish by the gradual reduction in the size of the dots as they approach the printing edges of the plate.

Wash drawing A drawing in monochrome in which tones are formed by washes of grey and black medium.

Web printing A continuous length of paper fed through a printing machine; the printing surface being rotary.

Wet plate The wet collodion plate.

Wetting agent Chemicals used to promote uniform wetting and drying.

Wood engraving The letterpress illustration method by hand engraving with a graver, used before the introduction of photo engraving.

Work and turn layouts One forme contains the material that is to be printed on both sides of the sheet. The forme is printed on one side of the sheet for half the number of impressions and the sheet then turned over sideways from left to right and the printing run completed on the reverse side. The turn is on the short axis, feeding into the same edge.

Work and tumble This describes printing one side of a sheet and turning it on its long axis and feeding into the other edge. The term 'work and flop' also indicates printing front and back on the same side of the sheet and then 'flopping' the sheet top to bottom and backing it up from the same plate. With 'work and turn' the difference is that the printed sheet is turned left to right for backing up.

Xerography Dry writing, invented by C. F. Carlson. The sensitive material consists of a plate carrying an electrical charge which is destroyed on exposure. Charged areas, representing the shadows, become the printing image in powdered pigment.

Index

Printed in Great Britain by
Butler & Tanner Limited
Frome and London